The Other Face

The Other Face

CATHOLIC LIFE UNDER ELIZABETH I

Collected and Edited by
PHILIP CARAMAN

SHEED AND WARD — NEW YORK

© PHILIP CARAMAN 1960

Library of Congress Catalog Card Number 61-11798

Manufactured in the United States of America

To

SHERMAN
JEANNE

JULIA

THOMAS

GEORGINA

HARRIET

ROBERT

STONOR

I know that no man can express a passion that he feeleth not, nor doth the pen deliver but what it copieth out of the mind.

ROBERT SOUTHWELL, *Mary Magdalen's Funeral Tears*

I was born in such a time when Holy Mass was in great reverence and was brought up in the same faith. In King Edward's time this reverence was neglected and reproved by such as governed. In Queen Mary's it was restored with much applause, and now in this time it pleaseth the State to question them, as now they do me, who continue in this Catholic profession. The State would have the several changes, which I have seen with mine eyes, good and laudable. Whether it can be so I refer to your Lordships' consideration. I hold me still to that wherein I was born and bred, and find nothing taught in it but great virtue and sanctity, and so by the grace of God I will live and die in it.

LADY CECILY STONOR, *questioned about her recusancy*

Contents

Introduction

This Elizabethan anthology began, almost accidentally, more than eight years ago as a collection of extracts from manuscripts and rare books that I happened to read. My only purpose then was to have at hand for my own reference and reading inaccessible but interesting passages drawn from papers and books that I was unlikely to use again. For the most part I found that I was choosing the little known but well written short story, the striking statement of conviction, the sharply defined character study, even the single stirring phrase. In its beginnings it was a personal and haphazard collection and extended beyond the Elizabethan period. Among other things, I was interested in the behaviour of priests, their jokes, the price paid to the hangman for their execution, their exits and their entrances. I noted also the authentic mystical experience of men like Fr. Alexander Bryant and Fr. Alexander Crowe; the comparison made by Robert Southwell between affliction and the crocodile: 'Fly, it pursueth and frights; followed, it flieth and feareth'; and the phrase with which Edmund Campion compared himself to an elephant. And there was the story of the two young English ladies who, on their way to a convent in Flanders, with a copy of Virgil, were found in bed at the London inn where they were waiting a passage to Dunkerque. Nearly all the incidents had a Catholic interest.

Later, after I had considered using the material for a social history of Catholicism, the following book suggested itself. It was not precisely a prose anthology, for most of the passages I had selected were little known; nor was it a source book, since my choice had in many instances been influenced by the literary appeal of the writers. My aim was to make it, as far as was possible, a reflection of the thoughts and emotions of Catholics, their anxieties and aspirations, their manner of life and suffering; and with this in view I read systematically. I was more anxious to show what passed in the mind of Catholics than to prove the validity of their belief. Thus the loyal statement of Catholic gentlemen at the time of the Armada revealed the fearful tension of conscience endured by their class. No matter what the modern scholar might think of Gregory Martin's strictures of the Bishops' Bible, they explain the suspicion with which Catholics regarded the Protestant Scriptures. Francis Wodehouse's tormented conscience and his physical suffering was a sad and not uncommon case. When I selected Fr. John Gerard's tribute to Sir Everard Digby, I wanted to give a contemporary sketch of a Catholic gentleman as well as an instance of the intimacy that existed between priest and people. It was unnecessary for the purpose of this book to establish whether the river Thames did or did not cease to ebb and flow on the day that Campion was executed: the fact that Catholics believed that it did was an unusual indication of the esteem in which Campion was held.

Ballads perhaps give the best indication of a popular mood, and it is for this reason, and not for their merit as verse, that I have drawn from them. Indeed, in contrast with the violence of anti-Catholic ballad-writers, they reveal a mind at peace with itself, sad yet always forgiving. Among the Catholic poets Southwell, Alabaster and others are represented. In as many ways as possible I have tried to expose the life of Catholics that lay below the surface of political events. Hence I have given much space to their prayers and devotional practices, to the ideals they held out to their children, their constant effort to forgive and to love their enemies. And as far as the sources allowed, I have shown them also at home, reading and letter-writing, at prayer, eating and entertaining, at school, in prison, in the convents and seminaries abroad, in their newly laid-out gardens, riding and in hiding, on the scaffold and at the assizes. I have tried to draw examples from every class of the population and from as many regions as possible; for the conditions of their life were different, for instance, in the Lancashire countryside and in the cities of southern England. I have tried also to show them not only as they appeared to themselves, but as others saw them. And I think there is revealed a picture of a brave and little known community, cruelly defined in the last thirty years of the reign, increasing in numbers, conscious of its strength of spirit, tenacious of all that it considered most traditional and English and best in the nation. This is 'the other face' of Elizabethan England.

In 1911 Professor Dover Wilson in compiling his anthology of Elizabethan England,[1] omitted any reference to religion, 'the greatest, and to Englishmen of that day, the most engrossing' of all topics. It

[1] John Dover Wilson, *Life in Shakespeare's England* (Cambridge University Press, 1911).

would be claiming too much for this book to say that it fills the gap left open by this now classic anthology; but it is perhaps the nearest approach to such a book. It might, of course, be said that I have portrayed only the Catholic side of the religious picture, but this is not altogether the case. Very many passages are drawn from the letters of the Protestant bishops and of other divines who endeavoured to supplant the old religion with the 'pure gospel of Christ'. Indeed full representation is given to their condemnation of the 'superstitious practices' of priests, whom Burghley branded as 'the vermin' of the nation. Their catechism is quoted, and their views on the crucifix, the Mass, the veneration of saints, and all that Catholics regarded as part of their religious inheritance. But it was only later that their forms of theological thinking were established and their Communion service became part of an English tradition. For the greater part of the reign the Protestant effort was directed to the negative business of uprooting the old worship. And on this account at least the book has some claim to be considered an anthology of religion under Queen Elizabeth.

No comment has been made on the extracts. Here and there I have added definition by means of a date or an identification that is missing in the original. Biographical notes on the principal persons occurring in the book are added after the list of references. In order to provide a setting for the religious scene I have inserted a short chronicle of events. This was particularly necessary for the first years of the reign. In greater part this chronicle is taken from Protestant writers, either contemporaries like Stow or others like Strype who drew on contemporary records. Without such an arrangement the book might have lacked both a framework and an introduction. In one or two instances only have I taken excerpts from the statutes, for these are already available in several collections. It is the impact of the statutes on the life and death of the people that I have been concerned to illustrate.

In a book of this kind it would be mistaken to underline, even in an introduction, the conclusions that emerge. It is for the reader to form his conclusions: but the anthology inevitably illustrates the confusion of the early years, the narrow margin by which the Elizabethan settlement succeeded, and the importance of the Bull, *Regnans in Excelsis*. There are few references to Scotland, which lay outside the Queen's dominions, and to Ireland, which is a subject to be treated separately. Half a dozen extracts only touch the religious situation in Wales.

In three further volumes I hope to continue this work into the Stuart period and beyond, possibly to the year of Catholic emancipation.

I am deeply grateful to Dame Edith Sitwell, who suggested the title of this book, to Mr. Thomas Raworth, my secretary, who patiently typed all the extracts, to Miss Benita Wells, for her assistance in arranging them; to the Rev. Hugh Montgomery, M.C. who proposed a number of titles; and to the authorities of the British Museum for permission to reproduce the decorative woodcuts, taken from sixteenth-century ballads in the Huth and Roxburghe Collections and also from the *Pontificale Romanum* (1520).

Farm Street   P.C.
30 September 1958

First Chronicle, 1558-1559

QUEEN MARY AND PRINCESS ELIZABETH

Queen Mary in her last sickness sent Commissioners to examine her about religion, to whom she answered, 'Is it not possible that the queen will be persuaded I am a Catholic, having so often protested it?' and thereupon did swear and vow that she was a Catholic. This is . . . confirmed by the Duke of Feria's letter to the king, who in this sickness of the queen visited the Lady Elizabeth. He certified him that she did profess the Catholic religion and believed the Real Presence, and was not like to make any alteration for the principal points of religion.

HENRY CLIFFORD, *The Life of Jane Dormer*

DEATH OF QUEEN MARY

i. On November 17, 1558, Queen Mary died; within twenty-two hours of her death, Cardinal Pole. Nearly at the same time died no less than thirteen Bishops, and a great number of the clergy, from quartan fever, then greatly prevalent. A great barrier to the revival of reforming views was thus removed.

ARCHDEACON SINCLAIR, *Memorials of St. Paul's Cathedral*

ii. She left this world . . . the 17th day of November, 1558. That morning hearing Mass, which was celebrated in her chamber, she being at the last point (for no day passed in her life that she heard not Mass) . . . she answered in every part with him that served the Priest; such yet was the quickness of her senses and memory. And when the Priest came to that part to say, *Agnus Dei, qui tollis peccata mundi*, she answered plainly and distinctly to every one, *Miserere nobis, Miserere nobis, Dona nobis pacem.* Afterwards seeming to meditate something with herself, when the Priest took the Sacred Host to consume it, she adored it with her voice and countenance, presently closed her eyes and rendered her blessed soul to God. This the duchess[1] hath related to me, the tears pouring from her eyes, that the last thing which the queen saw in this world was her Saviour and Redeemer in the sacramental species; no doubt to behold Him presently after in His glorious Body in heaven. A blessed and glorious passage. *Anima mea cum anima ejus.*

HENRY CLIFFORD, *The Life of Jane Dormer*

PROCLAMATION OF QUEEN ELIZABETH I

Queen Mary deceased the 17th day of November anno 1558, and about eleven or twelve o'clock aforenoon, the lady Elizabeth was proclaimed queen by divers heralds of arms, trumpets sounding, and many of the chiefest of the nobility present. . . . In the afternoon the bells in all the churches in London rung in token of joy; and at night bonfires were made, and tables set out in the streets, where was plentiful eating and drinking, and making merry. The next day being Friday, it was not thought decent to make any public rejoicings, out of respect, I suppose, to the day, being a fasting-day. But on the next, viz. Saturday, November 19, *Te Deum laudamus* was sung and said in the churches of London.

JOHN STRYPE, *Annals*

PROGRESS FROM THE CHARTERHOUSE TO THE TOWER

All the streets she was to pass, even to the Tower, were now gravelled. And so she rid through Barbican and Cripplegate, and along London-wall unto Bishopsgate, and thence up to Leaden-hall, and so through Grasschurch-street[2] and Fenchurch-street, turning down Mark-lane into Tower-street, and so to the Tower. Before her rode many gentlemen, knights, and nobles; after them came the trumpeters blowing; then all the heralds in array, my lord mayor holding the queen's sceptre, riding with garter: my lord of Pembroke bare the queen's sword. Then came her grace on horseback, apparelled in purple velvet, with a scarf about her neck: the sergeants of arms being about her person. Next after her rode Sir Robert Dudley, (afterwards Earl of Leicester,) master of her horse: and so the guard with halberds.

---

[1] Jane Dormer, Duchess of Feria.   [2] Gracechurch Street.

There was great shooting of guns, the like was never heard before. In certain places stood children, who made speeches to her as she passed; and in other places was singing and playing with regals.[1] Here at the Tower she lay until the 5th of December, which was the eve of St. Nicolas.

JOHN STRYPE, *Annals*

PREPARATIONS FOR THE CORONATION

In Christmas week scaffolds began to be made in divers places of the city, for pageants against the day the queen was to pass through to her coronation, which was to be January 14, and the conduits to be new painted and beautified.

Ibid.

THE PATRON OF MERCERS

On the 8th or 9th of January [1559] the image of St. Thomas, that is, Thomas Becket, the patron of the mercers, that stood over their chapel door, was thrown down and broken.

Ibid.

CORONATION OF QUEEN ELIZABETH I

On Sunday, 15th January [1559], Mass was sung for the coronation in Westminster Abbey, which was decorated with the handsomest and most precious tapestries that were ever seen, they having been purchased by Henry VIII, representing on one side the whole of Genesis, and on the other the Acts of the Apostles, from a design by Raffael d'Urbino; and the chambers were hung with the history of Caesar and Pompey. At one of the sides the buffet was prepared with its raised steps, on which were seen 140 gold and silver drinking cups, besides others which were below for the service. . . .

On her Majesty's arrival at the church, all the bells in London ringing, she ascended the lofty tribune erected between the high altar and the choir, being thus exhibited to the people, of whom it was asked if they wished her to be their crowned Queen? Whereupon they all shouted 'Yes'; and the organs, fifes, trumpets, and drums playing, the bells also ringing, it seemed as if the world were come to an end.

[1] *Regals*: small portable organs.

Descending from the tribune, the Queen placed herself under her royal canopy; and then the choristers commenced the mass, which was sung by the Dean of her Chapel, her Chaplain, the Bishops not having chosen to say mass without elevating the host and consecrating it with English words, as that worthy individual did; the Epistle and Gospel being recited in English after they had been sung in Latin.

Il Schifanoya, a Mantuan resident in London, to the
Castellan of Mantua,
23 January 1559

THE BISHOP OF CARLISLE

The day for opening Parliament now drawing near,[1] it was necessary that the queen should previously be crowned and anointed. The Archbishop refused to do this, having understood that something schismatical was going to be introduced into the ceremony. Many requests for the same object were made to him, but in vain. Others of the Bishops also refused, but at length the Bishop of Carlisle undertook the function, not as a favourer of heresy, but lest the queen should be angry if no one would anoint her, and be more easily moved to overthrow religion. Nor at this time were things so desperate, but that many hoped it might still be possible to turn her from her purpose. The rest of the Bishops assisted at the anointing, until they saw that part of the ancient rite in the celebration of the Mass was changed. For the queen had introduced a novelty, by ordering that the consecrated Host should not be elevated for the adoration of the people.

Dr. Nicolas Sander's Report to Cardinal Morone

INTIMATIONS OF CHANGE

On Wednesday the 25th [January 1559], St. Paul's Day, all the peers of this realm, both temporal and spiritual . . . awaited the arrival of her Majesty at the Church as usual for the mass of the Holy Ghost, which custom was not observed this year, the mass having been sung at an early hour in Westminster Abbey, without elevating the Sacrament, as is done in the Chapel Royal.

The Court having dined rather earlier than usual, her Majesty came to the Abbey, attended by all the gentlemen, both of the Court and of other conditions, and by all the peers in their coronation robes. . . .

[1] This is inexact. Parliament began before the Conferences.

As on her passage the populace knelt, shouting 'God save and maintain thee,' she turned first to one side and then to the other, answering 'Gramercy, good people,' and smiling most sweetly on all of them. . . .

On arriving at Westminster Abbey, the Abbot, robed pontifically, with all his monks in procession, each of them having a lighted torch in his hand, received her as usual, giving her first of all incense and holy water; and when her Majesty saw the monks who accompanied her with the torches, she said, 'Away with those torches, for we see very well'; and her choristers singing the litany in English, she was accompanied to the high altar under her canopy. Thereupon Dr. Cox, a married priest, who has hitherto been beyond the sea, ascended the pulpit and preached the sermon, in which, after saying many things freely against the monks, . . . he then commenced praising her Majesty, saying amongst other things that God had given her this dignity to the end that she might no longer allow or tolerate the past iniquities; exhorting her to destroy the images of the saints, the churches, the monasteries, and all other things dedicated to divine worship; proving by his own arguments, that it is very great impiety and idolatry to endure them; and saying many other things against the Christian religion.

Il Schifanoya to Ottaviano Viyaldino,
30 January 1559

IN THE QUEEN'S CHAPEL

The offices of the Church, and the ministration of the sacraments, continue in all the churches as during Queen Mary's reign, except in the Queen's Chapel, where, at the mass, they do not elevate the sacrament, and the litanies are said in the vulgar English, omitting the invocation of saints, and the prayers for the Pope; which practice is also observed by the incumbents of some few churches, but they are not compelled to do so. The Epistle and Gospel are also read in English, after the litanies.

Letter from London (writer unknown), 6 February 1559

DERISIVE PLAYS

There are yet many frivolous and foolish people who daily invent plays in derision of the Catholic faith, of the Church, of the clergy, and of religion, and, by placards posted at the corners of the streets they invite people to the taverns, to see these representations, taking money from their audience. Others rob the churches by night, break the windows, and steal whatever they can.

Il Schifanoya to Ottaviano Vivaldino,
6 February 1559

THE CHIEF AND THE COMMON PEOPLE

Although they [the Protestants] increase in number, they are not so powerful as the Catholics, who comprise the chief personages of the kingdom, with very great command of their estates, having also many followers; and the greater part of the common people, out of London, in several provinces, are much attached to the Catholic religion.

Venetian Ambassador's despatch, 21 March 1559

SACRILEGE AT ST. MARY-LE-BOW

These accursed preachers, who have come from Germany, do not fail to preach in their own fashion, both in public and in private, in such wise that they persuaded certain rogues forcibly to enter the church of St. Mary-le-Bow, in the middle of Cheapside, and force the shrine of the most Holy Sacrament, breaking the tabernacle, and throwing the most precious consecrated body of Jesus Christ to the ground. They also destroyed the altar and the images . . . breaking everything into a thousand pieces.

Il Schifanoya to Ottaviano Vivaldino,
28 March 1559

THE LAST DIRGE

April the 12th [1559], the corpse of Sir Rice Mansfield, knight, was brought from Clerkenwell unto the Blackfriars, with two heralds, and the rest of the ceremonies usual: twenty-four priests and clerks singing before him, all in Latin. The friars' church was hung with black and coats of arms. The *dirige* was sung both in the parish where he died, and likewise where he was buried. There were carried along with him four banners of saints, and many other banners. The morrow Masses were said in both churches. Afterward was his standard, coat, helmet, target, offered up at the high altar. And all this being performed, the company retired to his place to dinner. This was the common way of funerals of persons of quality in the popish times.

JOHN STRYPE, *Annals*

THE OLD BISHOPS

Queen Mary's bishops and prelates only sat in the house, from whom was to be expected all the opposition that could be against casting off the pope's usurpation, and restoring of true religion. They were indeed few, some being newly dead, as Canterbury, Salisbury, Norwich, Chichester, Rochester, and some others; several absent, who had sent their proxies, as Durham, Peterborough, Ely, (now abroad in an embassy,) Bath and Wells, St. David's.

Ibid.

YORK APPEALS TO THE QUEEN

Meanwhile, in order not to omit any part of his duty, Dr. Heath, Archbishop of York, one of the most prudent and best men living in England, by common consent of his episcopal brethren, went to visit the queen. . . . Being alone with the queen, he is said to have addressed her in this wise. Falling on his knees, he invoked with tears the name of Jesus Christ, and begged that she, being a woman, would refrain from interfering with the sacred mysteries. He said he had passed through every degree of the schools and had reached the highest honours, having been made a bishop under her father Henry and her brother Edward, and Archbishop and Lord Chancellor under Mary, and that from his experience in the course of a long life, to say nothing of his own studies, he had learnt that great mischief accrues to the State from frequent changes, even in the laws relating to the administration of justice. How much less then ought alterations to be attempted in religion, where evidence of antiquity was accounted so great a commendation? Now it was proposed to attempt this, not with any ceremony, but with the highest mysteries of the faith, which mysteries (as the name itself implies) should be reverenced in silence rather than be made the subject of popular debate. To call in question such sacraments, after such a length of time, and to do this in a kingdom in which, by a manifest marvel of God's providence, the late schism was but just removed, how could this fail to be injurious to the queen herself, grievous to the citizens and perilous to the whole kingdom? The most clement of princes, he said, should forgive him his freedom, for he was bound to speak on many accounts. For in a matter which touched her so closely her councillor ought not to be wanting to his prince, or its bishop to the see of York, or to the whole nation the sole archbishop who survived.

'But if (which may God avert) religion should unhappily be overthrown in this kingdom, I warn, I proclaim and declare beforehand, that I will not recede a nail's breadth in the least thing from the decrees of the Catholic Church, and in that quarrel I will resist every suggestion from others, and even from your Majesty, by every means in my power, to the last moment of my life.'

After he had said this, the queen, who had at once bidden him rise, comforted him with many words, and ended by declaring that she would do nothing which should not be approved of by many prudent men (among whom she regarded him as chief) and by the whole nation asembled in parliament.

Dr. Nicolas Sander's Report to Cardinal Morone

THE BILL OF UNIFORMITY

This 26th day, the bill for *uniformity* of common prayer, and service in the church, sent the day before from the commons, was read the first time in the lords' house. April the 27th the same bill was read the second time: April the 28th read the third time, and concluded; the bishops (as before) of York, London, Ely, Wighorn,[1] Landaff, Coventry and Litchfield, Exon, Chester, Carlisle, dissenting. The dissenting temporal lords were nine, viz. the marquis of Winchester, the earl of Shrewsbury, viscount Montague, barons Morly, Stafford, Dudley, Wharton, Rich, and North.

JOHN STRYPE, *Annals*

ST. MARK'S PROCESSION

The 25th [April 1559], St. Mark's day, was a procession in divers parishes of London, and the citizens went with their banners abroad in their respective parishes, singing in Latin the *Kyrie eleison* after the old fashion.

Ibid.

---

[1] *Wighorn:* Worcester.

MASS FOR THE DEAD

Mass for the dead was sung as usual, except that they said the Epistle and Gospel in English, and that they did not elevate the host.

Il Schifanoya to Ottaviano Vivaldino,
25 April 1559

ST. GEORGE'S DAY

The Queen would still wish to some extent to feign to profess the Catholic religion. . . . On St. George's Day [23rd April], the patron saint of the Knights of the Garter, she attended the ceremony. . . . During the procession not a single cross was displayed, and when the Queen asked where the crosses were, she was answered, that being of silver and gold they were deposited in the Tower, and could not be produced. On the morrow mass was sung as usual for the souls of the deceased knights, but the Queen, who was to have been present, altered her mind, and the mass was said without the elevation of the Host.

Paulo Tiepolo to the Doge and Senate,
4 May 1559

ASCENSION DAY

On Ascension Day, while the parish procession of the cathedral church of St. Paul was going round the precincts with a large company of people, a rascally lad-servant of these new printers against the Catholics violently and publicly took the cross out of the hand of the bearer, and struck it on the ground two or three times, breaking it into a thousand pieces. . . . Then he took a small figure from the said cross, and went off, saying, as he showed it to the women, that he was carrying away the Devil's guts (horrible and wicked words). Little less was done in another parish of London by two scoundrels, who, when the procession was about to issue forth from the church, placed themselves at the gate with naked swords in their hands, swearing that the ecclesiastics should not carry such an abomination, and that if they came forth, they should never re-enter.

Il Schifanoya to the Castellan of Mantua,
10 May 1559

THE CLERGY UNMOVED

Meanwhile we, that little flock, who for these last five years, by the blessing of God, have been hidden among you in Germany, are thundering forth in our pulpits, and especially before our queen Elizabeth, that the Roman pontiff is truly antichrist, and that traditions are for the most part mere blasphemies. At length many of the nobility, and vast numbers of the people, began by degrees to return to their senses; but of the clergy none at all. For the whole body remain unmoved.

Richard Cox to Wolfgang Weidner, 20 May 1559

THE NEW HARVESTERS

We are already endeavouring to break down and destroy the popish fences, and to repair under happy auspices the vineyard of the Lord. We are now at work; but the harvest is plenteous and the labourers few: let us ask the Lord to send labourers into his harvest.

Ibid.

THE UNIVERSITIES

Our universities are so depressed and ruined, that at Oxford there are scarcely two individuals who think with us; and even they are so dejected and broken in spirit, that they can do nothing. . . . You would scarcely believe so much desolation could have been effected in so short a time. So that, although it would give me the greatest pleasure, under other circumstances, to see even a dog from Zurich in England, yet I cannot at this time recommend you to send your young men to us, either for a learned or religious education, unless you would have them sent back to you wicked and barbarous.

John Jewel to Henry Bullinger, 22 May 1559

EDMUND BONNER, BISHOP OF LONDON

The Council nevertheless sent twice or thrice to summon the Bishop of London, to give him orders to remove the service of the mass and of the Divine office in that church; but he answered them intrepidly, 'I possess three things, soul, body, and property; of the two [last] you can dispose at your pleasure, but as to the soul God alone can command me.'

Il Schifanoya to the Castellan of Mantua,
30 May 1559

MASSES CEASE AT ST. PAUL'S

June the 11th [1559], being St. Barnabas-day, the apostle's mass ceased, and no mass was said any more at St. Paul's . . . And that afternoon was none of the old evensong there, and so abolished.

JOHN STRYPE, *Annals*

THE FAITH OUTLAWED

We have no longer masses anywhere except in the houses of the French and Spanish Ambassadors. All the friars and monks of every sort have received their passport; some of them have gone away, and will be followed by the others, although the Carthusians do not choose to depart till they are compelled to do so by force, which will soon be used.

Il Schifanoya to Ottaviano Vivaldino,
27 June 1559

CUTHBERT TUNSTALL, BISHOP OF DURHAM

As a young man he brought out an excellent book on arithmetic, and as an old man one on the reality of the Body of Christ in the Sacrament of the Altar. Being at length in decrepitude, he was excused from attending Parliament, nevertheless, he not only came to it with speed,[1] but preached on his journey, in spite of the prohibition of the queen, exhorting his people to remain constant in the Catholic faith. And when this worthy father came into the presence of the queen, he began severely to reprove her, because though a woman she had taken on herself to meddle in religion, and had deprived herself of Bishops the like of whom were hardly to be found in the Christian world. 'I confess,' said she, 'I am grieved for York and Ely.' 'But,' replied Tunstall, 'How can you grieve, when you have the remedy in your

---

[1] Sander is wrong here; Tunstall never came to Parliament. He reached London 20 July 1559, whereas Parliament was dissolved on May 8.

own hands? If you wish to be a Catholic, you can not only have these in your council, but many others besides.' Being then admonished in the council to change his religion, 'Do you think,' he said, 'that for me, who as a priest and a bishop have taught the faith for more than forty years, it would be right, after so many years of study, after such practice and experiences, on the very verge of the grave, to accept a rule of faith from laymen my juniors?' They blushed, and began to tender him the oath of the queen's supremacy. On his refusing it he was deprived of his episcopal dignity, and committed to the charge of the pseudo-bishop of Canterbury, where after a few days the blessed old man expired.

Dr. Nicolas Sander's Report to Cardinal Morone

Two Birthdays

To show the greater contempt for our Blessed Lady, they keep the birthday of queen Elizabeth in the most solemn way on the 7th day of September, which is the eve of the feast of the Mother of God, whose nativity they mark in their calendar in small and black letters, while that of Elizabeth is marked in letters both large and red. And, what is hardly credible, in the church of St. Paul, the chief church of London —whether elsewhere or not is more than I can tell—the praises of Elizabeth are said to be sung at the end of the public prayers, as the Antiphon of our Lady was sung in former days.

NICOLAS SANDER, *Anglican Schism*

Solemn Obsequies for Henry II of France

On Friday, 8 September [1559], when the hearse was solemnly brought into the Church and every man placed, whereas the ancient custom was for one of the heralds to bid aloud the prayer for the soul of the party departed, saying, Pray for the soul of, etc., now there was an alteration of the words. For York herald standing at the upper choir door, bad the prayer (as it used to be called, but now more properly the praise) first in English and after in French, *Benoit soit Eternel*, etc., *Blessed be the King of Eternal Glory, who through his divine mercy hath translated the most High Puissant and Victorious Prince Henry II, late the French King, from this earthly to his heavenly Kingdom.*

JOHN NICHOLS, *The Progresses of Queen Elizabeth*

CONSECRATION OF ANGLICAN BISHOPS

As to your expressing your hopes that our bishops will be consecrated without any superstitious and offensive ceremonies, you mean, I suppose, without oil, without the chrism, without the tonsure. And you are not mistaken; for the sink would indeed have been emptied to no purpose, if we had suffered those dregs to settle at the bottom.

John Jewel to Josiah Simler, 2 November 1559

2

The Bishops' Protest

BISHOP SCOT OF CHESTER

Now to speak of the matter, this I say,[1] that our faith and religion is maintained by no one thing so much as by unity; which unity is continued and maintained in Christ's church, even as concord and good order is maintained in a commonwealth. Wherein we see for civil quietness, there is appointed in every village one constable. And lest there should any variance fall amongst them, there is again in every hundred one head constable, in whom all the other inferiors be as knit in one. . . . The sheriffs likewise be joined in one prince, which prince being deprived of his princely authority, the unity and concord of that realm is dissolved, and every man chooseth himself a new lord. Even so it is in the church of Christ, according to the commandment of St. Paul. There is in every village at the least one priest; in every city, one bishop, in whom all the priests within the diocese be knit in one; in every province one metropolitan, in whom, for the avoiding of controversies, all the bishops of that province be joined; and for unity to be observed amongst the metropolitans, they be likewise joined in one high bishop, called the *pope*, whose authority being taken away, the sheep, as the scripture sayeth, be scattered abroad. For avoiding whereof, our Saviour Christ before his death prayed, that we might be all one, as his father and he be one; which thing cannot be, except we have all one head. And therefore Almighty God said by the prophet Ezechiel, *Suscitabo super eos pastorem unum; I will stir up over them one pastor.* And our Saviour in the gospel likewise saith, *There shall be one pastor and one sheepfold.* Which sentences peradventure some men will say to be applied only to our Saviour Christ, which in very deed I

[1] The speeches of Bishop Scot and Archbishop Heath were made in the House of Lords on 17 March 1559.

must needs grant to be so; yet this I may say, these places be applied to him only, as other like places of scripture be; for it is said in the scripture, that only God is immortal, and by participation with him, all we that be true Christian men be made immortal; only God forgiveth sin, and yet by commission from him, priests hath authority to forgive sin. He is only king, and by commission maketh kings; and likewise he is only priest after the order of Melchisedech, and by commission maketh priests: he of himself, and by none other; all the rest by him, and not of themselves. So he is our only pastor, and by commission hath made other pastors, and especially one to be vicar-general in earth, to govern and rule all his whole flock in unity and concord, and in avoiding of schisms and divisions. And likewise as he sent one Holy Ghost to rule and govern his people inwardly, so he appointed one governor to rule and lead them outwardly.

Which one head governor cannot be applied to any temporal prince: for then either must we needs grant that the church of Christ was not perfect, but rather a manke[1] body without a head by the space of three hundred years and more (for so long was it after the death of our Saviour Christ before there was any one Christian prince in all the world), or else, that Christ appointed an infidel, being no member of his church, to be head thereof; which both be absurdities. Again, that Christ appointed no temporal prince to be head of his church it appeareth, by that we see in divers kingdoms there be divers and sundry princes and rulers, so that there should by that means be many heads of one body, the which were a monstrous thing. Thirdly, that he appointed no temporal prince to be head of the church, it appeareth by the word itself, spoken by our Saviour Christ, *Pasce, Feed*, which he spoke not to Herod, Pilate, nor yet to Tiberius the emperor, but he spoke them unto Peter, saying, *Pasce oves meas*. And where peradventure some man will cavil and argue of the Greek word spoken by our Saviour Christ in that place, which doth signify not only to *feed*, but also to *rule* and *govern*; I answer, that I do not know where that word is applied unto any temporal ruler in the New Testament; and if it so were, yet it doth not prove their intent, for other manifest and plain places of scripture do exclude them from such authority, notwithstanding that the same scripture doth give them very great authority, commanding us to obey the same; declaring withal, that they bear the sword not in vain, nor without cause. But now mark this word *sword*, which princes had before the coming of our Saviour

[1] Manqué.

Christ; and that he did give them any further authority we read not, but left them as he found them. And as he did give them no *spiritual* authority, so I do not see that he did take any temporal rule from them. Wherefore he commanded Peter to put up his sword, because he had given him other instruments to use, wherein was included his authority, that is to say, the keys of the kingdom of heaven, saying, *Tibi dabo claves regni coelorum*. In these keys, and in exercising of the same, consisteth all authority ecclesiastical given by God unto any man. Unto whom he hath not by scripture given these keys, they have no right to it. Wherefore it followeth, that no temporal prince hath any authority ecclesiastical in or over the church of Christ, seeing that the keys were never given unto any of them.

JOHN STRYPE, *Annals*

ARCHBISHOP HEATH OF YORK

Now to the first point, wherein I promised to examine this forsaking and fleeing from the see of Rome. . . . It means we must forsake and flee from the unity of Christ's church, when St. Cyprian, that holy martyr, saith, *That the unity of the church of Christ doth depend upon the unity of Peter's authority*; therefore by our leaping out of Peter's ship, we must needs be overwhelmed with the waters of schism, sects, and divisions, when the same holy martyr St. Cyprian saith, in his third epistle *ad Cornelium*, that all heresies, sects, and schisms do spring only, for that men will not be obedient unto the head bishop of God. . . . And how true this saying of Cyprian is, it is apparent to all men that listeth to see by the example of the Germans,[1] and by the inhabitors of this realm. And this our forsaking and fleeing from the unity of the church of Rome, this inconveniency, amongst many, must consequently follow thereof, that either we must grant the church of Rome to be the church of God, or else a malignant church. If you answer, that it is of God, where Jesus Christ is truly taught, and all his sacraments rightly ministered; how then may we disburden ourselves of our forsaking and fleeing that church, whom we do confess and acknowledge to be of God, when with that church, which is of God, we ought to be one, and not to admit any separation? If you answer that the church of Rome is not of God, but a malignant church; then it will follow that we, the inhabitants of this realm, have not as yet received any benefit of Christ, when we have received no other

[1] *Germaynes* in original.

gospel, no other doctrine, no other faith, no other sacraments, than were sent us from the church of Rome; first, in king Lucius his days, at whose humble epistle the holy martyr Eleutherius, then bishop of Rome, did send unto this realm two monks, Faganus and Damyanus, by whose doctrine we were first put to knowledge of the faith of Jesus Christ, of his gospel, and of his most blessed sacraments. Second, holy St. Gregory, being bishop of Rome, did send into this realm two other holy monks, St. Augustine and Mellitus, to receive the very self same faith of Jesus Christ, that was before planted here in this realm in the days of king Lucius. Third and last, Paulus Tertius, being bishop of Rome, did send the lord Cardinal Pole's good grace, by birth a nobleman of this realm, as his legate, to restore us to the same faith that the blessed martyr Eleutherius and holy St. Gregory had planted here in this realm many years before. If therefore the church of Rome be not of God, but a malignant church, then we have been deceived all this while, when the gospel, the doctrine, faith, and sacraments, must be of the same nature that the church is of, from whence it came. And therefore in relinquishing and forsaking of that church, as a malignant church, the inhabitants of this realm shall be forced to seek further for another gospel of Christ, other doctrine, faith, and sacraments, than we hitherto have received. Which shall breed such a schism and error in faith, as was never in any Christian realm.

JOHN STRYPE, *Annals*

THE SECOND SPEECH OF SCOT

I have heard objected here of late against the supremacy of Peter and his successors divers reasons which appear unto me to have in them small substance. . . . The first doth consist in the wicked and evil lives, as it is alleged, of certain popes of Rome; which, as I do think, were nothing so wicked as they were reported to have been: but let that be, they were so; what then? A man is a man, and, as the scripture sayeth, *Quis est homo, qui non peccet? What man is he that sinneth not?* Again, if that our Saviour Christ had made the like warrant unto Peter and his successors, as concerning their conversation and living, as he did for the continuance and stability of their faith, and had said unto Peter, *Ego rogavi pro te ut non pecces; I have prayed for thee, that thou shalt not sin:* as he said, *Ego rogavi pro te ut non deficiat fides tua; I have prayed that thy faith shall never fail:* then their evil lives had been an argument to have proved, that they had not been the true successors of Peter, neither had had any such authority given unto them of God. But seeing that the warrant was made only for the continuance of their faith, wherein they have hitherto, and do yet most constantly stand, without any mention of their conversation and living, it is in my judgment no proof nor argument against the authority and supremacy of the see of Rome; as we see that the adultery and murder committed by king David, doth not diminish the authority of godly psalms written by him; neither the dissolute living and idolatry of king Solomon is prejudicial to divers books of scripture written by him, nor yet the covetousness of the prophet Balaam did let, in any condition, the virtue and strength of God, the blessing of God sent unto the children of Israel by him, nor the truth of the prophecy, as concerning the coming of our Saviour Christ, by him likewise pronounced: even so the lives of the popes of Rome, were they never so wicked, cannot be prejudicial to the authority given to Peter and his successors by the mouth of our Saviour Christ.

JOHN STRYPE, *Annals*

ABBOT FECKENHAM OF WESTMINSTER

Where in Queen Mary's days your honours do know right well how the people of this realm did live in an order, and would not run before laws; . . . there was no spoiling of churches, pulling down of altars, and most blasphemous treading down the sacrament under their feet, and hanging up the knave of clubs in the place thereof; there [was] no scrinching and cutting off the face and legs of the crucifix, there was no open flesh-eating nor shambles-keeping in the Lent and days prohibited. The subjects of this realm, and especially the nobility and such as were of the honourable council, did in Queen Mary's days know their way into churches and chapels, there begin their day's work with calling for help and grace by humble prayer and serving of God. But now since the coming reign of our sovereign lady Queen Elizabeth, by the only preachers and scaffold-players of this new religion, all things are changed and turned upside down.

Abbot Feckenham in the House of Lords

3

Second Chronicle, 1560-1577

THE NEW SERVICE BOOK

The 24th day of June [1559], being the festival of St. John Baptist, made a great alteration; that being the day appointed by the late parliament, from which the new service-book was to be only used in all the churches throughout England. . . . But the popish priests, that is, the majority of them, utterly refused.

JOHN STRYPE, *Annals*

THE OATH OF SUPREMACY

Soon after St. John Baptist's day [1559], commissioners were sent forth to visit the universities, the dioceses of bishops, cathedral churches, head cities and boroughs, to administer to them the oath of supremacy, and to see the order of parliament for uniformity in the use of the book set on foot, and observed.

Ibid.

CECIL'S PART

There was indeed great opposition now [1560] made to the reformation of religion by many men at court. And had it not been for Cecil's wisdom, diligence, and interest with the queen, in all likelihood it had not proceeded with that roundness it did. This I set down here, as a debt of gratitude owing from this church to his memory.

Ibid.

THE ANGLICAN EPISCOPATE

March 21 [1560], a bill was read now the second time, that the queen shall collate or appoint bishops in bishoprics being vacant, and that without rites and ceremonies.

JOHN STRYPE, *Annals*

THE UNIVERSITIES

In the mean time, our universities, and more especially Oxford, are most sadly deserted; without learning, without lectures, without any regard to religion.

John Jewel to Peter Martyr, 22 May 1560

REFORM AT ST. PAUL'S

That which was further done in this visitation in London was the pulling down and demolishing the roods, and taking away other things used for superstition in the churches. August the 15th [1560], the roods in St. Paul's were pulled down, and the high altar, and other things pertaining, spoiled. The 24th day, being St. Bartholomew's day, in Cheapside, against Ironmonger Lane and St. Thomas of Acres, as the lord mayor came home from Smithfield that fair-day and from the accustomed sports and wrestlings in Clerkenwell, were two great fires made of roods and images of Mary and John and other saints, where they were burnt with great wonder of the people. The 25th day, at St. Botolph's, Billingsgate, the rood and the images of Mary and John, and of the patron of that church, were burnt, with books of superstition: where at the same time a preacher standing within the church wall made a sermon; and while he was preaching, the books were thrown into the fire. They then also took away a cross of wood that stood in the churchyard. September 16, at St. Magnus, at the corner of Fish Street, the rood, and Mary and John were burnt, and several other things of superstition belonging to that church. This visitation did much good, and brought forward the religion very considerably throughout the nation.

JOHN STRYPE, *Annals*

ICONOCLASTS IN LONDON

The 24th [August 1560], being St. Bartholomew's day, and the day before and after, were burnt all the roods of St. Mary and St. John, and many other church goods, with copes, crosses, censers, altar-cloths, rood-cloths, books, banners, banner-staves, wainscot, with much other gear, in London.

JOHN STRYPE, *Annals*

DEPRIVATIONS

June the 12th, 1560, the friars of Greenwich were discharged, and went away.

June the 21st, the bishops of Litchfield and Coventry, of Carlisle, Westchester, and two bishops more, were deprived.

The 25th, the bishops of Lincoln and Winchester were brought to Mr. Haws the sheriff's house in Mincing-lane, and there were deprived. Winchester went to the Tower again; Lincoln was delivered, that is, set at liberty.

The 29th, bishop Bonner was deprived finally by the commissioners.

July the 5th, archbishop Heath and bishop Thirlby were deposed at the lord treasurer's place in St. Augustine's; that is, in Broad-street, where he had a house situate upon part of the Augustine friars.

The 12th, the Black friars in Smithfield went away; as the 4th day, the priests and nuns of Sion did, as also the monks of the Charterhouse; and the abbot of Westminster and his monks were deprived.

The 20th, the bishop of Durham came riding on horseback to London, with about threescore horse; and so to Southwark, unto one Dolman's house, where he remained.

September 29, the bishop of Durham was deprived.

Ibid.

THE DEATH OF THE BISHOPS

The end of the good bishops was this. Dr. Scot, Bishop of Chester, died at Louvain in Exile; Goldwell of St. Asaph at Rome; Pates of Worcester subscribed at the Council of Trent for the clergy of England, and never returned; Dr. Oglethorp of Carlisle, who consecrated the queen, died suddenly and shortly after his deprivation; learned and famous Tunstall died a prisoner at Lambeth; Bourne of Wells was prisoner to Carew, dean of the chapel; Thirlby of Ely was committed to the Tower and afterwards to Lambeth, where he died;

Abbot Fecknam, Bishop Watson, Bishop White and Bishop Bonner
died prisoners; and Prior Shelly in exile. This was the downfall of the
Catholic clergy, a thing incredible to posterity.

HENRY CLIFFORD, *The Life of Jane Dormer, Duchess
of Feria*

CONFUSION OF WORSHIP

Before long the Queen made a visitation . . . and made enquiries
touching the beneficed clergy who on the appointed day had not
adopted in their parishes the parliamentary rites; thereupon many of
these, fearing the loss of their goods and of their benefices, submitted. In the place of those who refused to conform she put ministers
of the new creation. . . . She also compelled the people to frequent the
churches as before, and, according to the act, inflicted a fine of one
shilling on everyone who should be absent on holy days. And by
force or fraud it came to pass that the largest portion of the Catholics
yielded by degrees to their enemies and did not refuse from time to
time publicly to enter the schismatical churches to hear sermons
therein and to receive communion in those conventicles.

At the same time they had Mass said secretly in their own houses by
those very priests who in church publicly celebrated the spurious
liturgy, and sometimes by others who had not defiled themselves with
heresy; and very often in those disastrous times they were on one and
the same day partakers . . . of the Blessed Eucharistic and the Calvinistic supper. Yea, what is still more marvellous and more sad, sometimes the priest saying Mass at home for the sake of those Catholics
whom he knew to be desirous of them, carried about him Hosts
consecrated according to the rite of the Church, with which he
communicated them at the very time in which he was giving to other
Catholics more careless about the faith, the bread prepared for them,
according to the heretical rite.

NICOLAS SANDER, *Anglican Schism*

WYKEHAMISTS KEEP THE FAITH

In Winchester school, when the head master was in prison, and the
schismatical master called them to the schismatical sermons, they were
so far from obeying that they kept away even from the public prayers,
and shut themselves up in their dormitories. When he found fault with
their disobedience, they asked if he wished to destroy the souls of

innocents. Then when the master attempted force, and called in the military commander from the nearest sea-port, about twelve of the boys took to flight; the rest, influenced by the prevalent terror, went most unwillingly to the church. Thus God 'out of the mouths of babes and of sucklings has perfected praise'; for in this persecution there is no order, or sex, or age, that has not nobly defended the Catholic faith.

Dr. Nicolas Sander's Report to Cardinal Morone, 1561

THE POOR OF WINCHESTER

Poor people, not having the means to pay the fines laid upon them because they would not enter the churches nor be present at the profane services of the Protestants, were by the sentence of the Judge long and piteously dragged, stripped of their clothes and cruelly whipped through the streets of Winchester.

NICOLAS SANDER, *Anglican Schism*

DEMOLITION OF THE ABBEY ALTARS

April the 16th [1562] were all the altars in Westminster abbey demolished; and so was the altar in the chapel of Henry VII where that king and king Edward VI lay buried. And all the stones thereof carried where the late queen Mary was buried: [perhaps toward the making of her monument with those religious stones.]

JOHN STRYPE, *Annals*

APPREHENSION OF CATHOLIC KNIGHTS

The 22nd April [1562] Sir Edward Walgrave, knight (who was a great officer in Queen Mary's court, and a privy counsellor,) and his lady, were carried to the Tower. It was for hearing mass, having a popish priest in their house. Others were brought to the Tower at that time; and, as it seems, for the same breach of the law. This knight and his lady had the character of very good alms-folks, in respect, no doubt, of their great liberality to the poor.

Ditto the 23rd, Sir Edward Hastings, Lord of Loughborough, Knight of the Garter, and another great counsellor with the late Queen Mary, was brought unto the Earl of Pembroke's [at Baynard Castle] for the same fault, I presume, in being present at mass.

Ibid.

THE EXTENT OF REFORM

The English common people consist of farmers, shepherds and artisans. The two former are Catholic. Of the others none are schismatics except those who have sedentary occupations, as weavers and shoemakers, and some idle people about the court. The remote parts of the kingdom are still very averse from heresy, as Wales, Devon and Westmorland, Cumberland and Northumberland. As the cities in England are few and small, and as there is no heresy in the country, nor even in the remoter cities, the firm opinion of those capable of judging is that hardly one per cent. of the English people is infected. Hence the Lutherans speak of their followers as 'the little flock.'

Dr. Nicolas Sander's Report to Cardinal Morone

NEW COLLEGE CUSTOMS, 1562

The Wardenship . . . being vacant by the resignation of Dr. Gervase . . . the government of that College continued still on Mr. William Hawle, then sub-warden, who being sufficiently known to be inclined to the Roman Catholic Religion, was not wanting in the vacancy to retrieve certain customs now by the Reformed accounted superstitions. Among such was the singing certain hymns in the College Hall round the fire on Holyday evenings and their Vigils, enduring from the Vigil of All Saints to the evening of the Purification: which custom being before annulled in Dr. Gervase his time, the Psalms of Sternhold and Hopkins were appointed in their places. . . . So it was that when Mr. James Leech, one of the junior fellows, had took the book into his hand, ready to begin one of the said Psalms, Mr. Hawle stepped from his place, offering to snatch the book from him, with an intent, as 'tis said, to cast it into the fire, adding moreover that neither he nor the rest would dance after his pipe. Which action of his and others in vindication of the Roman Catholic religion, gave encouragement and opportunity to the men of that party to take upon them and exercise their authority on the juniors that had not been trained up in that way.

A. WOOD, *History and Antiquities of the University of Oxford*

BURNING OF PAUL'S STEEPLE

June the 4th [1562], Corpus Christi eve, about four or five of the clock, the lightning took St. Paul's church, and entered at one of the holes in the outward part of the steeple, about two yards under the bells, and set the steeple on fire; and never left, till the steeple and bells, and top of the church, were all consumed, unto the arches; burning both wood and lead, and the bells, and the timber under which stood the great organs; and the chapel where the old bishop was buried.

JOHN STRYPE, *Annals*

FOXE'S 'MARTYRS'

About this year [1562] did the laborious John Fox set forth the first edition in English of his great book of Acts and Monuments, in one thick volume. . . . And for some reward of these his labours, the queen, in the sixth of her reign, gratified him with the prebend and parsonage of Shipton in the county of Oxon, belonging to the church of Sarum.

Ibid.

A STRANGE SEQUENCE

In the very same chapter and leaf concerning the severe punishment upon persecutors of God's People, [Foxe] hath committed a most egregious falsity in reporting that one Grimwood, of Higham, in Suffolk, died in a miserable manner, for swearing and bearing false witness against one John Cooper, a carpenter of Watsam in the same county, for which he lost his life. The miserable death of the said Grimwood was, as John Foxe saith thus: 'That when he was in labour, staking up a gosse of corn, having his health, and fearing no peril, suddenly his bowels fell out of his body, and immediately most miserably he died.' Now it so fell out that in the reign of Elizabeth, one Prit (or Prick) became parson of the parish where the said Grimwood dwelt, and preaching against perjury, being not acquainted with his parishioners, cited the said story of Foxe, and it happened that Grimwood being alive, and in the said church, he brought an action upon the case, against the parson, but Judge Anderson, who sat at the Assizes in the county of Suffolk, did adjudge it not maintainable, because it was not spoken maliciously.

ANTHONY WOOD, *Athenae Oxonienses*

THE BLINDNESS OF THE PAPISTS

But the popish party in England, blinded with old prejudices, would not see the present happiness of the English church; but laboured all they could to oppose and disparage and undermine this reformation: which they did partly by their writings privately dispersed. Thus when by lightning, on the 4th day of June this year, the steeple, the bells, and roof of St. Paul's church were burnt, a papist, soon after this accident, spread certain papers about at Westchester concerning it; wherein were these words: 'In St. Paul's church in London, by the decree of the blessed fathers, every night at midnight they had matins; all the forenoon, masses in the church, with other divine service, and continual prayer; and in the steeple, anthems and prayers were had at certain times. But consider how far now contrary the church hath been used: and it is no marvel, if God hath sent down fire to burn part of the church, as a sign of his wrath.'

JOHN STRYPE, *Annals*

PLAGUE IN LONDON

The 8th of August, Turner, commonly called Turner of Boulogne, for that he had been a preacher and minister among the soldiers at Boulogne, and had remained there so long as Boulogne was English, so that he was called the parson of Boulogne, preached at Paul's Cross, where he made two solemn petitions to my Lord Mayor of London. The one was that the dead of the city should be buried out of the city in the field; the other was that no bell should be tolled for them when they lay at the mercy of God departing out of this present life, affirming that the ringing or tolling of the bell did the party departing no good, neither afore their death nor after.

STOW, *Memoranda*

CATHOLICS BLAMED FOR THE PLAGUE

Anno 1564, on the Wednesday, being the 26th of January, was a solemn sermon made at Paul's Cross by Cole, Archdeacon of Essex, whereunto was warned the Lord Mayor of London with the Aldermen and Sheriffs, with also the crafts of the city in their liveries. Wherein the preacher did move the audience to rejoice that the plague was clean ceased, and that God had clean taken it away from us. He said the cause thereof was the superstitious religion of Rome, which was (as he said) so much favoured of the citizens. He gave us warning to beware thereof, calling it a false religion, worse than even the Turks' or the devils' religion. Moreover he said it stood upon four pillars which were rotten posts, that is to say, Images, Purgatory, the Sacrifice of the Mass, and Transubstantiation, against the which he did inveigh, and said that if we did not beware of false religion, all though God had clean taken away the plague, he would send a worse upon us, that is to say, fire and sword, which should slay the children at their mothers' breasts, the wives should be slain from their husbands, the husbands from their wives, and one neighbour should slay another to have his goods. But to conclude withal, he persuaded all states of the city to rejoice for that the plague was ceased, for now, said he, shall your mayor ride honourably accompanied with the aldermen and other their assistants the worshipful of the city; now should the lawyers be frequented and set awork, now shall the schools be opened, now should the merchants have free traffic into all countries and nations, whereas before all nations did abhor them, now shall you artificers rejoice, for you shall now sell your wares abundantly, and now shall you be set awork even thoroughly, whereas of long time you have had no work but lived in great penury. Now, O you artificers, shall you take money abundantly. O you prentices rejoice, for now shall you have your bellies full of meat, which of long time have been starved through your masters' scarcity.

STOW, *Memoranda*

CECIL'S FAST

The Protestants are forced also somehow or other, even now, to keep the fast formerly observed, though they do it very much against their will, for they complain loudly that the ordering of matters of this sort is contrary to Scripture and the liberty of the gospel. But the Queen, for the relief of their consciences herein, makes a proclamation at the beginning of Lent every year, that the fast is ordered to be kept not for the sake of religion, penance, or devotion, but simply for the good of the state; in order by the greater consumption of fish to furnish the fishermen, a large class of men in the island, with a livelihood, and to have during the rest of the year a more abundant supply of fleshmeat, and in particular for the necessary provisioning of the fleet.

Not deeming the abstinence of Friday and Saturday to be a sufficient support of the navy, the queen instituted a fast to be kept every Wednesday,[1] now commonly known as Cecil's fast, because it is regarded as his invention. Though the people, who despise these public fasts, are liable to heavy fines, very few observe them, and certainly not the bishops and the rest of the clergy, who are very much ashamed to find themselves under the law of fasting. But the Queen herself easily grants a dispensation in writing, upon cause assigned, to the lords and others, and the archbishop of Canterbury also on the payment of fees.

NICOLAS SANDER, *Anglican Schism*

THE VICARS OF RIPON MINSTER

The vicars on a night took the keys of the church from one John Day the sacristan there, and that night all the images and other trumpery were conveyed forth of the said church and bestowed by the said vicars where it is not knowen.

From a Visitation Book of Thomas Young,
Archbishop of York, 29 October 1567

DIOCESE OF CHICHESTER, 1569

In some places because the Rood was taken away, they painted in that place a cross with chalk, and because that was washed away with painting and the number of crosses standing at graves in the churchyard taken also away, they have since made crosses on the church walls within and without, and upon the pulpit and Communion Table in despite of the preacher. This was done of very late in Patching since I preached there. . . . In many places they keep their chalices, looking for to have Mass again. . . . Certain parishes keep Dr. Sander's book called *The Rock of the Church*, wherein he doth not account the bishops now to be any bishops—as Sir David Spencer, parson of Clapham, and Mr. King, parson of Stanmer—Many bring to church the old Popish Latin primers and use [them] all the time when the lessons are being read in the time of the Litany. In some places the rood lofts still stand, and those taken down still lie in the churches

[1] 5 Eliz., c.5.

ready to be put up again. Some old folks and women used to have beads in the churches, but these I took away from them, but they have some yet at home in their houses.

Archbishop Parker's report on the Diocese of Chichester

PLAIN SPEAKING

There be not ten gentlemen in all this country that do favour and allow of her Majesty's proceedings in the cause of religion; and the common people be altogether blinded with the old Popish doctrine.

Sir Ralph Sadler, Chancellor of the Duchy of Lancaster,
to Sir William Cecil, 6 December 1569

MONUMENTS OF IDOLATRY

As for our churches themselves, bells and times of morning and evening prayer remain as in times past, saving that all images, shrines, tabernacles, rood-lofts, and monuments of idolatry are removed, taken down, and defaced, only the stories in glass windows excepted, which, for want of sufficient store of new stuff, and by reason of extreme charge that should grow by the alteration of the same into white panes throughout the realm, are not altogether abolished in most places at once, but by little and little suffered to decay, that white glass may be provided and set up in their rooms.

WILLIAM HARRISON, *A Description of England*

THE QUEEN EXCOMMUNICATED

His Holiness [Pius V] has taken this step without communicating with me in any way, which certainly has surprised me, because my knowledge of English affairs is such that I believe I could give a better opinion on them and the course that ought to have been adopted . . . than anyone else.

Since, however, His Holiness allowed himself to be carried away by his zeal, he no doubt thought that what he did was the only thing requisite for all to turn out as he wished, and if such were the case, I, of all the faithful sons of the Holy See, would rejoice the most. But I fear that not only this will not be the case, but that this sudden and unexpected step will exacerbate things there and drive the Queen and her friends the more to oppress and persecute the few good Catholics remaining in England.

> *Philip II of Spain to Geran de Spes concerning the Bull,*
> *Regnans in Excelsis (1570)*

The Origin of the Name Recusant

The name of Recusant began then [1570], and first to be known in the world, and till then the Catholics were no more than Church Papists; but were commanded by the Pope's express letters to appear, and forbear church-going, as they tender their holy Father, and the holy Catholic Church their Mother: so that it seems the Pope had then his aims to take a true muster of his children; but the Queen had the greater advantage, for she likewise took tale of her apostate subjects, their strength, and how many they were that had given up their names unto Baal.

> SIR ROBERT NAUNTON, *Fragmenta Regalia*

Twelve Years Later

Therefore Christ gave us warning to beware of them that come in sheep's clothing, but inwardly are ravening wolves. . . . So (right reverend Father)[1] in these our days we have many, and specially of the clergy, [who] . . . draw nigh with tongue and pen unto us, but their hearts are at Rome. A number of them have gospel talk, but yet a Romish faith; an English Face, but Spanish hearts. . . . For they think now that if they subscribe, observe the order of service and wear a silk gown, a square cap, a cope and a surplice . . . they are good Protestants: yet all this while they run hugger mugger, a-whispering in corners, saying to simple people, 'Believe not this new doctrine. It is naught; it will not endure. Although I use order among them outwardly, my heart and profession is from them, agreeing with the mother Church of Rome. No, no (they say) we do not preach, nor yet teach openly. We read their new devised homilies for a colour, to satisfy the time for a season.'

> JOHN NORTHBROOK, *A Brief and Pithy Sum of the Christian Faith*
> *(1571)*

---

[1] Bishop Gilbert of Bath and Wells.

FURTHER MEASURES OF SUPPRESSION

No person or persons whatsoever shall wear beads, or pray, either in Latin or in English, upon beads, or knots, or any other like superstitious thing; nor shall pray upon any popish Latin or English Primer, or other like book, nor shall burn any candles in the church superstitiously upon the feast of the Purification of the Virgin Mary, commonly called Candlemas Day; nor shall resort to any popish priest for shrift or auricular confession in Lent, or at any other time; nor shall worship any cross or any image or picture upon the same, nor give any reverence thereunto, nor superstitiously shall make upon themselves the sign of the cross when they first enter into any church to pray, nor shall say *De profundis* for the dead, or rest at any cross in carrying any corpse to burying, nor shall leave any little crosses of wood there.

Archbishop Grindal's Injunctions to the Laity, 1571

CHURCHWARDENS' TASK

The churchwardens shall see that in their churches and chapels all altars be utterly taken down, and clear removed even unto the foundation, and the place where they stood paved, and the wall whereunto they joined whited over, and made uniform with the rest, so as no breach or rupture appear. And that the altar-stones be broken, defaced, and bestowed to some common use. And that the rood-lofts be taken down and altered. . . . And that all the boards, beams, and other stuff of the rood-lofts be sold by the churchwardens to the use of the church, so as no part thereof be kept and observed.

Ibid.

MR. AGLIONBY ADVOCATES TOLERATION

i. And for the other matter, concerning the receiving of the Communion, he argued that it was not convenient to enforce consciences; and for that purpose he showed the authority of doctors, which he vouchsafed without quoting the place or sentence. He said also it was the opinion of Fathers and learned men of this land, and therefore wished they might be consulted with. . . .

Matters of conscience did not concern the law-makers, neither were they to regard the error, curiosity or stiff-neckedness of the evil, ignorant or froward persons. For be it they did proceed orderly to the discharge of their own consciences, let them care for the rest whom it behoveth.

Edward Aglionby in the House of Commons, 11 April 1571

ii. Mr. Aglionby argued that there should be no human positive law to enforce conscience, which is not discernible in this world. . . . The conscience of man is eternal, invisible and not in the power of the greatest monarchy in the world, in any limits to be straitened, in any bounds to be contained, nor with any policy of man, if once decayed, to be again raised. He showed that neither Jew nor Turk do require more than . . . a convenient silence, as not to dislike what is publicly professed; but to enforce any man to do the act, which may tend to the discovery of his conscience, is never found. He showed out of St. Paul that we must not do ill that good may grow thereby; we must not take from him that is his, to the end thereby to make him do what is not in his power; to be fit for so great a mystery, God above of his free gift may make a man. . . .

He said there was no example in the primitive Church to prove a commandment for coming to the Communion, but an exhortation; he said St. Ambrose did excommunicate Theodosius and forbid him to come to the Communion, because he was an evil man. And for us to will and command men to come because they are wicked men, it is too strange for enforcement and without precedent.

Ibid., 21 April 1571

THE PORTUGAL EMBASSY, 1572

The Portugal ambassador, under pretence of having mass said privately in his family, by his privilege as ambassador, had now a good while entertained several mass-mongers in his house in Tower Street; which was now discovered, and a warrant was sent forth, to attach those of the queen's subjects that were present there against her laws. The bishop of London understanding that this ambassador had fostered these persons long time in his house, contrary to our laws, he and the rest of the commissioners for ecclesiastical matters required the sheriff of London, Mr. Pipe, to go and apprehend such as he should find there 'committing idolatry,' as the bishop of London expressed it in his letter to the lord treasurer: which warrant the said sheriff executed the 1st of March; 'and many he saw there ready to worship the calf.' He apprehended (the rest escaping by the ambassador's means) four students at the law, most of them Irish. These the bishops committed to the Fleet, until the lords' further pleasure were known. Francis Gerald (for that was the Portugal ambassador's name) offered to shoot dags (which we call pistols nowadays), and to smite with his dagger, and to kill, in his rage. There was found the altar prepared, the chalice of their bread-god, and a great many English hid in the house, that were minded to hear mass. The bishop gave commission to Norris the messenger to apprehend the Portugal and the mass-priest: but the messenger returned answer, that the Portugal was at the court, to complain. He cunningly told the tale first, and made himself plaintiff: so that the queen was somewhat offended with these proceedings against the ambassador.

JOHN STRYPE, *Annals*

THE QUEEN'S COMMISSIONERS AT OXFORD

Whereas by credible report we are informed that as yet there are remaining in your College divers monuments of superstition undefaced . . . [we] will and command you forthwith upon the sight hereof utterly to deface, or cause to be defaced, so that they may not hereafter serve to any superstitious purpose, all copes, vestments, albs, missals, books, crosses and such other idolatrous and superstitious monuments whatsoever, and within eight days after the receipt hereof to bring true certificate of their whole doing herein to us or our colleagues, whereof fail you not as you will answer to the contrary at your peril.

From Magdalen College in Oxford, 5 May 1573.

Laur. Humfrey.
Herbert Westfaling.
Jo. Kennall.
Wm. Cole.[1]

The Queen's Commissioners to the Fellows of Magdalen

DIOCESAN ENQUIRY

First all and every antiphoners, mass-books, grailes, portesses, processionals, manuals, legendaries, and all other books of late belonging

[1] Humfrey was President of Magdalen; Westfaling, Canon of Christ Church and afterwards Bishop of Hereford; Kennall, Canon of Christ Church, Archdeacon of Oxford, etc.; and Cole, President of Corpus Christi, Oxford.

to your church or chapel, which served for the superstitious Latin service, be utterly defaced, rent, and abolished; and if they be not, through whose default that is, and in whose keeping they remain? And whether all vestments, albs, tunicles, stoles, phanons,[1] pyxes, paxes, handbells, sacringbells, censers, chrismatories, crosses, candlesticks, holy-water-stocks, images, and such other relics and monuments of superstition and idolatry be utterly defaced, broken, and destroyed; and if not, where, and in whose custody they remain?

Whether your parson, vicar, curate, or minister, do wear any cope in your parish church or chapel, or minister the holy Communion in any chalice heretofore used at mass, or in any profane cup or glass, or use at the ministration thereof any gestures, rites, or ceremonies, not appointed by the book of Common Prayer, as crossing or breathing over the sacramental bread and wine, or shewing the same to the people to be worshipped and adored, or any such like, or use any oil and chrism, tapers, spattle,[2] or any other popish ceremony in the ministration of the sacrament of Baptism?

Whether any holy days or fasting days heretofore abrogated, or not appointed to be used as holy days or fasting days by the new kalendar of the book of Common Prayer, be either proclaimed and bidden by your parson, vicar, or curate, or be superstitiously observed by any of your parish, and what be their names that so do observe the same; and whether there be any ringing or tolling of bells to call the people together used in any of those days, more or otherwise than commonly is used upon other days that be kept as work days?

Whether, when any man or woman in passing out of this life, the bell to be tolled to move the people to pray for the sick person, especially in all places where the sick person dwelleth near unto the church; and whether, after the time of his or her passing out of this world, there be any more ringing but one short peal before the burial, and another short peal after the burial, without any other superfluous or superstitious ringing: and whether on All Saints' day after Evening Prayer there be any ringing at all, or any other superstitious ceremony used, tending to the maintenance of popish purgatory, or of prayer for the dead, and who they be that use the same; and whether there be any ringing or knolling of bells on Sundays or holy days between Morning Prayer and the Litany, or in any time of the Common Prayer, reading of the Homilies, or of preaching, except one bell in convenient time to

---

[1] *phanon:* the maniple used by the priest at Mass.   [2] *spattle:* spittle.

be rung or tolled before the sermon; or any other ringing used upon Saints' eves or festival days, saving to Common Prayer, and that without excess; and who doth ring or knoll otherwise?

Archbishop Grindal's Visitation, 1576

RECUSANTS IN YORKSHIRE

I have already laboured what I can since my coming hither, as well by persuasion as by execution of discipline, to reform them; but little have I prevailed, for a more stiff necked, wilful or obstinate people did I never know or hear of: doubtless they are reconciled to Rome and sworn to the Pope. . . . To some I have offered lodging and diet in my house, that I might have conference with them for their conformity; but they chose rather to go to prison.

Edwin Sandys, Archbishop of York to the Privy Council,
28 October 1577

4

The Old Priests

They [the clergy of the lower house of convocation] exhibited their articles conceived in the former session, which were read, and the bishops promised to present them to the upper house of parliament the next day. The articles were these:

I. That in the sacrament of the altar, by virtue of the words of Christ, duly spoken by the priest, is present *realiter*, under the kinds of bread and wine, the natural body of Christ, conceived of the virgin Mary, and also his natural blood.

II. That after the consecration there remains not the substance of bread and wine, nor any other substance but the substance of God and man.

III. That in the mass is offered the true body of Christ, and his true blood, a propitiatory sacrifice for the living and dead.

IV. That to Peter the apostle, and his lawful successors in the apostolic see, as Christ's vicars, is given the supreme power of feeding and ruling the church of Christ militant, and confirming their brethren.

V. That the authority of handling and defining concerning the things belonging to faith, sacraments, and discipline ecclesiastical, hath hitherto ever belonged, and ought to belong only to the pastors of the church; whom the Holy Ghost for this purpose hath set in the church; and not to laymen.

JOHN STRYPE, *Annals*

PRIESTS OPPOSE THE NEW PRAYER-BOOK, 1559

i. Now also, but especially a while after, when the parliament came together and by their authority a common form of prayers in the vulgar tongue was like to be brought in, instead of the old mass, the popish priests that could preach bestirred themselves everywhere in the churches, to prejudice the people against receiving it. Thus in February, John Murren, chaplain to the bishop of London and parson of Ludgate, was summoned before the lords of the council for preaching contrary to the queen's proclamation, and expounding the gospel in the church: which, when he was before them, he could not well deny. Wherefore he was committed to the Fleet, there to be kept without conference with any, until he were examined.

JOHN STRYPE, *Annals*

ii. The popish priests among us are daily relinquishing their ministry, lest, as they say, they should be compelled to give their sanction to heresies. Our enemies are many and mighty, but the Lord is mightier than all of them.

John Cox to Peter Martyr (after 21 December 1559)

SECRET ASSEMBLIES

i. Now that religion is everywhere changed, the mass-priests absent themselves altogether from public worship, as if it were the greatest impiety to have any thing in common with the people of God. But the fury of these wretches is so great that nothing can exceed it.

John Jewel to Peter Martyr, 1 August 1559

ii. There is everywhere an immense number of papists, though for the most part concealed: they have been quiet hitherto, except that they are cherishing their errors in their secret assemblies, and willingly shut their ears against the hearing of the word.

John Cox to Peter Martyr, 5 August 1562

iii. There be certain thought to have Masses in their houses, which come very seldom or not at all to church, which never received the Communion since the Queen Majesty's reign openly in the church, which keep, as it were, schools in their houses of Popery, deriding and mocking this religion and the Ministers thereof, which be a marvellous

stumbling to the Queen Majesty's loving subjects in this country. . . .
I confess that I am not able to reform these, except I should be mightily
backed by your honourable authority.

John Scory, Bishop of Hereford, to the Privy Council, 1564

A PRIEST AT BAY

In the year of our Lord 1562, the 8th day of September, was a
priest . . . taken by . . . my Lord of Ely's men for saying of Mass in
Fetter Lane at my Lady Cary's house, which priest was violently taken
and led, as ten times worse than a traitor, through Holborn, Newgate
market, and Cheapside to the Counter at the stocks called the Poultry,
with all his ornaments on him as he was ravished from Mass, with his
Mass-book and his porttoys[1] borne before him, and the chalice with the
pax[2] and all other things, as much as might make rude people to wonder
upon him. And the number of people was exceeding great that
followed him, mocking, deriding, cursing, and wishing evil to him,
as some to have set him on the pillory, some to have him hanged,
some hanged and quartered, some to have him burnt, some to have
him torn in pieces and all his favourers, with as much violence as the
devil could invent, and much more than I can write, but well was he or
she that could get a pluck at him or give him a thump with their fist
or spit in his face, and to scorn him with saying, *Ora pro nobis, Sancta
Maria* because it was our Lady's day of her nativity (but not kept holy)
and also they sang *Dominus vobiscum* and such like.

STOW, *Memoranda*

STRAGGLING DOCTORS

The straggling doctors and priests who have liberty to stray at their
pleasure in this realm do much hurt secretly and in corners: therefore
it were good that they might be called before the High Commission
and to show their conformity in religion by subscribing or open
recantation or else to be restrained from their liberty.

*Nicholas Bullingham, Bishop of Lincoln, to the Privy Council,
6 November 1564*

---

[1] A breviary.

[2] A tablet with a representation of the Crucifixion which was kissed by the officiating
priests and congregation at Mass.

HEREFORD CATHEDRAL, 1564

i. Besides mine own knowledge, Mr. John Ellis, dean of the said church, hath certified to me as followeth: that all the canons residentiary (except Jones, *qui dicit et non facit*, which is rash, hasty and indiscreet) are but dissemblers and rank Papists. And these have the rule of the church and of all the ministries and offices of the same and are neither subject to the ordinary jurisdiction, nor of the dean nor of the bishop. . . . So that they may now do as they list without controlment. They neither observe the Queen Majesty's injunctions given unto them in her Highness's visitation nor the Archbishop of Canterbury's injunctions given them in his visitation nor yet the injunctions of the Queen's Majesty's High Commissioners. . . . The Communion was not ministered in the Cathedral Church since Easter (as I am informed). The canons will neither preach, read homilies, nor minister the Holy Communion, nor do anything to commend, beautify or set forward this religion, but mutter against it, receive and maintain the enemies of religion. So that this church, which should be the light of all the diocese, is very darkness and an example of contempt of true religion, whom the city and country about follow apace.

John Scory, Bishop of Hereford, to the Privy Council,
1564

ii. Because I could not get any of the Canons that dwell in Hereford to read the first homily according to the . . . Order, I sent into Shropshire to one Parson Normecote, a Canon of that church of Hereford to come and read an homily according to the said Order: who did it and that very well, whereupon I thought that Mr. Luson[1] and the rest would have followed, but they did not nor will, except they be forced by authority.

Ibid.

RECOMMENDATIONS FOR REFORM

1. If Popish and perverse priests, which have forsaken the ministry and yet live in corners, are kept in gentlemen's houses and had in great estimation with the people, where they marvellously pervert the

[1] William Luson, Prebendary of Hereford.

simple and blaspheme the truth, were restrained of their liberty and put to the oath for the Queen Majesty's Supremacy;

2. If the Ministers of God's word were all compelled to consent in one truth and preach one doctrine, faithfully and prudently with all diligence to do their office and to live in good order,

I would not doubt but God should have his glory, this realm should flourish, the prince·live in great comfort and the people in good order and much quietness.

Edwin Sandys, Bishop of Worcester, to the Privy Council,
27 October 1564

Fr. Simon Southern

Being demanded whether he hath said Mass since her Majesty's coming to the Crown and since it hath been forbidden by the law, he answereth of his credit and honesty he hath not said any Mass since that time. And being demanded whether he hath shriven any or no, he sayeth that he hath shriven and absolved divers after the old manner when they have been sick.

The Examination of Fr. Simon Southern before the Bishop of
Winchester, 24 December 1582

Fr. John Pearson

John Pearson, a venerable old priest, was imprisoned for many years at Durham, for refusing to attend heretical services. After enduring with great patience the close confinement of an underground dungeon, he was removed to another far worse, and thrust among a set of thieves. This was done at a time when he was suffering from a burning fever. Here, as if the very filthiness of the place with its accompaniments were not torture enough to a refined man of advanced age, the thieves, out of mere malice, became his tormentors. For while he was taking his meals, they, like so many dogs utterly devoid of all sense of shame, did not hesitate, before his face, to yield to the necessities of nature, and thus by their open filthiness, caused him such nausea that he could not retain the poor nourishment he had taken. By this more than savage treatment received at the hands of these pitiless wretches, he was, before many days were passed, worn out, and so passed to a better life.

GRENE, *Collections*

Fr. John Acrige

John Acrige, priest, was born and brought up at Richmond, who, having good knowledge in music and competent understanding in the Latin tongue, was curate first at Wensley, under Parson Hyndmers, afterwards at a parsonage under Doctor Daykins, and last of all he did serve at Richmond, unto the rising of the earls, at which time he, repenting for his so long continuance in schism and heresy, did seek for reconciliation in God's Church again, which being obtained he did continue a firm member of the same Church until his death, passing abroad among Catholics as a poor pilgrim, until such time as he was apprehended at his sisters' in Richmond, where, being tried by an alderman, his kinsman, of the same town, and others, if he could [be] brought into schism or his former kind of dissimulation, he utterly detesting the same, and their persecution therein, was carried from thence to York, where, being brought to Mr. Hutton, he was asked if he was a priest. He answered, 'Yea, he thanked God, and that he thought that he also was a priest.' Mr. Hutton, like a heretic, made answer that he was a priest, but not a greased priest. The good simple man, knowing that he did speak that in a contempt of the unction of priests, said he was none of all them. He was committed to the Castle of York to be put in irons, being a priest, impotent and weak man, . . . where, and afterwards in the North Block-house and Castle of Hull, he did remain in prison until his death, which was in the year of our Lord 1585, March 2, at six o'clock after dinner. He did give all that he had unto Catholics, and wished to die rather in prison than in any other place.

GRENE, *Collections*

Father Moses

There is one Father Moses, sometime a friar in Chichester, and he runneth about from one gentleman's house to another . . . bearing a Popish Latin primer about with him, with Dirge and the Litany praying to dead saints, and in certain houses he maintained the popish doctrine of Purgatory and the praying to dead saints.

Archbishop Parker's report on the Diocese of Chichester (1569)

Recusants in Lancashire

On all hands the people fall from religion, revolt to popery, refuse to come at church; the wicked popish priests reconcile them to the Church of Rome, and cause them to abjure this Christ's religion and that openly and unchecked since Felton set up the excommunication. In some houses of great men . . . no service hath been said in the English tongue.

Richard Barnes to Sir William Cecil, 27 October 1570

MASSING ATTIRE

A note of such Massing attire as were found with . . . Sir James Stonnes at the time of his apprehension and acknowledged to be his own:

An alb; a girdle of thread; a stole; a Corpus and a Corpus case; a supaltar; three little pewter boxes in a leather case for oil and chrism; one cruet; a surplice or amice; a vestment; a flannel; a Chalice of tin and a cover; two little pewter bottles for wine; two little boxes for singing bread[1]; three crucifixes; one Agnus Dei[2]; a Porthowse with the Pope's name in the Calendar in many places; a piece of an old primer in parchment; a piece of an old book of sermons; an old Mass book.

Examination of a priest, Sir James Stonnes, ordained in
the reign of Henry VIII, and arrested in November 1585

[1] Altar breads.
[2] A disc of wax impressed with a cross and the figure of a lamb and blessed by the Pope. It was usually worn round the neck. In origin it goes back probably to the fifth century and symbolises Christ the Lamb of the New Testament.

5

The Image of Christ

BURNING OF CRUCIFIXES, 1560

Not long from the beginning of the queen's entrance upon her government, crucifixes were so distasteful to the people, that they brought many of them into Smithfield, and there broke them to pieces and burnt them.

JOHN STRYPE, *Annals*

UNGODLY DIGRESSION

When one of her chaplains, Mr. Alexander Nowell, dean of St. Paul's, had spoken less reverently in a sermon preached before her of the sign of the Cross, she called aloud to him from her closet[1] window, commanding him to retire from that ungodly digression and return unto his text.

HEYLYN, *History of the Reformation*

THE IMAGE OF THE CROSS

We are constrained, to our great distress of mind, to tolerate in our churches the image of the Cross and Him who was crucified: the Lord must be entreated that this stumbling-block may at length be removed.

Richard Cox, Bishop of Ely, to Peter Martyr
(after 21 December 1559)

THE CROSS IN THE QUEEN'S CHAPEL

i. Religion among us is in the same state which I have often described

[1] The Queen's private chamber for counsel or household devotions.

to you before. The doctrine is every where most pure; but as to
ceremonies and maskings, there is a little too much foolery. That little
silver cross, of ill-omened origin, still maintains its place in the queen's
chapel. Wretched me! this thing will soon be drawn into a precedent.
There was at one time some hope of its being removed; and we all of
us diligently exerted ourselves, and still continue to do, that it might
be so. But as far as I can perceive, it is now a hopeless case. Such is the
obstinacy of some minds.

John Jewel to Peter Martyr, 16 November 1559

ii. After I had written this, lo! good news was brought me, namely,
that the crucifix and candlesticks in the queen's chapel are broken in
pieces, and, as some one has brought word, reduced to ashes. A good
riddance to such a cross as that! It has continued there too long already,
to the great grief of the godly, and the cherishing of I know not what
expectations in the papists.

John Parkhurst, Bishop of Norwich, to Henry Bullinger,
20 August 1562

iii. I wrote you word that the cross, wax candles, and candlesticks
had been removed from the queen's Chapel; but they were shortly
after brought back again to the great grief of the godly. The candles
heretofore were lighted every day, but now not at all. The lukewarm-
ness of some persons very much retards the progress of the gospel.

Ibid., 26 April 1563

AT HAMPTON BISHOP

In Hampton Bishop in Herefordshire a young man searching his
father's house, happened to find a great crucifix, whereat the blasphemous fellow swore, saying, 'What, standeth thou here idle?'
Whereupon he took the crucifix and hanged it up upon a pear-tree to
fright away the birds, the pears being now almost ripe. The pear-tree
was the night following strucken half dead, the one side being clean
withered away, and the other side bearing fruit withered and of a sour
and saltish taste. This tree stood many years after, one half withered,
the other half bearing the most unsavoury fruit, . . . Mr. John Scuda-
more and Mr. John Harper Esquires did see this. Besides it is known
to the whole shire.

GRENE, *Collections*

THE SIGN OF THE CROSS

A poor man was presented at Durham because he had his shirt marked with a cross, and was amerced and enforced to pay 2s. for the same.

An Ancient Editor's Note Book

UPON THE ENSIGNS OF CHRIST'S CRUCIFYING

O sweet and bitter monuments of pain,
Bitter to Christ who all the pain endured,
But sweet to me, whose Death my life procured,
How shall I full express, such loss, such gain?
My tongue shall be my pen, mine eyes shall rain
Tears for my ink, the Cross where I was cured
Shall be my book, where having all abjured
And calling heavens to record in that plain
Thus plainly will I write: *no sin like mine.*
When I have done, do thou Jesus divine
Take up the tart sponge of thy Passion
And blot it forth: then be thy spirit the quill,
Thy blood the ink, and with compassion
Write thus upon my soul: *thy Jesu still.*

WILLIAM ALABASTER

CROSS AND CROWN

21 November 1581. Alexander Briant, for shaving the crown of his head that he might appear at his trial in the character of a priest, and for making a wooden cross, which he carried openly to the courts, was compelled for two days to wear the iron shackles.

EDWARD RISHTON, *Tower Journal*

VILLAINOUS TYRANNY

One of the sheriff's men standing in the cart with M. Filby, said unto him, 'What hast thou there in thy handkerchief?' And therewithal taking the handkerchief from him found a little cross of wood within it, which he holding up in his hands said, 'O what a villainous traitor is this, that hath a cross,' divers times repeating it, and divers of the people saying the same. Whereunto M. Filby answered nothing.

WILLIAM ALLEN, *Brief History*

6

Wales, Ireland and Scotland

'MASS-SAYERS' IN THE WELSH MARCHES

The Papists were busy in these parts: Mass was said in the house of one Edwards, beads for pardon of sins were distributed about to the people, and *Agnus Dei's*; baptized persons were christened over again; and some buried secretly by night, to avoid the office of burial, with other matters, wherein the Papists exercised their superstitions: which were discovered to him and the Council there in the month of January. The particulars of their dealings he sent to the Privy Council in a memorial, which was as followeth.

At Eyton, 15 January, 1578. *Memorandum*, That Thomas Laurence, head schoolmaster of Salop, and Richard Atkys, a third schoolmaster there, came before me George Bromley,[1] and uttered their knowledge concerning certain disorders committed in the house of John Edwards, of Thirsk, in the county of Denbigh, and elsewhere by him and others resorting to his house. In short, the sum of the articles were, 'That the Lady Throgmorton, wife of Mr. Justice Throgmorton, and others, heard Mass in that house. That those that said Mass were five, and so apparelled that they could not be known. That one Hughes was the chief sayer of Mass: and that he came from beyond seas: that he taught the son of Sir John Throgmorton. That these Priests delivered to them that heard Mass certain beads, called *pardon-beads*. And that they ministered a corporal oath to such as they could draw to their religion and hearing of their Mass. That they christened children anew; and swore their parents that they should not come to church. That they buried children and other persons by night, because they would not admit nor receive the service now used. That upon St. Winifrid's

---

[1] A lawyer, and one of the Council for the Marches of Wales.

day, Mrs. Edwards went to Holywell by night, and there heard Mass in the night season. That they carried thither with them by night, in mails and cloak-bags, all things pertaining to the saying of Mass. And that at these Mass-sayings their audience used to receive holy water, and come to confession.'

So that these parts of Wales were very much warped towards Popery, and the Popish Mass and ceremonies took place among them, and many converts were made by the Popish Priests that sheltered themselves there, by the favour of connivance of the magistrates thereabouts inhabiting; until the Vice-President now began to stir vigorously against this important matter, wherein the state of religion was so much concerned. He sought therefore, from the Council, for a special commission to him and some of the Welsh Bishops, exclusive of others, to be his assistants; not trusting perhaps to some of the gentlemen, nor to the Justices themselves.

JOHN STRYPE, *Life and Acts of Archbishop Whitgift*

INDECENT VIGILS AND WATCHES

Right honorable, I thought it some part of my duty to certify your honour . . . that in these three shires called Carnarvon, Anglesey and Merioneth through the wisdom and careful diligence of Mr. George Bromley, chief justice, the people live in much obedience, freedom and quiet, so that toward their prince they are like to continue faithful subjects, and among themselves peaceable neighbours.

But touching the Welsh people's receiving of the Gospel, I find by my small experience among them here that ignorance continueth. . . . For the most part of the priests are too old (they say) now to be put to school . . . For there are not six that can preach in these three shires. I have found since I came to this country images and altars standing in churches undefaced, lewd and undecent vigils and watches observed, much pilgrimaging and many candles set up to the honour of saints, some relics yet carried about, and all the countries full of beads and knots besides divers other monuments of wilful serving of God. Of the which abuses some (I thank God) are reformed, and other (my hope is) will daily decay by the help of the worshipful of the countries who show some better countenance to the Gospel, by the godly zeal of the Chief Justice whose counsel and aid I have in such matters, all which I trust almighty God will turn to his own glory and the salvation of his people.

Thus I am bold to open unto your honour the pitiful case of a poor people not obstinate to hear, nor dull to understand, neither careless in that he knoweth, but for want of knowledge now a long time seduced.

Nicholas Robinson, Bishop of Bangor, to Sir William Cecil,
7 October 1567

PENCARS OR HEAD-MINSTRELS

The people naturally are very devout, having in heart doubtless engrafted as great fear, regard and reverence of a supernal power as any people in the world elséwhere have, but more than the name of God they know nothing at all; and therefore as utterly ignorant of him or their salvation, do still, in heaps, go on pilgrimage to the wonted wells and places of superstition, and in the nights, after the feasts when the old offerings were used to be kept at any idol's chapel, albeit the church be pulled down, yet do they come to the place where the church or chapel was, by great journeys barefoot, very superstitiously, etc. The mean for the meeting and knowledge of the time when the pilgrims shall come is chiefly wrought by their pencars[1] or head-minstrels, who at the direction of some old gentlewoman do ordinarily give the summons of the time certain for such meetings.

Truly at this day if you look thoroughly to the whole number of gentry and others of all sorts in North Wales, you shall scarcely find any (the Bishops and some few others excepted) yet in any sort well instructed in the faith of Christ: for of the whole multitude, such which be under thirty years of age seem to have no show of any religion, the others well near generally all dare to profess and to maintain the absurdest points of popish heresy.

ANONYMOUS, *Report on Wales, 1575*

THE SHIRE OF BRECKNOCK

There resteth yet one matter amiss, that is, an extreme want of learned and godly preachers to instruct the people in the knowledge and fear of God: for in this whole shire of Brecknock there are scarce two learned and sufficient pastors, and for a great part some one slender chaplain, which can but read the divine service, doth serve two, some three parishes, and those two or three miles asunder at the

[1] *penbards*, chief bards.

least. Whereby the common people are so rude and ignorant in the most necessary points of the Christian faith, that over many of them cannot as much as say the Lord's Prayer and Articles of the Belief in any language that they understand. And therefore it is no marvel that they are very injurious one to another, and live in contempt both of the laws of God and man; as in keeping, one his brother's wife, another his wife's daughter, and living and dwelling with them (as many doth most abominably) seeing they are not instructed in the fear of God.

Richard Price of Brecknock to Lord Burghley,
31 January 1575

ADVICE ON IRELAND

I take it to be against good policy for a great prince to keep a long and lingering war with a subject nation, though the people be never so base; for it teacheth them to be skilful, stout and resolute, as appeareth by the Low Countries. God grant it may not appear in Ireland! The people there are grown very valiant and desperate, and, being able to abide all kind of hardiness, take the benefit of the country, of woods and bogs, and are like to hold out a long time, without the loss of more noblemen and captains than may well be spared in England. Besides that, many of our English nation (*nescio quomodo*) are very unwilling to go thither; and many tall men at home, when they come there, prove cowards, and the very country consumeth them. Therefore (in mine opinion) it were not amiss for you of her Majesty's Council to think rather of an honorable peace, than to endanger so many noblemen, valiant captains and dutiful subjects, and perhaps (in time) the loss of that great kingdom. You and I are men of peace, and therefore I am bold to write unto you, being near to her Majesty, etc.

Matthew Hutton, Archbishop of York, to John Whitgift, Archbishop of
Canterbury, 20 May 1600

JAMES MAXWELL, EARL OF MORTON

About a month since (7th December) James Maxwell, Earl of Morton, the Scottish King's Lieutenant General, was slain in pursuing the Lord Johnston to arrest him according to the King's warrant, and the Catholics made much note of his death.

Not many years since, the Earl of Morton, though he was a Catholic, had been persuaded to sign the articles expressing conformity and directed against the Catholic religion. But at 12 o'clock that day, being alone in his room, an angel appeared to him in the form of a youth who said, 'My Lord, do not as your kinsmen would persuade you; for if you do you shall lose the hand with which you sign, and your days shall end with shameful death.' Moved by this appeal, the Earl again put on the gold crucifix and an *agnus dei* which he used to wear round his neck, but had taken off when he abandoned his former professions. He then told the principal kinsmen who had persuaded him to sign how remorseful he was for his error, and what the angel had told him; and in order that God's mercy might for ever be remembered by his house, he added to his arms the figure of an angel. He refused also to sign the articles declaring himself an enemy of the ministers.

But after a time he was greatly moved by his kinsmen, and the King himself made him many offers, creating him his Lieutenant General, so that at last he gave way and signed the articles. But shortly afterwards going to arrest the Lord Johnston with 5000 soldiers he met with the end the angel foretold him.

For when he came up the Lord Johnston, taking advantage of the ground, had posted 600 horsemen in three squadrons in a triangle at some little distance from each other. The Earl of Morton's regiment entering into their midst, Lord Johnston and his men who were on one side threw themselves with such fury upon the Earl's men that they broke and fled; and the Lord Johnston, reaching the Earl, at the first blow smote off his right hand, and at the second cut off a leg. Then being thrown from his horse, the Earl was cut into a thousand pieces.

Stories from Scotland

7

Compulsory Church-going

PERSONS ON FREEDOM OF CONSCIENCE

In what miserable case standeth many a man in England at this day, which take oaths, receive sacraments, go to church and commit many a like act against their own consciences and against their own knowledge: nay, what a case do they stand in, which know such things to be directly against other men's consciences and yet do compel them to do it: as to receive against their will, to swear against their will and the like. Surely, as I am now minded, I would not for ten thousand worlds, compel a Jew to swear that there was a Blessed Trinity. For albeit the thing be never so true, yet should he be damned for swearing against his conscience, and I for compelling him to commit so heinous and grievous a sin.

ROBERT PERSONS, *A Brief Discourse*

FIFTY THOUSAND IN A MONTH

We hear that one month since more than fifty thousand names of persons who refused to go to the heretical churches were reported. Many more, I fancy, have been discovered since.

Robert Persons to Fr. Agazarri, 17 November 1580

REASONS FOR RECUSANCY

i. Persons who refuse to come to Church with their reasons.
20 November (1576)

Walmegate Ward

All Hallows on the Pavement.

Elizabeth Wilkinson, wife of William Wilkinson, milner, sayeth she cometh not to the church, because there is neither priest, altar nor sacrifice.

Katherine Wildon, wife of John Wildon, tailor, sayeth she cometh not to the church, because there is neither altar nor sacrifice.

Margaret Taylor, wife of Thomas Taylor, tailor, sayeth she cometh not to the church, because there is not a priest as there ought to be; and also that there is not the sacrament of the altar.

The same Thomas Taylor sayeth, his substance is very small and liveth on his credit, and so we think; he is a very poor man and little worth of his own goods.

Elizabeth Porter, widow, sayeth she cometh not to the church, because the service there is not as it ought to be, nor as it hath been heretofore; and she sayeth she is a poor woman and of no substance, but we think her worth in clear goods 40s.

Isabel Addenall, widow, sayeth she cometh not to the church, because her conscience will not serve her; and that she hath little or nothing to live upon, and so we think.

St. Dionys Parish.

Agnes Wiggan, widow, sayeth she cometh not to the church, because there is neither priest nor sacrament; she is nothing worth, as we think.

Richard Brafferton, baker, who was lately presented for not coming to the church, is gone forth of this City, to what place we know not.

St. Mary's in Castlegate.

Isabel Porter, wife of Peter Porter, tailor, sayeth that she cometh not to the church, because her conscience will not serve her; for things are not in the church as it hath been aforetime in her forefathers' days.

Gregory Wilkinson, feltmaker, sayeth he cometh not to the church because his conscience will not serve him so to do, for he will remain in the faith that he was baptised in.

St. Margaret's Parish.

Thomas Pearson, weaver, sayeth he cometh not to the church for his conscience will not serve him; because there lacketh the sacrament, the priest and the altar; and sayeth he is worth in clear goods 20s., and so we think; which Thomas is now in ward.

Monkward

Christs Parish.

Frances Hall, wife of George Hall, draper, sayeth she cometh not to the church because she is persuaded otherwise to do, and believeth in the faith that she was baptised in.

Janet Geldart, wife of Percival Geldart, butcher, sayeth she cometh not to the church because her conscience will not serve her so to do, and sayeth there can be no greater cause for the same than her conscience.

Jane West, single woman, servant to George Hall, draper, sayeth she cometh not to the church, for she thinketh it is not the right church, and that if she should come there it would damn her soul.

Margaret Clitheroe,[1] wife of John Clitheroe, butcher, cometh not to the church, for what cause we cannot learn, for she is now great with child and could not come before us.

St. Maurice Parish.

John Wood, tailor, cometh not to the church, for what cause we know not, for he cannot be had, and as for his substance he is worth little or nothing.

Miklythward

Trinities of Miklegate.

Janet Strickett, widow, sayeth she cometh not to the church because her conscience will not serve her; for the bread and wine is not consecrate, as it hath been in time past.

York Civic Records

ii. William Bowman, locksmith, sayeth he refuseth to come to the church because he thinketh it is not the Catholic Church, for there is neither priest, altar, nor sacraments, and sayeth that he is worth in clear goods not above 40s., and so we think.

Isabel Bowman, wife of the said William Bowman, sayeth she cometh not to the church, for her conscience will not serve her, because there is not the Sacrament hung up and other things as hath been aforetime.

Ibid.

IF ANY MAN BUT YIELD

If any man but yield to go to Church all treasons are remitted.

An Ancient Editor's Note Book

[1] In the margin 'in prison.'

THE CASE OF FRANCIS WODEHOUSE

I will mention no other case here, apart from this. Although I never had any previous doubt about it—I had it first on the testimony of a large number of witnesses—later on I heard everything I am going to tell you from the man himself when he came to see us at Wisbech.

'That proclamation of the Queen,' he said, 'did not touch me lightly. On the contrary, it lay like a load on my mind. It was not a matter merely for myself, not just a question of imprisonment. My wife, my children, my whole family and fortune were concerned. At a single blow all would be gone together. Yet, if I submitted, I would have to face perpetual disgrace in the eyes of decent men: and not that only, but infamy and the stigma of cowardice as well, and, before God, the assured and inescapable jeopardy of my soul. And on top of it all,' he continued, 'came the entreaties and prayers of my friends—friends, that is, who regularly set more store by the things of this world than by those of God. They exaggerated infinitely the importance of these passing possessions, and insisted how rash and regrettable it would be to refuse to purchase immunity from disaster by a single visit to church. Finally,' he said, 'I was timid. I saw the best course, and followed the worst. I decided, just once, to rig my conscience, and throw my scruples to the wind. The feast day came when I had to be present. Immediately I entered the church—it was quite foreign to me, a novelty which I had shunned already for many years—my bowels began to torture me. A fire seemed to kindle in them and in a few moments flared up. The torment was acute. The flame rose right into my chest and the region of my heart, so that I seemed to be steaming and boiling in some hellish furnace. And it did not stop there; it mounted to my head and rose so high above it, that from time to time I raised my hand to see whether it was a real flame that I felt. At last all my intestines seemed one furnace of fire. I was at a loss what to do, for I no longer had strength enough to endure the flames. To go out and leave the pestilential meeting when its business was only half through would avail me nothing, or rather place me in an even worse position than before.'

So he held on, doing violence to himself to master his agony, until the profane prayers were ended. Outside the church, so it seemed to him, he was carrying about within himself an unendurable hell. Afflicted with a searing thirst, he entered the first tavern he saw, and ordered a drink to be brought. And—this may seem incredible—he emptied to the dregs so many mugs one on top of the other, that he put down about eight gallons in all. And he felt no discomfort or nausea. It was like pouring water into a raging furnace; all the liquor was immediately taken into his stomach and absorbed. Yet, in spite of this, the secret fire was not extinguished, and he got no relief. In desperation he returned home, with a justifiably sad heart and countenance. His wife looked him all over. She saw he had altered altogether and asked him what was wrong. What had he done? He told her, therefore, his whole sad story from the beginning—what had happened to him at the heretical meeting and the acute physical and mental anguish he had been through. Now she was not only a good Catholic but a sensible woman also. She comforted her husband in every way she knew; she soothed him with wise words and with hope of better times, and, what was most important, ordered a priest to be called in at once, in order that the inpouring of the grace of the Holy Spirit might, better than any medicine, heal his soul's distemper and deep distress. With every day his condition became easier and less acute. Finally, he was totally restored to his former good health. After this, he visited the pseudo-bishop of the place and told him how, to meet the wishes of the Queen, he had compromised his conscience and been to church. And he explained all that had taken place there. 'I desire you to know,' he said, 'that not only do I regret what I have done, but I am determined never to do it again. You can do or command me anything you wish. That is my resolve.' But the tale the man told did not stir the bishop at all. Neither did he commiserate with him nor show him the slightest sympathy. But, there and then he clapped him into prison. And with a brave heart he suffered there for four whole years, not minding so much the lack of personal freedom as the loss of his home and family.

WILLIAM WESTON, *Autobiography*

EFFECTS OF THE POPE'S BULL

Most of the Papists of England did come to our Church and heard divine service till the eleventh year of the Queen when the Bull of Pope Pius Quintus enforced not only their wilful obstinate separation, but drew on and necessitated many of those laws which were afterwards made against them.

Journals of all the Parliaments of Elizabeth

THE MEASURE OF CONFORMITY

The heretics, when they throw Catholics into prison, only ask them one thing,—to come to their churches, and to hear sermon and service. It was even lately proposed to certain noblemen to come, if it were only once a year, to church, making, if they pleased, a previous protestation that they came not to approve of their religion or doctrines, but only to show an outward obedience to the queen; and yet all most constantly refused. A certain noble lady was offered her choice, either to stay in prison, or simply to walk through the church without stopping there, or exhibiting any signs of respect; but she declared that she never would. A boy, of, I believe, twelve years, who had been cheated by his friends into walking to church before a bride (as the custom here is), and had been afterwards blamed by his companions, was perfectly inconsolable till he found me a few days after, when he threw himself down at my feet, and confessed his sin. A thousand similar instances might be given.

Robert Persons to Claude Aquaviva, 17 November 1580

GOD'S SERVANTS FIRST

In the beginning of this persecution, there were some people in a certain county who were frightened, and promised to go to the Protestant church; but their wives stood out against them, and threatened to leave them if they, for human respect, left off their obedience to God and the Church. Many like things have taken place among boys, who for this cause have separated themselves from their parents.

Ibid.

IN DEFENCE OF RECUSANCY

Let us suppose the case thus: I know in England certain places where at certain times and days assemblies are made by certain men, in shew, to honour and commend, but in my conceit, to dishonour, dispraise and impugn the majesty of the most dread sovereign Lady, the Queen. And I am invited thither to hear the same by my parents, kinsmen and acquaintance: nay, I am enforced thither by the greatest authority that under her Majesty may command me. Tell me now: if I should go thither under any pretence whatsoever of gratifying my friends or by commandment of any her inferior powers, can her Majesty take it well or account of me better than a traitorous caitiff, for yielding myself to stay there, to hear them, to countenance their doings with my presence, to hold my peace when they speak evil of her, to hold my hands while they slander her and, finally, to say nothing whiles they induce other men to forsake her and her cause? And if her Majesty or any other Prince in the world could not bear at their subjects' hands any such dissimulation, treachery or treason, how much less shall the omnipotent Majesty of God (who requireth and deserveth much more exact service at our hands) bear this dissimulation and traitorous dealing of ours, if we be content, for temporal respects and for satisfaction of any mortal power less than himself, to present ourselves to such places and assemblies, where we shall hear his Majesty dishonoured, his Son slandered, his Holy Word falsified, his Church impugned, his saints and martyrs discredited, his bishops and pastors reviled, and all the whole ecclesiastical hierarchy rent, broken, dis-severed and turned upside down, and his people (purchased with his Blood and dearer unto him than his own life) excited and stirred up against him and his ministers, and by sweet words and gay benedictions stocked away to the slaughter house of heresy.

ROBERT PERSONS, *A Brief Discourse*

LADY MONTEAGLE

The Lady Monteagle was accustomed to have the Protestant service read to her by a chaplain in her house, and afterwards to hear Mass said privately by a priest. But as soon as she understood the unlawfulness of this practice, she would never be present at the Protestant service any more.

Lives of Philip Howard and Anne Dacres

COMPULSORY CHURCH-GOING

15 January 1581. Edward Hopton, the Lieutenant of the Tower, having forced us to church by means of the military, publicly protested that he had no one in his custody who did not willingly go to the Protestant worship.

5 February 1581. John Nicholas, formerly a Calvinistic minister,

and afterwards a pretended Catholic, mounted the pulpit to inveigh against the Roman pontiff, at whose expense he boasted that he had for some years lived in Rome. All the prisoners were carried by force to hear him, but they interrupted him more than once in the midst of his raving, and, when his sermon was finished, hooted him away.

EDWARD RISHTON, *Tower Journals*

8

The Queen

Queen Elizabeth to the Deprived Bishops

Sirs, As for your entreaty for us to listen to you, we waive it; yet do return you this our answer. Our realm and subjects have been long wanderers, walking astray, whilst they were under the tuition of Romish pastors, who advised them to own a wolf for their head (in lieu of a careful shepherd), whose inventions, heresies and schisms be so numerous that the flock of Christ have fed on poisoned shrubs for want of wholesome pastures. And whereas you hit us and our subjects in the teeth, that the Roman Church first planted the Catholic faith within our realms, the records and chronicles of our realms testify the contrary. . . . And whereas you would frighten us, by telling us how Emperors, Kings and Princes have owned the Bishop of Rome's authority, it was the contrary in the beginning. For our Saviour paid his tribute unto Caesar, as the chief superior, which shows that your Romish supremacy is usurped. . . . We give you warning, that for the future we hear no more of this kind, lest you provoke us to execute those penalties enacted for the punishing of our resisters, which out of our clemency we have foreborne.

Letters of Queen Elizabeth

The Queen to Her Clergy

No prince herein, I confess, can be surer tied or faster bound than I am with the link of your good will, and can for that but yield a heart and a head to seek for ever all your best. Yet one matter toucheth me so near as I may not overskip—religion, the ground on which all other matters take root, and, being corrupted, may mar all the tree. And there be some fault-finders with the order of the clergy, which so may make a slander to myself and the Church, whose over-ruler God hath made me, whose negligence cannot be excused, if any schism or errors heretical were suffered. . . . All which if you my Lords of the clergy do not amend, I mean to depose you. Look you therefore to your charges. This may be amended without heedless or open exclamations. I am supposed to have many studies, but most philosophical. I must yield this to be true, that I suppose few (that be no Professors) have read more. And I need not tell you that I am not so simple that I understand not, nor so forgetful that I remember not; and yet amidst my many volumes I hope God's Book hath not been my seldomest lectures, in which we find that which by reason (for my part) we ought to believe. . . . I see many overbold with God Almighty, making too many subtle scannings of his blessed will, as lawyers do with human testaments. The presumption is so great that I may not suffer it (and yet mind I not hereby to animate Romanists, which what adversaries they be to mine estate is sufficiently known) nor tolerate new-fangleness, I mean to guide them both by God's holy true rule.

Queen Elizabeth to the House of Lords, 20 May 1585

A Call to Order

The queen lays down for her clergy a rule of life, outside of which they dare not move, not only in those things which Protestants call indifferent, but in all matters of faith, discipline, and doctrine, in virtue of that supreme spiritual power with which she is invested: she suspends her bishops when she pleases, she grants a licence to preach, either to those who are ordained according to her rite or to simple laymen, and in the same way at her pleasure reduces whom she will to silence. To show her authority in these things, she occasionally, from her closet, addresses her preacher, and interrupts him in the presence of a large congregation, in some such way as this: 'Mr. Doctor, you are wandering from the text, and talking nonsense, return to your subject.'

NICOLAS SANDER, *Anglican Schism*

The Dean on the Carpet

Dean Nowell, so often noted for his frequent preaching before the Queen, preached on the festival of the Circumcision, being New Year's Day [1562], at St. Paul's, whither the Queen resorted. Here a remarkable passage happened. . . . The dean, having gotten from a foreigner several fine cuts and pictures, representing the stories and passions of the saints and martyrs, had placed them against the Epistle and Gospels of the Festivals in a Common Prayer Book; and this book he had caused to be richly bound and laid on the cushion for the Queen's use, in the place where the company sat, intending it for a New Year's gift to her Majesty, and thinking to have pleased her fancy therewith. But it had not that effect, but the contrary; for she considered how this varied from her late open injunctions and proclamations against the superstitious use of images in churches, and for the taking away all such reliques of popery. When she came to her place, she opened the book and perused it, and saw the pictures; but frowned and blushed and then shut it (of which several took notice); and calling the verger, bad him bring her the old book, wherein she was formerly wont to read. After sermon, whereas she was wont to get immediately on horseback or into her chariot, she went straight to the vestry and applying herself to the dean, thus spoke to him:

Q. Mr. Dean, how came it to pass that a new service book was placed on my cushion? To which the Dean answered:

D. May it please your Majesty, I caused it to be placed there. Then said the Queen:

Q. Wherefore did you so?

D. To present your Majesty with a New Year's gift.

Q. You could never present me with a worse.

D. Why so, Madam?

Q. You know I have an aversion to idolatry, to images and pictures of this kind.

D. Wherein is the idolatry, may it please your Majesty?

Q. In the cuts resembling the angels and saints; nay grosser absurdities, pictures resembling the Blessed Trinity.

D. I mean no harm: nor did I think it would offend your Majesty when I intended it for a New Year's gift.

Q. You must needs be ignorant then. Have you forgotten our proclamation against images, pictures and Romish reliques in churches? Was it not read in your deanery?

D. It was read. But be your Majesty assured, I meant no harm, when I caused the cuts to be bound with the service book.

Q. You must needs be very ignorant after our prohibition of them.

D. It being my ignorance, your Majesty may the better pardon me.

Q. I am sorry for it: yet glad to hear it was your ignorance rather than your opinion.

D. Be your Majesty assured, it was my ignorance.

Q. If so, Mr. Dean, God grant you his spirit, and more wisdom for the future.

D. Amen, I pray God.

Q. I pray, Mr. Dean, how came you by these pictures? Who engraved them?

D. I know not who engraved them. I bought them.

Q. From whom bought you them?

D. From a German.

Q. It is well it was from a stranger. Had it been any of our subjects, we should have questioned the matter. Pray let no more of these mistakes, or of this kind, be committed within the churches of our realm for the future.

D. There shall not.

This matter occasioned all the clergy in and about London and the churchwardens of each parish to search their churches and chapels: and caused them to wash out of the walls all paintings that seemed to be Romish and idolatrous; and in lieu thereof suitable texts taken out of the Holy Scriptures to be written.

JOHN NICHOLS, *The Progresses of Queen Elizabeth*

BEWARE, ON MY WORD

I thank God that you beware so soon of Jesuits, that have been the source of all these treacheries in this Realm, and will soon spread like an evil weed, if at the first they be not weeded out. . . . What religion is this, that they say that the way to salvation is to kill the Prince for a merit meritorious? This is what they have all confessed without torture or menace. I swear it, on my word.

Queen Elizabeth to James VI, King of Scotland

NO MASS FOR MONSIEUR D'ANJOU

So our meaning is to be declared plainly to Monsieur de Anjou, that we cannot permit him at his coming to have the use of any private Mass, which speech we have plainly uttered unto him, because there should be no misgiving gathered of our answer, whereby the Duke might hope for a sufferance.

The Letters of Queen Elizabeth, 2 September 1571

THE QUEEN'S PURPOSE

The Queen feels no great interest in any faith or any sect, . . . she has no other thought than to keep herself on the throne in whatever way she can, and by means of whatever religion . . . may best serve her purpose.

John Baptista Castagna, Nuncio at Venice, to the
Cardinal of Como, 11 June 1575

'MADAM I MAY NOT CALL YOU'

But now though this Archbishop [Parker] dissembled not his marriage, yet Queen Elizabeth would not dissemble her dislike of it. For whereas it pleased her often to come to his house, in respect of her favour to him (that had been her mother's chaplain) being once above the rest greatly feasted; at her parting from thence, the Archbishop and his wife being together, she gave him very special thanks, with gracious and honourable terms, and then looking on his wife, 'And you,' saith she, 'Madam I may not call you, and Mrs. I am ashamed to call you, so I know not what to call you, but yet I do thank you.'

SIR JOHN HARINGTON, *Nugae Antiquae*

'OH BOY, I DIE'

[Richard Fletcher] being Bishop of London and a widower, he married a gallant lady and a widow, sister to Sir George Gifford the pensioner, which the Queen seemed to be extremely displeased at. . . . But certain it is that the Queen being pacified, and he in great jollity, with his fair lady and her carpets and cushions in his bed-chamber, he died suddenly, taking tobacco in his chair, saying to his man that stood by him, whom he loved very well, 'Oh boy, I die'.

Ibid.

FR. PERSONS TO THE QUEEN

Jesus Christ, in abundance of mercy, bless your Majesty, to whom (as he knoweth) I wish as much good as to mine own soul: persuading myself that all good Catholics in England do the same. And they which go about to insinuate the contrary are, in mine opinion, but

appointed instruments by the common enemy, to despoil your
Majesty of your strongest pillar and best right hand, as . . . shall be
more manifest before the last tribunal seat, where we shall all be
presented shortly, without difference of persons and where the cogitations of all hearts shall be revealed and examined, and in justice of
judgment rightly rewarded. Now matters are craftily clouded up and
false vizards put upon every action. Then all shall appear in sincerity
and truth, and nothing avail but only the testimony of a good conscience. The which Catholics by suffering do seek to retain, and which
God, of his infinite goodness, inspire your Majesty, graciously without
enforcement, to permit unto them still.

ROBERT PERSONS, *A Brief Discourse, 1580*

RICHARD SHACKLOCK TO THE QUEEN

Truly, most noble Queen, this one saying[1] doth encourage many of
your Grace's faithful and learned subjects on this side of the sea to
writing: some to make new works never seen before, some to translate
books which have been made of others. Some to write in Latin, some
in English, some in verse and other some in prose. All whose diligence
and study intendeth nothing less than to write one word willingly
which might displease your Majesty, which may sow any seeds of
sedition, which may disquiet the peace of our native country (as in your
grace's dear sister's days divers seditious sectaries did) but only to
further and to prefer as much as is possible this princely desire of
knowing the truth, which we hear with great joy to be reported of
your Majesty.

RICHARD SHACKLOCK, *The Hatchet of Heresies*

THE MIRROR OF TRUTH

Sir Christopher Hatton and another knight made challenge who
should present the truest picture of her Majesty to the Queen. One
caused a flattering picture to be drawn; the other presented a glass,
wherein the Queen saw herself, the truest picture that might be.

Diary of John Manningham, 12 February 1602

---

[1] Shacklock had heard that the Queen, taking account each night how she had spent
the day, if she found that she had been unable to learn a single lesson out of a godly
author, used to say, 'This day I have lost, for I have learned never a lesson.'

LORD BURGHLEY

i. The Queen's Highness doth often speak of him in tears and turn aside, when he is discoursed of; nay even forbiddeth any mention to be made of his name in the Council. This I learn by some who are in good liking with Lord Buckhurst.

Robert Markham to John Harington, 1598

ii. I do see the Queen often . . . Burghley's death doth often draw tears from her goodly cheeks: she walketh out but little, meditates much alone, and sometimes writes in private to her best friends.

Sir Robert Sydney to John Harington, 1600

ALL FRESH AND LUSTY

Here is no news that I can learn, for we live all as it were in a wilderness. Her majesty hath been in danger by a short sickness, but thanks be to God well recovered, and was yesterday at the triumphs all in yellow, that it was comfortable to behold her so fresh and lusty.

Henry Garnet to Robert Persons, 19 November 1594

THE QUEEN AT GREENWICH, 1598

Next came the Queen, in the 65th year of her age (as we were told), very majestic; her face oblong, fair but wrinkled; her eyes small, yet black and pleasant; her nose a little hooked, her lips narrow, and her teeth black, (a defect the English seem subject to, from their too great use of sugar); she had in her ears two pearls with very rich drops; her hair was of an auburn colour, but false; upon her head she had a small crown, reported to be made of some of the gold of the celebrated Luneburg table; her bosom was uncovered, as all the English ladies have it till they marry; and she had on a necklace of exceeding fine jewels; her hands were slender, her fingers rather long, and her stature neither tall nor low; her air was stately, her manner of speaking mild and obliging. That day she was dressed in white silk, bordered with pearls of the size of beans, and over it a mantle of black silk shot with silver threads; her train was very long, the end of it borne by a marchioness; instead of a chain, she had an oblong collar of gold and jewels. As she went along in all this state and magnificence, she spoke very graciously, first to one, then to another (whether foreign ministers, or those who attend for different reasons), in English, French, and Italian; for besides being well skilled in Greek, Latin, and the languages I have mentioned, she is mistress of Spanish, Scotch, and Dutch. Whoever speaks to her, it is kneeling; now and then she raises some with her hand. While we were there, William Slawata, a Bohemian baron, had letters to present to her; and she, after pulling off her glove, gave him her right hand to kiss, sparkling with rings and jewels—a mark of particular favour. Wherever she turned her face as she was going along, everybody fell down on their knees. The ladies of the court followed next to her, very handsome and well-shaped, and for the most part dressed in white. She was guarded on each side by the gentlemen pensioners, fifty in number, with gilt halberds. In the ante-chapel, next the hall where we were, petitions were presented to her, and she received them most graciously, which occasioned the acclamation of *God save the Queen Elizabeth!* She answered it with *I thancke you myn good peupel.*

Journal of Paul Hentzner

FACTA AND FACIENDA

I have not dared in particular to propound it[1] to the Queen, lest she should not assent unto it, being apter to approve *facta* than *facienda*.

Sir Robert Cecil to Sir George Carew, 24 October 1602

BEDIZENED MAJESTY

It was commonly observed this Christmas that her Majesty, when she came to be seen, was continually painted, not only all over her face, but her very neck and breast also, and that the same was in some places near half an inch thick.

Anthony Rivers to Robert Persons, 13 January 1601

[1] Sir George Carew's visit to England.

9

Ministers and Preachers

THE COMMONS' REQUEST, 1585

In that great and weighty charge which in the Book containing the form and Ordering of Priests . . . is prescribed to be delivered to all such as shall be received into the Ministry, they are admonished that they be the messengers, the watchmen, the pastors and stewards of the Lord, to teach, to premonish, to feed and to provide for the Lord's family, to seek for Christ's sheep that be dispersed abroad and for his children that be in the midst of this naughty world, to be saved through Christ for ever, with other remembrances of other sundry weighty parts of their duties; it may like their Honours to consider of some good order to be given that none hereafter be admitted to the Ministry but such as shall be sufficiently furnished with gifts to perform so high and so earnest a charge.

The humble Petition of the Commons to the House of Lords,
25 February 1585

THE VICAR OF TRUMPINGTON

The Vicar of Trumpington understood not *Eli, Eli, lama sabacthani* when he read the Passion upon Palm-Sunday. Coming to which place he stopped, and calling the church-wardens, said, 'Neighbours, this gear must be amended. Here is *Eli* twice in the book. I assure you, if my Lord of Eli come this way and see it, he will have the book, [since his name was in it.] Therefore by mine advice we shall scrape it out, and put in our own town's name, *viz. Trumpington, Trumpington, lama sabacthani.*' They consented, and he did so, because he understood no better.

JOHN STRYPE, *The Life of Bishop Aylmer*

Travellers' Talk

If you that be Ministers would travel by land or by sea, yourselves should surely hear your own sinful trespasses all truly told and uttered. For whereas sometimes men travelling [were] accustomed, by telling of histories and tales, to avoid the weariness of their long ways and journey: in these days they have none other news nor any other history than the telling of the mad touches of Ministers, insomuch that whether he be a child, a young man, of middle age or aged, he is sure able to say that this Minister or that Minister hath committed this evil deed or that, and one mischievous fact or another.

ANONYMOUS, *A Brief Admonition unto the new made Ministers*

The Parson of St. Mary Abchurch

Anno 1563, the 26th June, was a minister, parson of St. Mary Abchurch, of St. Martin's in Ironmonger Lane, and of one other benefice in the country, taken at Distaff Lane using another man's wife as his own, which was daughter to Sir Miles Partridge and wife to William Stockbridge, grocer, and he being so taken at the deed doing (having a wife of his own) was carried to Bridewell through all the streets, his breeches hanging about his knees, his gown and his . . . hat borne after him with much honour; but he lay not long there, but was delivered without punishment and still enjoyed his benefices. They were greatly blamed that apprehended him and committed him.

JOHN STOW, *Memoranda*

The New-made Ministers

If you mark the young sort of new made Ministers you shall find in them such folly and pride, such wilfulness and wantonness, that woeful it is to hear it. They be in their attire and apparel so ruffed, welted, jagged and stitched as meeter to be minstrels than ministers. They do no sooner attain this one new only order, but then busily seek they for some bussing girl to make up their new godliness. . . . Seek further what your gravest fathers and new named Bishops have been, and you shall find that . . . they were those, for whom the whole clergy were accused of incontinence, that they were but the riff-raff amongst the religious: that they were but truants in comparison of the true Catholic teachers: that they were the very worst of all those which professed priesthood and sanctity, and that they were but the very dregs of the divines and doctors of our days. Behold of them some, who having lived this long time without any matching in marriage, do now in their old age fall to such folly and doting as their mere mad doings must well declare what kind of faith they seek to maintain and also what manner of life they heretofore have led. These be not of their simple sorts, for they be of their Bishops, and they be of their new godly, devout and (as the Protestants can call them) most grave fathers. But is it gravity for a Bishop with a grey beard in his extreme age to wax wanton and to wade in love with a light maid of his host his kitchen, with whom he has made such haste to marry? I shall not need to trouble you with his name, for the city and county do well know it. Yet if any far dweller hereof do doubt, let him trust that it be as true as that Bath and Wells be within one Bishopric.

ANONYMOUS, *A Brief Admonition unto the new made Ministers*

WITH WIVES FROM COLMAN'S HEDGE

I would you could but see the manner of the lives of the blessed Capuchins, which here to recount would be so long, and hardly could I reckon up all their holy exercises of mortifications, or of the happy Fathers of the Society of Jesus, and of other such like. Oh, what fasting, what prayer, what meditation, what contemplation, . . . what watching, what visiting the sick, what teaching of the ignorant, what rebuking of sinners, what comforting of the afflicted should you behold! They pray whilst your ministers play; these fast whilst they feast; these meditate the contempt of the world, whilst they beat their brains to compass worldly commodity; these watch and sing praises to God in the night, whilst they in a warm bed hug their sweetheart in their arms. Who is he amongst you which seeth not and is not ashamed of the lives of your ministers? Are not some of them almost in every circuit hanged for robberies, for rapes, imprisoned for sodomy, for having divers wives at once, for debt, and for other knaveries? The law bindeth them to have but one wife at once and she must be viewed by two justices of peace, to see that she be a maid forsooth. But do they not now and then take their wives from Colman's hedge, and some, other common strumpets? . . . An hundred examples I could here allege to prove these things, but I will not pollute my paper at this time with such filthy matter.

THOMAS HILL, *A Quatron of Reasons*

COLD GOSPELLERS

For come into a church on the sabbath day, and ye shall see but few, though there be a sermon: the alehouse is ever full. Well worth the papists therefore in their kind: for they be earnest, zealous and painful in their doings; they will build their kingdom more in one year with fire and fagot, than the cold gospellers will do in seven. A popish summoner, spy, or promoter will drive more to the church with a word to hear a latin mass, than seven preachers will bring in a week's preaching to hear a godly sermon.

JAMES PILKINGTON, *Exposition upon the Prophet Aggeus*

ARCHBISHOP WHITGIFT

[This was] his thesis when he kept his act for Doctor in Divinity, *viz.*, that *the Pope is Antichrist*.

JOHN STRYPE, *Life and Acts of John Whitgift*

10

Anabaptists and Others

AT THE CART'S TAIL

The tenth day of April [1561] was one William Geoffrey, an heretic, whipped at a cart's arse from the Marshalsea in Southwark to Bethlem without Bishopsgate of London, for that he believed one John More to be Christ, the Saviour of the world. He was very sore whipped, and on his head were pinned papers, and also about the cart were hanged the like papers, wherein was written as followeth: "William Geoffrey, a most blasphemous heretic, denying Christ our Saviour in heaven." And when he the said William Geoffrey was brought to Bethlem gate, there the Marshal's servants caused the cart to stay and John More to be brought out of Bethlem, which John More did profess himself to be Christ the Saviour of the world. And after examination and his answers, which were very doubtful, he was likewise stripped and tied at the cart's arse and whipped a birdbolt shot beyond Bethlem and so back again, and sent into Bethlem prisoner again. And William Geoffrey was sent again to the Marshalsea. They had been in the prisons before named nigh a year and a half before this time, the one for affirming himself to be Christ, the other affirming himself to be St. Peter the Apostle of Christ.

JOHN STOW, Memoranda

UNSPOTTED LAMBS OF THE LORD

About that time [July 1567] were many congregations of the Anabaptists in London, who called themselves Puritans or Unspotted Lambs of the Lord. They kept their church in the Minories without Aldgate. Afterwards they assembled in a ship or lighter in St. Katherine's Pool, then in a chopper's house,[1] nigh Wall Quay in Thames Street, where only the goodman of the house and the preacher, whose

---

[1] *chopper*: one who buy sand sells.

name was Brown (and his auditory were called the Brownings), were committed to ward; then afterward in Pudding Lane in a minister's house in a blind alley, and seven of them were committed to the Counter in the Poultry.

JOHN STOW, *Memoranda*

MR. BLOSSE

One Blosse, alias Mantel, was in the month of January [1573] taken up, for affirming King Edward VI was yet alive; and that Queen Elizabeth was married about the year 1564 to the Earl of Leicester, and had four children by him: and he had confidently told the same many times.

JOHN STRYPE, *Annals*

THE FAMILY OF LOVE

Divers other odd sects, about these times [1575], bearing pretty fantastical names, had their proselytes: as the 'family of the mount', the 'family of the essentialists', etc. All which seemed to be no other than some subdivision and slips of the 'family of love'. And of these, some were ministers. . . .

The sectaries of the 'family of the mount' held all things common, and lived in contemplation altogether; denying all prayers, and the resurrection of the body. They questioned whether there were an heaven or an hell but what is in this life. And they said, that what the scriptures spake of, was begun and ended in men's bodies here, as they do live. As heaven was, when they do laugh and are merry; and hell, when they are in sorrow, grief, or pain. And lastly, they believed that all things came by nature. This was acknowledged by one that had been of their society, to be held by them when he kept them company; and many other things as bad, or worse.

The 'family of the essentialists' had their opinions from one Mrs. Dunbar, a Scotchwoman. These held there was no sin at all: but what is done, God doth all, in what kind soever it be. One Lockley, a tailor, one of these, used to say, '*Sin? What sin, man? There is no man sinneth at all.*' He said further, in contempt of the holy altar in the church, where the Lord's supper is celebrated, that the altar did stand like a cook's dresser-board. This man had many meetings up and down, and would spend £20 or £30 at a sitting.

These, and the like, were the spawn and improvements of this 'family of love'.

Ibid.

A Flat Arian

And in the very next diocese, that of Ely, there were some heresies and dangerous opinions sprung up already, and maintained. One Wilkinson, of that diocese (who wrote a book against the 'family of love'), mentioned one in Cambridgeshire that was a flat Arian; and that under his own hand, and before some men of worship, anno 1574, March 24, in Cambridge, he denied Christ to be God equal with his Father. Moreover, that he asserted children were not by nature sinful, neither ought to be baptized, till years of discretion. And further affirmed, that the regenerate sin not: and that Paul's epistles were not to be more accounted of than the letters of private men. This man once recanted his errors; but since fell into the same again. His name was W. H. of B. i.e. Balsham, I suppose.

JOHN STRYPE, *Annals*

John Lewes

On the eighteenth day of September [1583], John Lewes, who named himself Abdoit, an obstinate heretic, denying the godhead of Christ, and holding divers other detestable heresies (much like to his predecessor Matthew Hamont) was burned at Norwich.

RAPHAEL HOLINSHED, *Chronicles*

'The Dogs of Tottenham'

The Archbishop did enjoin an exemplary penance upon one Joseph Leak, of Edmonton in Middlesex, for a most scandalous crime against not only the Protestant, but the Christian religion; intending, as it seems, thereby to make a mock of the holy Communion, as administered by the reformed Churches. The case was this. A company of people met together in some place in that parish, upon the marriage of a couple of ordinary people, where they spent the whole day in piping and dancing. And when night came, this man would needs have the company withdraw into a barn, where they continued their exercise till one or two after midnight. And when they were ready to depart, saith Joseph Leak, 'Nay, but we will first have a *communion*, and so farewell.' Thereupon he caused one of the rabble to go to the next alehouse for bread and beer. Which being brought, he appointed one to be the clerk, whose name was Edward Smith, to deliver to the company the beer, which he termed wine; and another to be sexton, to follow the clerk, and to fill the cup when it was empty. And when he had thus appointed his officers, he made himself a square cap, and cut the bread for the communion. And this done, he, playing the part of the minister, went before, and delivered to the company the bread, abusing the words of our Saviour, *Take, eat,* etc., taking the bread out of a hat, which he carried under his arm. The clerk and sexton followed with their wine, according to his appointment. And when their communion was ended, they sung, instead of a Psalm, a vile profane song, called, *The Dogs of Tottenham,* etc.

JOHN STRYPE, *Life and Acts of Archbishop Whitgift*

FRANCIS KETT

He denied the divinity of Christ and the Holy Spirit, and the Motherhood of the Blessed Virgin; and he prohibited the taking of oaths, the existence of magistrates, and the baptism of children—after the manner of anabaptists. Condemned to death by those who were very little different from himself, he was burnt at the stake—with a great show, I am told, of stubborn and misguided zeal. Yet a little while after, there was nothing to be seen of his bones and even of his ashes; these foes of holy relics were so eager to get possession of his remains.

Robert Southwell to Claude Aquaviva, 26 August 1587

Persecution

Our Counts are Cast

The persecutors be now no stronger than they were of old. The Church is no weaker than she had wont to be. Her assistant and defender is as near her as ever he was. We less fear death and less store set by our lives than ever before. Our counts are cast and allowed: it is better to die in this apostolical fight and combat, *quam videre mala gentis nostrae et sanctorum*, assuring ourselves that to be undoubted which St. Leo writeth . . . the religion founded in the sacrament of Christ's cross can be destroyed by no kind of cruelty. The Church is not diminished by persecutions, but increased. And that St. Augustine saith, *Nemo delet de caelo constitutionem Dei: nemo delet in terra Ecclesiam Dei.*

WILLIAM ALLEN, *A True and Sincere Defence*

Men Appointed to Death

Our days cannot be many, because we be men: neither can it be either godly or worldly wisdom, for a remnant of three or four years and perchance not so many months, to hazard the loss of all eternity. . . . No martyrdom of what length or torment soever can be more grievous than a long sickness and a languishing death: and he that departeth upon the pillow hath as little ease as he that dieth upon the gallows, block, or butcher's knife. And our Master's death, both for pains and ignominy, passed both sorts, and all other kinds either of martyrs or malefactors. Let no tribulation then, no peril, no prison, no persecution, no life, no death separate us from the charity of God, and the society of our sweet Saviour's passions, by and for whose love we shall have the victory in all these conflicts. Nevertheless, if by God's suffering, for causes hidden unto us, any shrink (which Christ forbid) for fear of death, torments, or tribulations, from the fellowship of your happy confession and crowns prepared for the same, as in the time of St. Cyprian and always divers did, and as one of the 40 did, whose glorious fight St. Basil describeth, and the Church celebrateth the 9th of March: be not scandalised or troubled thereat, but use such with all lenity, taking compassion of their infirmity, considering that yourselves also, or any of us all, may be tempted and overthrown with Peter, and by God's grace afterward repent and rise with him again, though it be perilous to presume thereon, many more following him in his fall and misery, than attaining to his martyrdom and mercy.

WILLIAM ALLEN, *Admonition to English Catholics*

PALM SUNDAY

There was on Palm Sunday last, at one hour, at four sundry masses, in four sundry places, and out corners of the city of London, fifty-three persons taken; whereof the most part were ladies, gentlewomen, and gentlemen. Two and twenty of them stood stoutly to the matter; whereof the lady Morley and the lady Browne (who had paid before a hundred marks for her offence) were the chief. The priests gloried in their doings, and affirmed that there were five hundred masses in England said that day.

George Gardiner, Dean of Norwich, to John Parkhurst,
Bishop of Norwich, 8 April 1574

A HUNDRED MORE RACKS

The Fathers of the Society are sought for most diligently: nevertheless by the singular providence of God they are yet free. One of them in the same room of Fr. Robert was seized not long ago: but the Father himself was not then present. But one Bryant, who had been an alumnus of our college at Rheims, living in a certain chamber adjoining, was also taken, and was twice most cruelly tortured on the rack, and for this purpose that he might disclose where that Jesuit was, but so far was he from making known anything concerning this matter, that he derided his torturers, and though almost killed with suffering said, 'Is this all that you can do? If the rack is nothing more than this let a hundred more come for this purpose.'

William Allen to Alphonsus Agazarri, 23 June 1581

THE EDGE ON OUR ZEAL

At no hour are we certain to survive, but as we make no account of living, the expectation of death only puts an edge on our zeal. Twice very recently we almost fell into their hands, but we escaped, for God was pleased to allow their mind and eyes to be cheated. I have lost everything, but 'the earth is the Lord's' and we can lack nothing we need.

William Weston to Robert Persons, 1586

THEY BRAG NO MORE

Of their martyrs they brag no more now; for it is now come to pass, that for a few apostates and cobblers of theirs burnt, we have bishops, lords, knights, the old nobility, patterns of learning, piety, and prudence, the flower of the youth, noble matrons, and of the inferior sort innumerable, either martyred at once, or by consuming prisonment dying daily. At the very writing hereof, the persecution rages most cruelly. The house where I am is sad; no other talk but of death, flight, prison, or spoil of their friends; nevertheless they proceed with courage. Very many, even at this present, being restored to the Church, new soldiers give up their names, while the old offer up their blood; by which holy hosts and oblations God will be pleased, and we shall no question by Him overcome.

Edmund Campion to Claude Aquaviva, 17 November 1580

IMMEASURABLE SUFFERING

The days that followed the Parliament[1] were bitter days for Catholics and filled with immeasurable suffering. Earlier, indeed, there had been great cruelty. Many had been broken. But now the fury of the persecution burst upon them more savagely still. It was the power held by the Earl of Leicester that was responsible, combined with Cecil's counsel, for these two men were in control under the Queen. Catholics now saw their own country, the country of their birth, turned into a ruthless and unloving land. All men fastened their hatred on them. They lay in ambush for them, betrayed them, attacked them with violence and without warning. They plundered them at night, confiscated their

---

[1] William Weston refers to the Parliament of 1584-5. On 14 December 1584 a bill was introduced 'For the utter extirpation of Popery against Jesuits and others.' It received royal assent on 29 March 1585.

possessions, drove away their flocks. stole their cattle. Every prison no matter how foul or dark, was made glorious by the noble and great-hearted protestations of saintly confessors, and even martyrs. In the common thoroughfares and crossways watchmen were abruptly posted, so that no traveller could pass peacefully on his way or escape stringent scrutiny. On the same night and at the same hour, now a single town, now several throughout the kingdom, experienced the sudden incursion of secret spies: inns, taverns, lodging-houses, bed-chambers, were searched with extreme rigour, and any suspected person, unable to give a satisfactory account of himself, was put in prison or under guard until morning; or until he could clear himself before the magistrates of the suspicion that he was a Catholic, and, in particular, a Catholic priest. Untrue reports were set in motion that a hostile Armada was being prepared, even approaching England; counterfeit letters were written, purporting to come from Catholics, disclosing plots against the Queen—it was the fashion to believe they planned the Queen's death. Some spies, in fact, went so far as to dis-guise themselves as Catholics and get themselves arrested and im-prisoned in order to confess their guilt and inflame the people's passion against the Catholics, and so have sharp vengeance demanded on them.

In London sometimes—I witnessed this myself and listened to Catholics groaning and grieving over it—a report would go round and be confirmed as certain fact, that the Queen's Council had passed a decree for the massacre of all Catholics in their houses on this or that night. Then many people would abandon their homes and lodgings and pass the night in the fields; others would hire boats and drift up and down the river. And a rumour was afoot, supposed to come from the lips of Cecil himself, that he was going to take steps to reduce Catholics to such destitution that they would be incapable of helping one another and, like swine, would be grateful if they could find a husk on which to appease their hunger. In fact, it appeared to me that the prophecy of our Saviour was then fulfilled, 'They will put you out of the synagogues: and whosoever killeth you will think that he doth a service to God.'

I have no misgivings in not speaking here of the arrest of priests and other men, their imprisonment and violent deaths, which took place some in London, some at York, Winchester, Canterbury and other cities. These events have been carefully chronicled in histories of their own, arranged in order of time, and described in all their circum-stances. It was then that new prisons were provided and established—

at Wisbech, Ely and Reading—and for the greater part were filled with high-born and illustrious men. When the Queen was asked to make the same provision for women, she is said to have answered, 'You have had your way with the men. Would you have me shut the women up too—like nuns in a convent? A fine thing that would be!' and she withheld her consent. Nevertheless, in Yorkshire there were public gaols in which the wives of several men of rank were imprisoned.

WILLIAM WESTON, *Autobiography*

POLICY OF PERSECUTORS

Persecutors . . . at the beginning use, of purpose and policy, gentle allurements hoping that way to gain the grace of all sorts, which is the reason that Julian the Emperor at the beginning was much noted of clemency; but . . . when he saw he could not extinguish the Christian faith by art, his former hypocritical lenity was at length turned into extreme fury.

WILLIAM ALLEN, *A True and Sincere Defence*

A GIRL OF RESOLUTION

The adversaries are very mad that by no cruelty can they move a single Catholic from his resolution, no, not even a little girl. A young lady of sixteen was questioned by the sham Bishop of London about the Pope, and answered him with courage, and even made fun of him in public, and so was ordered to be carried to the public prison for prostitutes. On the way she cried out that she was sent to that place for her religion, and not for immodesty.

Robert Persons to Claude Aquaviva, November 1580

JANE WISEMAN

'The sentence is that the said Jane Wiseman shall be led to the prison of the Marshalsea of the Queen's Bench, and there naked, except for a linen cloth about the lower part of her body, be laid upon the ground, lying directly on her back; and a hollow shall be made under her head and her head placed in the same; and upon her body in every part let there be placed as much of stones and iron as she can bear and more; and as long as she shall live, she shall have of the worst bread and water of the prison next her; and on the day she eats, she

shall not drink, and on the day she drinks she shall not eat, so living
until she die.'

Sentence passed on Jane Wiseman

The Poor and Penniless

i. For the poor Catholics in our parish of Hemingborough, the
persecution has been greater than I can relate, for no Catholic could
keep any goods, no, not the poor folks keep a cow to give their children
milk, but it was taken from them; and of late years they forced them to
pay 12*d*. every Sunday. And of such as had not money, they take their
goods, and of the poor that had not great goods, they took such things
as they found in their houses, as their vessels, of some their porridge
pots, and of others clothes off their beds, and if they had more coats
than that on their backs, they took them, and of one that had, with
her work in the summer, got a piece of cloth to clothe her children
with, they took it from her; and those they could get nothing of, they
sent to prison.

LADY BABTHORPE, *Recollections*

ii. A father in London caused his son to be whipped and burnt
through the ear for being a Catholic.

An Ancient Editor's Note Book

iii. An alms of milk being given to one, Mother Taylefathes, aged
and decrepit, one Rogers, a persecutor . . . took this milk from the
poor woman, and washed his hands in it, saying she was unworthy to
have alms, and that whosoever gave her anything should repent it all
the days they had to live.

Ibid.

iv. The same time [*c*. 1588] a poor man [Alan Blake] that was an
ostler in Gray's Inn Lane was hanged with a title over his head because
he had lodged a priest in his house.

GRENE, *Collections*

v. At this time [*c*. 1588] Nicholas Horner, a tailor, was condemned
to be hanged for that he had made a jerkin for a priest. The evidence

against him was only given by Topcliffe and Young. He was executed in Smithfield.

GRENE, *Collections*

OUR FORLORN ESTATE

Such is now our forlorn estate, that we are not only prisoners at every promoter's pleasure, and common steps of contempt to tread upon; but men so neglected by our superiors, and so left to the rage of pitiless persons, that contrary to the course of all Christian laws we are by the extremest tortures forced to reveal our very thoughts. It is not enough to confess we are priests, for that is seldom denied; but we must be urged upon the torture with other odious interrogatories far from our knowledge, much farther from our action: we are compelled to accuse those whom our conscience assureth us to be innocent, and to cause their overthrows by our confessions, to whose souls we were pastors, and they the fosterers of our bodies; and if we do not, because without untruth or injury we cannot answer, we are so unmercifully tormented, that our deaths, though as full of pangs as hanging, drawing and unbowelling us quick can make them, are unto us rather remedies than further revenges, more releasing than increasing our miseries. Some are hanged by the hands, eight or nine, or twelve hours together, till not only their wits, but even their senses fail them; and when the soul, weary of so painful an harbour, is ready to depart, they apply cruel comforts, and revive us, only to martyr us with more deaths; for eftsoons they hang us in the same manner, tiring our ears with such questions, which either we cannot, because we know not, or without damning our souls we may not satisfy. Some are whipped naked so long and with such excess, that our enemies unwilling to give constancy her right name, said, that no man without the help of the devil could with such undauntedness suffer so much. Some, besides their tortures, have been forced to lie continually booted and clothed many weeks together, pined in their diet, consumed with vermin, and almost stifled with stench. Some have been watched and kept from sleep, till they were past the use of reason, and then examined upon the advantage, when they could scarcely give account of their own names. Some have been tortured in such parts, as is almost a torture to Christian ears to hear it; let it then be judged what it was to chaste and modest men to endure it, the shame being no less offensive to their minds than the pain (though most excessive) to their bodies. Divers have been thrown into unsavoury and dark dungeons, and brought so near starving, that some for famine have licked the very moisture of the walls; some have so far been consumed that they were hardly recovered to life. What unsufferable agonies we have been put to upon the rack, it is not possible to express, the feeling so far exceedeth all speech. Some with instruments have been rolled up together like a ball, and so crushed, that the blood spouted out at divers parts of their bodies. To omit divers other cruelties, better known by their particular names to the rack-masters and executioners than to us, though too well acquainted with the experience of their smarts: it is not possible to keep any reckoning of the ordinary punishments of Bridewell, now made the common purgatory of Priests and Catholics, as grinding in the mill, being beaten like slaves, and other outrageous usages. For to these are we forced at the discretion of such, as being to all other despised underlings, take a felicity in laying their commandments and showing their authority upon us to whom every warder, porter and jailer is an unresisted lord.

ROBERT SOUTHWELL, *An Humble Supplication*

12

The Mass

SACRIFICE AND PRIESTHOOD

If then they will stand upon their later translations and refuse to justify the former, let us demand of them concerning all their English translations, why and to what end they suppress the name priest, translating it *Elder*, in all places where the Holy Scripture would signify by *Presbyter* and *Presbyterium*, the Priests and Priesthood of the New Testament?

Understand, gentle reader, their wily policy therein is this. To take away the holy sacrifice of the Mass, they take away both altar and priest, because they know that these three (priest, sacrifice and altar) are dependents and consequences one of another, so that they cannot be separated. If there be an external sacrifice, there must be an external priesthood to offer it, an altar to offer the same upon. So had the Gentiles their sacrifices, priests and altars: so had the Jews: so Christ himself, being a priest according to the order of Melchisedeck, had a sacrifice, his body, and an altar, his Cross: upon which he offered it.

And because he instituted this sacrifice to continue in his Church for ever in commemoration or representation of his death, therefore did he withal ordain his Apostles priests at his last supper, there and then instituted the holy order of priesthood (saying, *hoc facite*, Do this) to offer the self-same sacrifice in a mystical and unbloody manner, until the world's end.

To defeat this and to take away all external Priesthood and sacrifice, they by corrupt translation of holy Scriptures, make them clean dumb as though they had not a word of any such Priests or Priesthood as we speak of. Their Bibles (we grant) have the name of priests very often, but that is when mention is made either of the priests of the Jews or of the priests of the Gentiles (specially when they are reprehended and blamed in the holy Scriptures) and in such places our adversaries have the name Priests in their translations to make the very name of Priest odious among the common ignorant people. Again they have also the name Priests, when they are taken for all manner of men, women or children, whereby our adversaries would falsely signify that there are no other priests, as one of them of late freshly avoucheth, directly against St. Augustine, who in one brief sentence distinguisheth Priests properly so called in the Church and Priests as it is a common name to all Christians (Lib. 20 *De Civitate Dei*, cap. 10). This name then of Priest and Priesthood properly so called (as S. Augustine saith, which is an order distinct from the laity and vulgar people, ordained to offer Christ in an unbloody manner to his heavenly father for us, to preach and minister the sacraments, and to be the Pastors of the people) they wholly suppress in their translations, and in all places where the Holy Scripture calleth them, *Presbyteros*, there they never translate *Priests* but *Elders*, and that they do observe so duly and so warily and with so full and general consent in all their English Bibles, as the Puritans do plainly confess, and M. Whitgift denieth it not, that a man would wonder to see how careful they are that the people may not once hear the name of any such Priest in all the holy Scriptures.

But, alas, the effect of this corruption and heresy concerning Priests, hath it not wrought within these few years such contempt of priests, that nothing is more odious in our country than that name: which before was so honourable and venerable, and now is among all good men? . . . Sacrifice and priesthood go forgotten, and therefore were both honourable together: so when they had according to Daniel's prophecy, abolished the daily sacrifice out of the Church, what remained but the contempt of Priests and Clergy and their offices, so far forth that, for the holy Sacrifice sake, Priests are called in great despite 'Massing Priests.'

GREGORY MARTIN, *A Discourse of the Manifold Corruptions*
of the Holy Scriptures

THE PROTESTANT CATECHISM

i. *Master*. Of this that thou hast said of the Lord's Supper, meseems I may gather that the same was not ordained to this end, that Christ's body should be offered in sacrifice to God the Father for sins.

Scholar. It is not so offered. For he, when he did institute his supper, commanded us to eat his body, not to offer it. As for the prerogative of offering for sins, it pertaineth to Christ alone, as to him which is the eternal Priest; which also when he died upon the cross, once made that only and everlasting sacrifice for our salvation, and fully performed the same for ever. For us there is nothing left to do, but to take the use and benefit of that eternal sacrifice bequeathed us by the Lord himself, which we chiefly do in the Lord's Supper.

ALEXANDER NOWELL, *Catechism, 1570*

ii. *Master.* Dost thou then, . . . imagine the bread and wine to be changed into the substance of the flesh and blood of Christ?

Scholar. There is no need to invent any such change. For both the Holy Scriptures, and the best and most ancient expositors, do teach that by baptism we are likewise the members of Christ, and are of his flesh and bones, and do grow into one body with him, when yet there is no such change made in the water.

Ibid.

CATHOLICS AT MASS

No one is to be found here who complains of the length of services. If a Mass does not last nearly an hour, many are discontented. If six, eight, or more Masses are said in the same place, and on the same day (as often happens when there is a meeting of priests), the same congregation will assist at all. When they can get priests they confess every week. Quarrels are scarce known amongst them. Disputes are almost always left to the arbitration of the priest. They do not willingly intermarry with heretics, nor will they pray with them, nor do they like to have any dealings with them.

Robert Persons to Fr. Agazarri, July 1581

BISHOP JEWEL ON THE MASS

Our papists oppose us most spitefully. . . . This it is to have once tasted of the mass! He who drinks of it is mad. Depart from it, all ye who value a sound mind; who drinks of it is mad.

John Jewel to Peter Martyr (no date)

TOUCHING THE DREADFUL SACRIFICE

The same night on which he [Edmund Gennings] came to the city, he repaired to a Catholic house in Holborn, where he found M. Polidore Plasden, a very virtuous and godly priest. After a friendly and kind congratulation with some discourses of each other's success in the harvest of England, they began to confer of that which ever was and still is the chief joy of all true zealous priests and their only felicity, to wit, touching the offering of the dreadful sacrifice, where they might serve God together the next day and say Mass. At length they concluded to say their Matins together and celebrate the next morning at M. Swithun Wells his house, being in the upper end of Holborn.

Life and Death of M. Edmund Gennings

As Sure as in a Castle

He said Mass daily in his chamber and the heretics knew it well and yet he would never leave it, although the Doctors[1] willed him not to be so bold. Once being at Mass with him, an heretic lodged in the next room having perceived he struck fire,[2] did call the rest of his friends and had thought to have taken us all, who were eight in number, and came and bounced at the door several times so hard as the door was like to be laid on the floor. Mr. Woodhouse turned unto us before consecration, and bade us be of good cheer for (his life upon it) they should have no power to take us: after which words we all thought ourselves so sure as if we had been in a castle, and as he promised we were safe, for they went away.

Relation of the sufferings of Mr. Thomas Woodhouse

Mass in a Barn

A certain priest, unknown, said a private Mass on 11 April 1590 at Lea in the barn of James Catforth. James Catforth of Lea, husbandman, John Ryley of Clifton, labourer, Edmund Fidler of Lea, webster, . . . and William Houghton of Lea, alehousekeeper, with other persons unknown, were then present and heard Mass and procured the priest for saying Mass contrary to the statute.

Presentments before Session of the Peace, Lancaster,
16 July 1590

No Priest, no Mass

It is related that Edmund Plowden once came within danger of the law. One day some evil-disposed persons told him that Mass was about to be celebrated in a certain house in the neighbourhood in case he

---

[1] Doctors of Divinity, *i.e.* 'Henry Cole, Doctor of Divinity, Dean of Paul's, Dr. John Harpsfield, Archdeacon of London, Dr. Nicholas Harpsfield his brother, Dr. Dracot, Dr. Harcourt'.

[2] Presumably to light the candles for Mass.

might wish to assist thereat. Edmund accepted the invitation, attended the service, and was seen to make the sign of the Cross and use his prayer-book. Shortly afterwards, he was summoned and tried for the offence, but being suspicious of foul play somewhere or other, he cross-examined the witnesses, and amongst others the supposed priest who had officiated. He demanded of this man whether he would swear to being a priest, and upon his answering in the negative, 'Then,' quoth Plowden, 'the case is altered; no priest, no Mass; no Mass, no violation of the law.' 'The case is altered, quoth Plowden' became a common proverb.

Plowden family papers

MEMENTO, DOMINE

One day my mother, Lady Arundell, begged Father Cornelius to offer up Mass for the soul of her son John, Lord Stourton, which he consented to do. When at the altar he remained a considerable time in prayer between the consecration and the memento for the dead. After Mass he made an exhortation on the words, *Beati mortui qui in Domino moriuntur*, and then told us that he had just seen a vision. Before him was presented a forest of immense size, in which all was fire and flame, and in the midst he perceived the soul of the deceased Lord. . . . Father Cornelius wept much in relating his vision to us, and all the household, who to the number of about eighty persons were listening to him, united their tears with his. The server of the Mass [John Carey], afterwards a sufferer for the faith with Father Cornelius, saw and heard all that passed in the vision; but as for myself and the rest of those present, we only perceived, while it was manifested, a glimmering reflection like that of live coals on the wall against which the altar stood.

DOROTHY ARUNDELL, *Life of Fr. Cornelius*

ATTENDANCE TO NO OTHER THING

The Catholic religion teacheth the Holy Mass to be a sacrifice in which the very Body and Blood of our Saviour is offered up, which maketh people so devout and reverent at the service thereof, as that they kneel altogether, pray continually, give attendance to no other thing for that time, and thereupon it cometh that they bear such respect and reverence to priests; but the Protestant, allowing nothing but certain chapters, psalms and collects to be read in the vulgar tongue, giveth the people occasion to be undevout, irreligious and unreverent for that they see nothing worthy of reverence. Hereupon you may see the people at the Protestants' service, some staring about them without book or bead in their hands, some walking, some talking, some wrangling, but none kneeling or praying or using any reverence at all, either to service or minister, and no marvel when every one of them, if he can but read, can play the minister at home as well as the best curate of them all.

THOMAS HILL, *A Quatron of Reasons*

IN THE COUNTY OF LANCASTER

In the county of Lancaster they have arrested sixty men for attending mass. When the order arrived the people in the neighbourhood said that if the Queen was going to punish them for that, she would have to imprison all the country.

Bernardino de Mendoza to the King of Spain,
26 June 1580

HOW TO RECEIVE COMMUNION

1. Let the hands be held before the breast, nor lifted so high that they may hinder the priest.
2. Let the head be conveniently lifted up, and inclined to neither side, that without difficulty the mouth may be reached.
3. Let the eyes be shut or bent downward: for it is unseemly at that time, either to look upon the priest or to turn the eyes otherwhere.
4. Let the mouth be altogether quiet, without any reading or moving of lips, reasonably open and not gaping.
5. Let the tongue touch the side of the lip (not too much put forth) that it may receive the host and may bring it into the mouth. . . . For it is not to be chewed with the teeth, nor brought to the roof of the mouth, but to be swallowed (if it may be) before the ablution.
6. Let the whole body be erect and quiet without any motion, sighings, blowings, groanings, knocking of the breast, exclamations, vocal prayers, and other like things, which oftentimes bring danger either to the fall of the host, or of the touching of the teeth or lips in the time of receiving, are to be omitted.
7. After the receiving of the host, let the head not indecently be cast down, but remain erect with the hands joined before the breast until the ablution, which everyone ought to take.

HENRY GARNET, *The Society of the Rosary*

13

Douai and Rome

The Increase of Workmen

And shortly again in the year 1580, at the instance of M. D. Allen in the name of English Catholics, Father General of the same Society,[1] agreed also to send English Jesuits into this harvest, and presently sent the same Fr. Persons and Fr. Campion, both men of most excellent good talents. And the next year very notable men also, Fr. Heywood and Fr. Holt, and so continually the like missions are maintained still. Then the seminaries and the Society, with other priests remaining of the old store, laboured jointly and merrily together, for the conversion of our country *unanimes in domo Dei*. There were in England before this year, of the College of Douai, about seventy priests (which were not for every shire two) and as yet none of the College of Rome. But of this year 1580 entered the realm, of both the colleges, and of the Society, and other priests, that had lived before in Rome and elsewhere privately, near forty. And the next year about forty more. Which great increase of workmen, especially the coming in of Jesuits (whom the heretics little expected, and less wished) wrought diverse effects. Some stormed, others admired; some sought to entrap them in snares; others to be instructed and spiritually relieved by them; some imagined to dispatch all Jesuits and seminary priests out of the realm again by public proclamations and more severe parliament statutes, and greater persecution of all Catholics. But no malice being able to overthrow the work of God, still Catholics increased in number and in courage, and more were willing to suffer and to die for their faith than before; more and more were incensed with desire to go to the seminaries; and some immediately to the holy Society, that so they might enter into

[1] The Society of Jesus.

the same work, and be participant of the same glorious reward. Of which sort some be already in heaven, others yet labouring in the vineyard.

THOMAS WORTHINGTON, *A Relation of Sixteen Martyrs*

UNDERHAND EGGING

In the year 1568 (if we remember well) began the Seminary of Doway by Doctor Allen afterwards Cardinal, and divers other grave men joined with him, who seeing the ruin of Catholic religion to grow daily in England, went over the sea, placed themselves in divers universities, wrote books in confutation of English heretics, and some other attended to the setting forward of this Seminary, for maintaining and restoring both of religion and a Catholic new clergy in England.

When the Council of England did hear of [this Seminary] and of their designments . . . [they] applied themselves wholly to persecute the same as well by egging underhand some other Catholics in England to mislike of it, as a thing that would exasperate the State and hinder their peace in England as also by procuring the heretics and rebels of Flanders to drive the same out of their countries as they did about the year 1577, and they fled to Rheims in France.

When the Council thus understood of their new pitch in France they dealt effectually with the King (Henry the third) to drive them also from thence and had effectuated, as is thought, their desire, if Pope Gregory XIII had not earnestly opposed himself by intercession with the King, as also the Duke and Cardinal of Guise, in whose government the city and university of Rheims was.

Therefore when this attempt took no place, they resolved to begin another way of persecution, which was to put sedition among ourselves, by sending over spies and traitors to kindle and foster the same, such as was one Bayne, who besides other ill offices, was to poison also Dr. Allen at that time in the seminary of Rheims, as himself confessed, and when afterwards in the year 1578, they understood that a new seminary was instituted also in Rome, other like people were directed thither to like effects, as John Nicols, Salomon Aldred, Monday, Sled and others, who having sowed such seed of sedition as they could at their being in Rome, returned to England and showed themselves for open enemies.

Epistle of the English priests to Clement VIII, 20 July 1601

THE BROOD OF SEMINARISTS

The councillors of Elizabeth at first despised the poor beginnings of the seminary at Douai. They thought, and they said so too, that those who might be trained in the college, or even become priests, would, compelled by want or tempted by gain, return some day to England, accept a benefice, and minister in the Anglican churches according to the laws and teaching of the state. But if any among them should be obstinate, and refuse to conform, they would be able to do nothing; for what could a few poor and homeless men—such is the judgment of the world—do against their new Church, which was under the protection of so mighty a queen, guarded by such severe laws, watched over by such diligent ministers, and so effectually defended on every side? But before many years were over it was observed that very many young men, possessed of great gifts, went from the schools and the universities to the colleges beyond the seas, and came back before long as priests to their native land, where by preaching, by their writings and example, by the ministration of the sacraments in secret, by reconciling men to the Church, by withdrawing them from schism, and from their attendance upon the sacrilegious rites of the heretics— for many Englishmen at that time, men who in their hearts believed aright, had thus defiled themselves through fear of the laws—they made a great impression upon innumerable souls. Then the queen's advisers, when they saw this, and that the country, the towns, the universities, the houses of the nobility, and even the court itself, were full of converts, began to bewail their mistake, and by cruel laws,[1] by every human means and contrivance, and by spreading terror far and near, to set themselves against the work, which we believe to be the work of God.

NICOLAS SANDER, *Anglican Schism*

WE STRIVE IN VAIN

Some of the Queen's counsel showed themselves of the same opinion in this case, judging it vain to kill priests in England, so long as more come after them from the seminaries, and from a noble Society that dieth not. And amongst others, one M. Fleetwood, a

---

[1] 27 Eliz. c.2, 'An Act against Jesuits, seminary priests, and other suchlike disobedient persons'.

justice of the peace in his country, and a hot Protestant, when sitting upon causes of religion, he heard that there was one M. Laurence Johnson, a young man and a seminary priest (afterwards a martyr) come into the same Province, 'Nay then,' saith he, 'we strive in vain. We hoped these old Papistical priests dying, all Papistry should have died, and ended with them; but this new brood will never be rooted out, it is impossible ever to be rid of them nor to extirpate this Papistical faith out of the land.' And much more many heretics despaired of ever effectuating this their desire, to abolish the Catholic religion in England, when they saw this new fire of the Society of Jesus seize upon English hearts. Whereupon many of all other sorts of people, and some also of their Rabbins and greatest Doctors dissuaded, so much as they could, from rigorous persecution of Jesuits, seminary priests and of all other Catholics; for that the more they should blow this fire, the more it would burn. As namely Doctor Humfrey of Oxford, did so much dislike the putting to death of Fr. Campion, that he could not dissemble his counsel and opinion (no, not after the martyr's death, when it was too late to recall him to life again) but in his book entitled *De praxi Romanae Curiae* bewailed the oversight of those that caused his death, affirming that the common proverb, *Mortuus non mordet*, was not true in Campion, *Campianus enim mortuus adhuc mordet*. For Campion (saith he) *being dead doth yet bite*.

THOMAS WORTHINGTON, *A Relation of Sixteen Martyrs*

EDMUND GENNINGS AT DOUAI

Now he began to meditate on the exceeding dignities and prerogatives of priesthood, of the great charge he was to undertake, and of the exact account he was to render; yea he shaked and trembled at the words of the Prophet Malachy, *Labia Sacerdotis custodient scientiam, et legem requirent ex ore eius*; *quia Angelus Domini Exercituum est*, The lips of the priest shall keep knowledge, and men shall require the law of God from his mouth, because he is the angel of the Lord of Hosts. The apprehension of which was so vehement that it put him into a continual shaking of his flesh, as it were a palsy, which continued with him even to his dying day. And many there did note the cause, but more here in England did see the effect, and I myself at first sight did wonder at the same.

Life and Death of M. Edmund Gennings

Do It by Your Lives

It was credibly reported in the College of Douay, that in the last Parliament [1601], great complaints being made of the recusants how they increased, that her Majesty answered in these words, viz.: 'If you will have them decrease do it by your good lives and work, for I will persecute no more than I have already.'

Report on Douai

The Queen's Spies

The Queen maintains such a multitude of spies in France to dog the footsteps of the English Catholics there, that it is not possible for their friends to send them a penny without her hearing of it. They therefore constantly have recourse to me, and I send the money as if it were my own. I have now 10,000 crowns which they have asked me to send to Rouen and Paris.

Bernardino de Mendoza to the King of Spain, 6 May 1583

Roman Life

The English College is a house both large and fair, standing in the way to the Pope's palace, not far from the Castle St. Angelo. In the College, the scholars are divided, by certain number into every chamber, as in some four, in some six, or so many as the Rector thinketh convenient, as well for the health of the scholars, as the troubling not much room. Every man hath his bed proper unto himself, which is, two little trestles, with four or five boards laid along over them, and thereon a quilted mattress as we call it in England, which, every morning after they are risen, they fold up their sheets handsomely, laying them in the midst of the bed, and so roll it up to one end, covering it with the quilt, that is their coverlet all the night time.

First in the morning, he that is the porter of the College ringeth a bell, at the sound whereof every student ariseth and turneth up his bed, as I have said before. Not long after the bell ringeth again, when as everyone presently, kneeling on his knees, prayeth for the space of half an hour: at which time the bell being tolled again, they arise and bestow a certain time in study, everyone having his desk, table and chair to himself very orderly; and, all the time of study, silence is used of everyone in the chamber, not one offering molestation in speech to another.

The time of study expired, the bell calleth them from their chambers, down into the Refectorium, where everyone taketh a glass of wine and a quarter of a manchet,[1] and so he maketh his collation. Soon after, the bell knowleth again, when as the students, two and two together, walk to the Roman College, which is the place of school or instruction, where everyone goeth to his ordinary lecture, some in divinity, some to physic, some to logic, and some to rhetoric. There they remain the lecture time, which being done, they return home to the College again; where they spend the time till dinner in walking and talking up and down the gardens. . . .

Having recreated themselves somewhat, either in the house or in the gardens, [they] are now at the sound of the bell come into the Refectorium to dinner. The custom is, that daily two of the students take it by turns to serve all the other at the table, who, to help them, have the butler, the porter, and a poor Jesuit, that looketh to all the scholars' necessaries, to bring them their clean shirts, and foreseeth that neither their gowns, cassocks, doublets, breeches, hose, nor shoes, want mending. These bring in their hands, each of them, a round board, which hath a staff about half a yard long made fast through the middle of it, and round about that board is set little saucers wherein the cook shareth every man a little quantity, which they bring, and hold over the table, when as every man taketh his own mess.

As for their fare, trust me, it is very fine and delicate, for every man hath his own trencher, his manchet, knife, spoon, and fork laid by it, and then a fair white napkin covering it, with his glass and pot of wine set by him. And the first mess, or antepast, as they call it, that is brought to the table, is some fine meat to urge them to have an appetite, as sometimes the Spanish anchovies, and sometimes stewed prunes and raisins of the sun together, having such a fine tart syrup made to them, as I promise you a weak stomach would very well digest them. The second is a certain mess of pottage of that country manner, no meat sod in them, but are made of divers things whose proper names I do not remember, but methought they were both good and wholesome. The third is boiled meat, as kid, mutton, chicken, and such like, every man a pretty modicum of each thing. The fourth is roasted meat, of the daintiest provision that they can get, and sometimes stewed and baked meat, according as pleaseth Master Cook to order it. The fifth and last is sometime cheese, sometime preserved conceits, sometime figs, almonds and raisins, a lemon and sugar, a

[1] *manchet*: a loaf of wheaten bread.

pomegranate, or some such sweet geete, for they know that English-men love sweetmeats.

And all the dinner while, one of the scholars, according as they take it by weekly turn, readeth, first, a chapter of their Bible, and then, in their Martyrologium, he readeth the martyrdom of some of the saints, as St. Francis, St. Martin, St. Longinus, that thrust the spear into Christ's side, St. Agatha, St. Barbara, St. Cecilia, and divers others, among whom they have imprinted the martyrdom of Dr. Storie, the two Nortons, John Felton, and others, calling them by the name of saints, who were here executed at Tyburn for high treason.

The dinner done, they recreate themselves for the space of an hour, and then the bell calleth them to their chambers, where they stay awhile, studying on their lectures given them in the forenoon; anon the bell summoneth them to school again, where they stay not past an hour, but they return home again, and, as soon as they be come in, they go into the Refectorium, and there everyone hath his glass of wine and a quarter of a manchet again, according as they had in the morning.

Then they depart to their chambers, from whence at convenient time they are called to exercise of disputation: the divines to a lecture appointed for them, and every study to a several Jesuit, where they continue the space of an hour, and afterward, till supper time, they are at their recreation.

After supper, if it be in winter time, they go with the Jesuits and sit about a great fire talking. . . .

After they have talked a good while, the bell calleth them to their chamber, the porter going from chamber to chamber, and lighteth a lamp in every one. So, when the scholars come, they light their lamps, lay down their beds, and go sit at their desks and study a little, till the bell rings, when everyone falls on his knees to prayers.

Then one of the priests in the chamber, as in every chamber there is some, beginneth the Latin litany,' all the scholars in the chamber answering him. And so they spend the time till the bell rings again, which is for everyone to go to bed.

ANTHONY MUNDAY, *The English Roman Life*

DEFENCE OF THE ENGLISH STUDENTS

Now whereas we are most uncourteously called 'a multitude of dissolute young men,' we desire no other evidence to disprove this accusation than an indifferent censure. For first before our departure out of the realm, we must resolve to abandon our country, friends, and all such comforts as naturally all men seek and find in their native soil: we must relinquish all possibilities of favour, riches, and credit: we must limit our minds to the restrained and severe course of the Society of Jesus, or the seminaries; where the place is in exile, the rules strict, the government austere, our wills broken, the least faults chastised, and a most absolute virtue exacted. And who can imagine those to be of so dissolute humours, who thus determine to abridge themselves of all causes of dissoluteness, and to imprison their affections within the precinct of a regular and strait order? And lest haply it may be imagined that we say more than in proof we find, it is known to thousands, and daily seen and witnessed by travellers that we are there tied to so precise terms in diet, apparel, exercise, and all other things, that we are much more shortened of our scope than in any college of our English universities. I omit the prayers, fastings, hair-cloths, and other chastisements of the body, which being voluntary, yet usual, are to any (if not more than partial judges) invincible grounds against this slander of our being dissolute, that being by the laws, by examples, by common experience taught, with what bloody conflicts they are here to encounter, and how many fears, dangers, and bloody agonies both in life and death they are undoubtedly to expect, are notwithstanding contented, for the reclaiming of souls into God's fold, willingly to yield their bodies to the hazard of all these miseries foreseen and foreknown, and advisedly chosen before all worldly contentments.

ROBERT SOUTHWELL, *An Humble Supplication*

DEFEND THIS COLLEGE

All Catholics here lift up their hands and thank God and his Holiness for founding such a college at Rome, beyond all their hopes; and they beseech his Holiness, by the bowels of the mercy of our Saviour, to defend the college, and to enlarge it for the needs of the present time.

Robert Persons to. Claude Aquaviva, November 1580

CAUGHT ON THE JOURNEY

Here were lately fifteen or sixteen youths of good houses taken as they were going over to the seminaries.

John Chamberlain to Mr. Dudley Carleton, 27 May 1601

COUNTER-MISSIONARIES

Some of the chief heretics here have held a conference, and have resolved, in reprisal for the priests who have come to preach here, to send Englishmen to sow the weed of heresy in Spain.

Bernardino de Mendoza to the King of Spain,
1 October 1581

AQUAVIVA CONCURS

Dr. Allen coming to Rome not many months after upon the year 1579 made together with Fr. Persons a perfect union and correspondence between the two seminaries, how scholars should depart from the one to the other, how they should be sent to England and the like.

But his special consolation was that he had obtained of Pope Gregory that some of the English Fathers of the said Society should for time to come be sent into England together with the priests of the seminaries. For obtaining which point the said Doctor had laboured much and alleged many reasons, and (among others) that it would be a notable encouragement and help to the seminaries to have the said religious men of the Society, not only to assist them abroad in their studies and institution of life, but also at home in this war and combat against the sectaries, which war growing now more sharp than before had need of more men and assistance; and that it would animate the Catholics in England to see religious men to return thither again after a long exile, and especially such religious men as could pretend the recovery of no temporal possessions from any man and whose institute was proper for this purpose to be sent in missions; and that God had concurred with them hitherto in all other countries as well of Europe, Asia and Africa and the Indies; and finally that this was the desire of all good Catholics of our country.

These and like reasons being proposed and urged by the said Dr. Allen both to the General and the Pope as before has been said, albeit the said General with his Assistants and Counsellors found divers difficulties in the matter in respect of the novelty thereof, especially about their manner of living there in secular men's houses in secular apparel, diet and conversation and the like, as also how their rules and orders for conservation of religious spirit might be there observed, whereof they had more care then than of any corporal dangers to their bodies; yet understanding afterward that the Pope was much inclined to have this suit granted [he consented]. Wherein the Father that was then Provincial of the Roman Province and afterwards General, Fr. Claudius Aquaviva, did not a little help forwarding the matter, not only favouring the said mission but offering himself also to go therein. But Almighty God that had appointed to take unto himself the very next year that blessed man Everard Mercurianus, had designed also that this man should succeed him in his place and perfect that which the other had begun, which he hath now done with all affection for the space of 24 years and hath profited the English mission much more absent by his authority and favour than if he had been employed there in person himself.

ROBERT PERSONS, *First Entry of the Fathers of the Society*

ON THE ROAD FROM ROME

But Father Campion . . . had a fashion to leave the rest of the company every morning after the *Itinerarium* was said and to get him before for the space of some half a mile or more, to the end that he might with more freedom make his prayers alone and utter his zealous affections unto his Saviour without being heard or noted by his fellows. And this he used throughout all the way, which endured more than a month, and would not suffer himself to be overtaken until he had fully finished his devotions, which was commonly one hour before dinner, and then he would stay to go in company with the rest and would be so merry and talk of suffering for Christ with such comfort . . . as a man might easily perceive with whom he had had conversation in his prayers before.

ROBERT PERSONS, *Life of Edmund Campion*

A LAST MESSAGE TO THE ENGLISH PRIESTS

I cannot but advertise you, my loving brethren that be priests, of this one thing, that I would have you use great compassion and mercifulness towards such of the laity, especially as for mere fear or saving their family, wife and children from ruin, are so far only fallen as to come sometimes to their churches or be present at the time of their service. For though it be not lawful to do so much, nor yet in itself in any ways excusable, yet such necessity in that kind of men maketh the offence less and more compassionable, yea, and more easily by you to be absolved. And therefore be not hard nor rough nor

rigorous nor *morosi* in receiving again and absolving them when they
confess their infirmities. . . . Which mercy you must use, though they
fall more than once, and though perhaps you have some probable fear
that they will of like infirmity fall again; whereof we yet cannot be
assured, because God may give them more strength. . . . Yet, on the
other side, you and all my brethren must have great regard that you
teach not nor defend that it is lawful to communicate with the Protestants in their prayers or service or conventicles, where they meet to
minister their untrue sacraments; for this is contarry to the practice of
the Church and the holy Doctors in all ages who never communicated
or allowed any Catholic person to pray together with Arians, Donatists or what other soever. Neither is it a positive law of the Church,
for so it might be dispensed withal upon some occasion; but it is
denied of God's own eternal law, as by many evident arguments I could
convince. . . . To make all sure, I have demanded the Pope's Holiness
that now is his sentence; who expressly told me that to participate with
the Protestants either by praying with them or coming to their
churches or service or such like was by no means lawful or dispensable,
but added withal, that such as of fear and weakness or other temporal
force or necessity should do it, ought to be gently dealt withal and
easily absolved, as said before. This is his Holiness's express will . . . in
which I desire all my loving fellows to agree, *ut non sint in vobis schismata.*

Cardinal Allen to the Catholics of England

14

Secret Arrivals

THE LANDING OF FR. GERARD AND FR. OLDCORNE

In the year 1588, he and Father Gerard were received together into the Society by the Rev. Father Claudius Aquaviva, General of the same, upon the Assumption of our Blessed Lady; and within five or six weeks after were sent together into England, in company with two other Priests who were not of the Society. By the way Father Oldcorne gave very great edification unto all his company with his religious behaviour, showing in all his actions great humility and readiness to help and assist any of them in their needs. When they came to the sea-side, they understood of the extraordinary difficulty to pass into England, and of such persecution in England at that time, as had not been of long time before, the Earl of Leicester (who then ruled and overruled all under Queen Elizabeth) having made a solemn vow, that within a twelvemonth he would not leave one Papist in England; but God with His mercy prevented the malice of that persecutor, and called him out of this life within half the time that he had limited for the life of others. But in the meantime he caused divers to be put to death, both Priests and others, and set watch and ward in every town, so that none could pass the country that were not known, and could not satisfy the officers of their dwelling and manner of life. In which regard those Fathers of the College where Father Oldcorne and Father Gerard stayed[1] whilst a passage was preparing, would not by any means let them pass, thinking it impossible they should land safely and get safely to London.

Whereupon they wrote back to Rome, to know their Superiors' mind, yet with earnest suit that it might please them to permit their

[1] St. Omer.

going forward. They received answer from Father Persons, that the times were much more periculous than was expected when they went from Rome, yet sith the cause was God's, and their will so good to prefer the safety of others' souls before the safety of their own bodies, they might in the name of God proceed, if their desire still continued; but that it was left unto their own election. These letters were received with great joy, and the two Fathers, within few days after, got a ship wherein they embarked, thinking to have landed in the north parts of England; but sailing along the coast of England one evening, and seeing a shore where they might be set on land, and no town nor house near them to see where they landed, they resolved to commit themselves to the providence of God, and caused the sailors to cast anchor until it was dark, and then in a cock-boat to set them on land. When they were landed, having first commended themselves to God, they purposed to have gone forward in the first way they could find, to get as far from the sea-side before morning as they could; but they found that every path did lead them to some house or other, where the dogs making a noise, they durst proceed no further in that course; but got them into a wood, and there stayed all night, whilst it rained a good pace. But yet they were as merry as might be, and well contented with their wet lodging, as I have heard one of them affirm from whom I have these particulars. Towards day they commended their business earnestly to God, and, after their prayers, resolved not to adventure both to go one way to London, but to take several courses, that so if one were taken in the time of danger, the other might scape. They therefore looked into their provision of money, and he that had more gave it unto the other to make it equal, and then they embraced and gave one the other their benediction; and one went out on the one side of the wood, the other went out of the other hand. They never had been in that country before, nor knew any one person in the country, nor the way to London, where they promised to meet. But God provided for them both.

JOHN GERARD, *Narrative of the Gunpowder Plot*

FR. GENNINGS LEAVES FOR ENGLAND, 1590

He took his leave of all the Superiors and scholars, who weeping even as those good Christians did for the departure of St. Paul and falling upon his neck they kissed him with tears and many of them brought him forth to the gates of the city, with divers others his companions in that journey, as F. Tho. Stanney of the Society of Jesus, M. Singleton, M. William Mush and M. Robert Clinch, all priests. Within a few days they came to Tréport in Normandy, where presently they endeavoured to procure a speedy and (if it might be) a safe passage. And behold, after two or three days' abode there, they found an unexpected and altogether unwonted vessel fraught for England, whose master was a Frenchman and in religion well affected. This man imagining (as it may be supposed) what they were, offered them unrequested safe passage, and to set them ashore by night, if they so pleased. . . .

On the next morning committing themselves to the tuition of their high Protector God Almighty, they took shipping, and wind and weather being both prosperous, they sailed along the coast of England and meant to have landed on Essex side: but for their sakes the master of the bark lingered that evening until it was two hours within the night, and being come near unto Scarborough, there came out a little boat with divers rovers or pirates in it, to have surprised them, who shot at them divers times with muskets, but had no harm; for the wind being then somewhat contrary, the master turned his ship and sailed back into the main sea, where in foul weather they remained three days; and so at last being driven eastward, they landed near unto Whitby in Yorkshire on the side of a high cliff, with great danger to their lives. At last they came to Whitby, where going into an inn they found there one Ratcliffe, a pursuivant, who after an exact view of them all, questioned with them about their arrival in that place, whence they came and whither they would? They answered that, coming from Newcastle, they were by tempest driven thither. And so after refreshing of themselves, they all went to a Catholic gentleman his house (whose name for divers respects I suppress) within two or three miles of Whitby, by whom they were directed some to one place, some to another, according to their own desires.

Thus being each one sent to several places, M. Gennings with one other kept together, who travelling by the way, determined at last to separate themselves . . . and so severally to commit themselves to the protection of God and their good angels. And whiles they thus resolved, they came to two fair beaten ways, the one tending north-east and the other south-east, and there (it being in the night) they stayed and fell both down on their knees, making a short prayer together, that Almighty God of his infinite mercy would vouchsafe to respect his humble servants and send them peaceable passage into the thickest of his vineyard. Then rising up they embraced one another with tears trickling down their cheeks. Thus Edmund took his leave.

Seeing (quoth he) we must now part, through fear of our enemies and for our greater security, farewell, sweet brother in Christ and most loving companion. God grant that as we have been friends in one College and companions in one wearisome and dangerous journey, so we may have a merry meeting once again in this world to our good comfort (if it shall please Him) even amongst His and our great adversaries. . . . And also, as we began, so we may end together in Jesus Christ.

Thus being not able to speak one word more for grief and tears, they departed with mutual silence, the one directing his journey towards London, because he was born there, the other northward, because he was affected that way.

Life and Death of M. Edmund Gennings

SAFE ENTRY OF PRIESTS, 1581

Thirty priests at least have entered England since Easter, nor was any one of them hindered at the port, or afterwards taken, blessed be God!

William Allen to Fr. Agazarri, 23 June 1581

IN COMELY APPAREL

And furthermore, because it is known and proved by common experience . . . that they do come into the same [realm] by secret creeks, and landing places, disguised both in names and persons; some in apparel as soldiers, mariners, or merchants, pretending that they have heretofore been taken prisoners, and put into galleys, and delivered. Some come in as gentlemen, with contrary names, in comely apparel, as though they had travelled into foreign countries for knowledge: and generally all, for the most part, are clothed like gentlemen in apparel, and many as gallants; yea in all colours, and with feathers and such like, disguising themselves; and many of them in their behaviours as ruffians, far off to be thought or suspected to be friars, priests, jesuits, or popish scholars.

The Proclamation against Jesuits, 21 November 1591

FR. WATKINSON REACHES LONDON

I was acquainted with a niece of Mr. Robert Watkinson, who told me that he came from Rome into England for his health before he had ended his studies, and that soon after his arrival, walking in London streets, he met a poor man unknown to him, who welcoming him into England said, 'Sir, you are come hither for your health. Within a month you shall be rid of all diseases.' Mr. Watkinson, wondering to hear this from a stranger, put his hand into his pocket for to give him an alms, but the poor man was vanished, and soon after Mr. Watkinson was apprehended for a priest and within a month crowned a martyr.

Thomas Carey to Martin Greene, 4 June 1566

By Tottenham High-cross

I came over a little before the last statute made against the coming in of priests,[1] and by reason thereof I found everybody so fearful as none would receive me into their houses. Wherefore I, with another priest called John Taddy, hired a chamber in a poor cottage in the wood, by Tottenham High-cross, where we remained close for six or seven months, sending the poor man to the city for victuals.

Confession of John Brushford

Fr. Roger Dickenson's Defence

I came into the realm, my native country, to give myself to study, to prayer and devotion and to use my function, and that, I hope, is no treason.

GRENE, *Collections*

[1] 27 Eliz., 1585.

15

The New Priests

THE COMING OF THE JESUITS AND CERTAIN STRANGE THINGS

i. But as for the common people they were yet much more moved with this matter and as it were amazed, not knowing what to say or think of the same: for on the one side they were told of certain strange named men called Jesuits that were come into the land and were enemies to her Majesty and to the now established religion and to the state of the realm, and that they were sought for diligently as the most perilous persons to the weal public; and yet upon the other side they understood that they were ecclesiastical men that came without weapons only to preach and teach the old ancient doctrine of their forefathers, fasting, praying, confession, restitution of goods wrong-fully taken away, and the like, and to dispute with their ministers about these points, whose lives they well knew to be far distant from any of these things: so as they remained doubtful what would be the event and whether any change would follow or no in matters of religion.

And much more particularly were the vulgar sort moved to these imaginations by certain strange things that had fallen out in England about the very same time of Father Campion's entering, I mean, in the months of April, May and June 1580, which wonders I shall briefly touch here according to the substance of that which John Stow chronicler of England setteth down in his Annals written and printed this very year of 1580, to wit, within very few days after the said events fell out, and published by public approbation of the Queen's privilege and dedicated to the Earl of Leicester, where he saith as follows.

First, that upon the 6th of April in this year 1580 being Wednesday in Easter week about 6 of the clock towards evening a strange and sudden earthquake happened in London and in many other parts of England all at one hour; the great clock-bell of Westminster struck of itself with shaking against the hammer as also did many other clocks and bells of the city and other places. The gentlemen students of the Temple being at supper, seeing the tables move, ran out of the Hall with their knives in their hands: a piece of the Temple Church fell down as did also a piece of Christ's Church at sermon time and slew two persons: other earthquakes followed saith John Stow in the month of April and the next of May which put men generally in exceeding great fear and amazement.

Secondly, the same historiographer writes that the next month after, to wit, June, there followed such tempests of lightning and thunder and monstrous hailstones as was wonderful, and that presently after one of these tempests a woman named Alice Perin of the age of 80 years was delivered of a strange and hideous monster (for so are his words) whose head was like a headpiece of harness, his face resembled a man's face, but his mouth was very small and round like unto the mouth of a mouse: the former or upper part of his body was like also a man's body but that it had eight legs, not one like to another, and besides all this he had a tail of half a yard long and that not long after this there was another monster born of one Agnes the wife of William that was male and female and had his mouth and eyes like a lion and other parts no less monstrous.

Thirdly, the same author writeth that upon the 18th day of May of this year about one hour before sun setting, divers gentlemen of worship and credit riding from the town of Bodmin in Cornwall they saw risen in the north east over the sea a great mist or fog much like unto the sea, and therein the form of a cloud like some great castle with flags and streamers thereon, vanishing away there succeeded another cloud in place thereof like unto a great argosal furnished with masts and other necessaries and her sails full of wind, having also flags and streamers very warlike and two boats at every stern, and she made her way on the south-west of the said castle with another argosal after her furnished as the other: and after this came again 3 or 4 gallies with their masts and flags at their sterns in very warlike fashion and this sight endured for the space of an hour.

Moreover the same author writeth that at the very same time, to wit, the very self day that the first earthquake was, by report of many honest men there was heard five miles from Blonsdon in Wiltshire a cry of hounds in the air and the noise thereof was so great that they seemed three or four score couple of hounds, whereat divers men took their greyhounds to go and course for that they supposed that some gentlemen had been hunting in the chase, but at length finding no such matter, some of them looking up into the air saw divers hounds perfectly to be discerned in the same.

Fifthly, the same writer reporteth that about the same time a certain worthy gentleman of the country did write to a right good gentleman in the court (for so are his words) that there was seen upon a down called Brodwels Down in Somerset 60 personages all clothed in black a furlong only in distance from those that beheld them: and after their appearing and a little while tarrying and encountering the one the other they vanished away, but immediately another strange company of like attire, colour and number appeared in the self same place and they encountered the one the other and after vanished away: and then the third time appeared the like number but all in bright armour and harness and encountered the one the other as before and so vanished away. And for the truth of this, saith John Stow, four honest men that saw the sight were examined upon their oaths before Sir George Norton Knight and they deposed in all respects as hath been rehearsed. This writeth John Stow and before him Thomas Churchyard: and it is to be noted that these things are to be found only in the Chronicles of Stow set forth in the year 1580, dedicated, as I said, to the Earl of Leicester, but in his later edition of the said Chronicle which he published in 1592 and is dedicated to Whitgift that calleth himself Archbishop of Canterbury, he setteth not down these stories at length but saith thus: This year were many monstrous births and strange sights to be seen, which I overpass in this place, for that I have partly touched them in my summary.

These strange things then being published among the people as well by writing, printing and reporting presently after they had happened, which was the very same time that our arrival was divulged in England, men could not tell what to think: and divers made sundry commentaries and expositions upon these accidents. For some men said that those earthquakes, extraordinary tempests and monstrous births were warnings to the Protestants to look about to the monstrous doctrine compounded of all variety of ancient heresies as hermaphroditus was of diverse sexes; and that those argosies and gallies, which are foreign kind of vessels, that came to assault the castle did signify these worthy champions of Christ that were newly come from beyond the seas to batter the castle of sin and heresy in England: and that the sight of hounds in the air imported the like, for that as S. Gregory in his *Morals* saith the name of hounds in Scripture is taken oftentimes for preachers that bark against wickedness and with the virtue of their tongues do heal the sores of sins as the others' tongues do heal wounds. And finally the last sight of three score persons in black attire encountering the one the other so many times, might more manifestly be interpreted of the combat between these priests coming from foreign countries and the Ministers and clergy of England and their last encounter the third time in bright harness signifieth that this contention is not to surcease quickly but to endure and every day wear hotter and hotter until at last the conquest remain on the one side or the other.

Such were the discourses and interpretations of each man concerning these affairs as either his judgment or affection did lean him. But the ignorant people stood astonished and knew not what to believe or say: and for that most part of them, especially those that live in the country out of towns, are generally well affected to the Catholic religion and out of conceit with the life of their Ministers, they were glad to hear of the coming of these other preachers and desirous to hear them until at length the fury of persecution making their cause to be treason and their aiders or receivers to be traitors did terrify the weak sort as afterwards will appear.

ROBERT PERSONS, *Life of Edmund Campion*

ii. This year April 6 [1580] between five and six of the clock in the afternoon Oxford was sorely shaken with an earthquake, being Wednesday in Easter week. All people being amazed left their houses and ran into the open places. The birds that had taken up their nests in the holes and roofs of houses, suddenly fled, and others of the air settled on the earth. The cows and oxen at the sudden alteration lowed, and other cattle were much affrighted. Oxford was not the sole sharer of this earthquake, but also all England, France, Flanders and other regions. At the same instant of time, as 'twas generally supposed, the sea was so much tossed and troubled that the mariners expected sudden destruction. In many places the earth shook twice in one night, and in Kent some thrice in a fortnight, and the first time so much that not only the foundations of houses and churches, but also the roofs suffered great damage.

ANTHONY WOOD, *History and Antiquities of the University of Oxford*

iii. He [Edmund Gennings] loved greatly to behold the heavens, and therefore he usually went forth in the evening to delight himself with the sight of the skies bedecked with stars. And on a time in these his tender years going forth at night according to his custom this strange spectacle appeared to him in the air. He saw, as it were, armed men with weapons killing and murdering, others that were disarmed and altogether destitute of like furniture and a great store of blood running everywhere about them.

This strange sight put the child into a great fear, which caused him to run in hastily to tell his mother, being then a widow, what he had seen, and she presently went forth with three or four of her neighbours who that night had supped with her, and they were all eye-witnesses of the same spectacle. Thus much I myself have heard them report, who also affirmed that myself was then present, but being very young I cannot remember it. This happened in the beginning of our chiefest persecution, not long before the glorious death of Blessed Father Campion about the year 1581.

Life and Death of M. Edmund Gennings

ON HORSEBACK I MEDITATE

I ride about some piece of the country every day. The harvest is wonderful great. On horseback I meditate my sermon; when I come to the house, I polish it. Then I talk with such as come to speak with me, or hear their confessions. In the morning, after Mass, I preach; they hear with exceeding greediness, and very often receive the sacrament, for the ministration whereof we are ever well assisted by priests, whom we find in every place, whereby both the people is well served, and we much eased in our charge. . . . I cannot long escape the hands of the heretics; the enemies have so many eyes, so many tongues, so many scouts and crafts. I am in apparel to myself very ridiculous; I often change it, and my name also. I read letters sometimes myself that in the first front tell news that Campion is taken, which, noised in every place where I come, so filleth my ears with the sound thereof, that fear itself hath taken away all fear. My soul is in mine own hands ever. . . . Marry, the solaces that are ever intermingled with the miseries are so great, that they do not only countervail the fear of what punishment temporal soever, but by infinite sweetness make all worldly pains be they never so great, seem nothing. A conscience pure, a courage invincible, zeal incredible, a work so worthy the number innumerable, of high degree, of mean calling, of the inferior sort, of every age and sex.

Here, even amongst the Protestants themselves that are of milder nature, it is turned into a proverb, that he must be a Catholic that payeth faithfully what he oweth, insomuch that if any Catholic do injury, everybody expostulateth with him as for an act unworthy of men of that calling. To be short, heresy heareth ill of all men; neither is there any condition of people commonly counted more vile and impure than their ministers, and we worthily have indignation that fellows so unlearned, so evil, so derided, so base, should in so desperate a quarrel overrule such a number of noble wits as our realm hath. Threatening edicts come forth against us daily; notwithstanding, by good heed, and the prayers of good men, and, which is the chief of all, God's special gift, we have passed safely through the most part of the island. I find many neglecting their own security to have only care of my safety.

Edmund Campion to Claude Aquaviva, 17 November 1580

Campion's Challenge

Right Honourable:

Whereas I have come out of Germany and Boëmeland, being sent by my Superiors, and adventured myself into this noble Realm, my dear country, for the glory of God and benefit of souls, I thought it like enough that, in this busy, watchful and suspicious world, I should either sooner or later be intercepted and stopped of my course. Wherefore, providing for all events, and uncertain what may become of me, when God shall haply deliver my body into durance, I supposed it needful to put this writing in a readiness, desiring your good Lordships to give it your reading, for to know my cause. This doing, I trust I shall ease you of some labour. For that which otherwise you must have sought for by practice of wit, I do now lay into your hands by plain confession. And to the intent that the whole matter may be conceived in order, and so the better both understood and remembered, I make thereof these ix points or articles, directly, truly and resolutely opening my full enterprise and purpose.

1. I confess that I am (albeit unworthy) a priest of the Catholic Church, and through the great mercy of God vowed now these viii years into the Religion of the Society of Jesus. Hereby I have taken upon me a special kind of warfare under the banner of obedience, and

eke resigned all my interest or possibility of wealth, honour, pleasure, and other worldly felicity.

2. At the voice of our General Provost, which is to me a warrant from heaven, and Oracle of Christ, I took my voyage from Prague to Rome (where our said General Father is always resident) and from Rome to England, as I might and would have done joyously into any part of Christendom or Heathenness, had I been thereto assigned.

3. My charge is, of free cost to preach the Gospel, to minister the Sacraments, to instruct the simple, to reform sinners, to confute errors —in brief, to cry alarm spiritual against foul vice and proud ignorance, wherewith many my dear countrymen are abused.

4. I never had mind, and am strictly forbidden by our Father that sent me, to deal in any respect with matter of State or Policy of this realm, as things which appertain not to my vocation, and from which I do gladly restrain and sequester my thoughts.

5. I do ask, to the glory of God, with all humility, and under your correction, three sorts of indifferent and quiet audiences: *the first* before your Honours, wherein I will discourse of religion, so far as it toucheth the common weal and your nobilities: *the second*, whereof I make more account, before the Doctors and Masters and chosen men of both Universities, wherein I undertake to avow the faith of our Catholic Church by proofs innumerable, Scriptures, Councils, Fathers, History, natural and moral reasons: *the third* before the lawyers, spiritual and temporal, wherein I will justify the said faith by the common wisdom of the laws standing yet in force and practice.

6. I would be loth to speak anything that might sound of any insolent brag or challenge, especially being now as a dead man to this world and willing to put my head under every man's foot, and to kiss the ground they tread upon. Yet have I such a courage in avouching the Majesty of Jesus my King, and such affiance in his gracious favour, and such assurance in my quarrel, and my evidence so impregnable, and because I know perfectly that no one Protestant, nor all the Protestants living, nor any sect of our adversaries (howsoever they face men down in pulpits, and overrule us in their kingdom of grammarians and unlearned ears) can maintain their doctrine in disputation. I am to sue most humbly and instantly for the combat with all and every of them, and the most principal that may be found: protesting that in this trial the better furnished they come, the better welcome they shall be.

7. And because it hath pleased God to enrich the Queen my Sovereign Lady with notable gifts of nature, learning, and princely education,

I do verily trust that—if her Highness would vouchsafe her royal person and good attention to such a conference as, in the second part of my fifth article I have motioned, or to a few sermons, which in her or your hearing I am to utter,—such manifest and fair light by good method and plain dealing may be cast upon these controversies, that possibly her zeal of truth and love of her people shall incline her noble Grace to disfavour some proceedings hurtful to the Realm, and procure towards us oppressed more equity.

8. Moreover I doubt not but you her Highness' Council being of such wisdom and discreet in cases most important, when you shall have heard these questions of religion opened faithfully, which many times by our adversaries are huddled up and confounded, will see upon what substantial grounds our Catholic Faith is builded, how feeble that side is which by sway of the time prevaileth against us, and so at last for your own souls, and for many thousand souls that depend upon your government, will discountenance error when it is bewrayed, and hearken to those who would spend the best blood in their bodies for your salvation. Many innocent hands are lifted up to heaven for you daily by those English students, whose posterity shall never die, which beyond seas, gathering virtue and sufficient knowledge for the purpose, are determined never to give you over, but either to win you heaven, or to die upon your pikes. And touching our Society, be it known to you that we have made a league—all the Jesuits in the world, whose succession and multitude must overreach all the practices of England—cheerfully to carry the cross you shall lay upon us, and never to despair your recovery, while we have a man left to enjoy your Tyburn, or to be racked with your torments, or consumed with your prisons. The expense is reckoned, the enterprise is begun; it is of God, it cannot be withstood. So the faith was planted: so it must be restored.

9. If these my offers be refused, and my endeavours can take no place, and I, having run thousands of miles to do you good, shall be rewarded with rigour, I have no more to say but to recommend your case and mine to Almighty God, the searcher of hearts, who send us his grace, and set us at accord before the day of payment, to the end we may at last be friends in heaven, when all injuries shall be forgotten.

Edmund Campion to the Privy Council

THE SOULS OF CATHOLICS

The souls of Catholics are more precious than our bodies; and when we reckon the price at which they were bought, it should not seem much to endanger our lives for their salvation. That Sacred Blood is still warm, those wounds still open, and those bruises may still be seen, with which God redeemed the souls that we are tending. At such a sight dangers may well be scorned, lest such precious pearls be lost.

Robert Southwell to Claude Aquaviva, 21 December 1586

CANTICLES IN A STRANGE LAND

We have altogether, with much comfort, renewed the vows of the Society, according to our custom, spending some days in exhortations and spiritual conferences. *Aperuimus ora et attraximus spiritum.* It seems to me that I see the beginnings of a religious life set on foot in England, of which we now sow the seeds with tears, that others hereafter may with joy carry in the sheaves to the heavenly granaries.

We have sung the canticles of the Lord in a strange land, and in this desert we have sucked honey from the rock and oil from the hard stone. But these our joys ended in sorrow, and sudden fears dispersed us into different places; but, in fine, we were more afraid than hurt, for we all escaped.

Robert Southwell to Claude Aquaviva, 8 March 1590

THE BASE BIRTH OF PRIESTS

And for the baseness of their birth . . . I mean not to dwell long upon it: for the thing neither importeth any offence to God, nor crime against your Majesty, nor greatly abaseth them, whom excellent virtues (the only true measures of worthiness) have ennobled. . . . How many of them are Knights' and Esquires' sons, and otherwise allied both to worshipful and noble houses, and heirs to fair revenues, let their own friends and parents dispersed through the whole realm bear witness! This only we may say in answer to our objected baseness; that in the small number of the Catholic priests of our nation (which reacheth not to the tenth of the Protestant ministry) there are very near as many, yea happily more gentlemen, than in all the other clergy of the whole realm.

ROBERT SOUTHWELL, *An Humble Supplication*

NO BREAD WITHOUT FEAR

The fruit that priests do is unspeakable. . . . It is a singular comfort to see how willingly they venture their lives, never sleeping one night in security, nor eating a bit of bread without fear, but like men ever in hazard of their liberties and lives, they are still in expectation of the persecutor: yet nothing dismayed with all these frights, they still pursue their labours and attend to gain souls, riding, going, toiling, and wearying themselves in all kinds of travails.

And God hath so framed the minds of Catholics that, notwith-standing all dangers, they are, in regard of their conscience, contented to venture their lives and livings for priests' safety; rather hazarding that they *have* than that they *are*, and preferring God and their soul before all earthly things.

The reverence and respect of Catholics to priests is very much; and whereas there are now no prelates nor bishops to honour the clergy, God hath so disposed their minds that every priest is as much rever-enced as heretofore bishops.

They so much esteem the blessing of a priest that they not only ask it every day, at their first meeting with priests and their last parting from them, but if any other come between these times to ask bene-diction, they all ask with them, never weary, yea never almost satisfied with being blessed.

A report from England (undated)

A WAY TO DEAL WITH ALL SORTS

As soon as any father or learned priest has entered an heretical country he should seek out some gentleman to be his companion. This man should be zealous, loyal, discreet and determined to help him in this service of God, and should be able to undertake honourably the expenses of them both. He should [be] knowledgeable about the country, the roads and paths, the habits and disposition of the gentry and people of the place, and should be a man who has many relations and friends and much local information. He should associate himself with a man of this sort so as to be able with his aid to appear and mix freely everywhere, both in public and in private, dressed as a gentleman and with various kinds of dress and disguises so as to be better able to have intercourse with people without arousing suspicion: and he should also frequently change his name, his dress, his horse, and not come needlessly to places where search is being made for him, and still less tell anyone, without due consideration, especially other people's servants or even his own, what road he is going to take or for

what house or place he is making; and when information is desired
beforehand about the road, it should be sought in course of conversation with the gentlemen who are living in that part of the country,
mentioning such and such a heretic and such and such a Catholic,
asking what their reputations are, how far distant they are from one
another; and having thus learnt the name of some heretic or country
seat which is near to the house of the Catholic, he can enquire how
many miles away it is, and what is the usual road used to get there; and
then, when he has come close to the Catholic house, he can make more
detailed inquiry from some boy or woman or yokel. But to do away
with much trouble of this sort it will be necessary to have a map of the
country and villages, for there will not often be an opportunity of
getting information from anyone. In this way, when the heretics seek
to take him, it will be more easy for him to slip out of their hands and
travel without being recognised. . . .

When any Father or priest, who is a preacher, comes to the house of
a Catholic, he should send around the neighbourhood for the latter's
relations and friends and dependants—Catholic or heretic, so long as
they are trustworthy—to hear the sermon, so that there will be a suitable number, and so that the priest may not in that case be too much
delayed by making it a stopping place and lingering in houses and
places that are close to one another, thus giving rise to suspicion and
causing him to be detected sooner. It will be necessary also for the
priests to be stationed in various parts of the country and for each of
them to stay at the house of some gentleman or other, as though he
were a relation, friend or steward, or in some office of dignity but
little work, so as not interfere with his own calling; and he should
also undertake the charge (unless the family with whom he is staying
is a very large one) of a certain district in the neighbourhood, or of a
number of neighbouring families, because it will be very difficult to
find priests enough for every family; and if families in the neighbourhood were to come often to the house at which he is stopping, the
priest would soon be noticed by the heretics. It will be convenient also
that, after a priest has stayed and exercised his functions in a house for
some time, he should change places with another priest and go and
stay with another Catholic, and send the priest he finds there to the
place from whence he has come. This exchange will be useful in
various ways: it will give better chance of escape to the priests, and
the houses of Catholics will remain free from suspicion; it will give
rise to a new spirit of devotion in the priests, causing them to perform

their office with all diligence, seeing that they will have to deal with persons whom they do not know interiorly; their judgment will improve and they will gain experience by having to deal with a variety of cases of conscience, temperaments and personalities; and the Catholics also will be more careful and vigilant about their behaviour and imperfections when they have to put themselves under the care of another priest.

Memorandum of George Gilbert, 1583

RICHARD COWLING IN LANCASHIRE

As for me, at the earnest request of good priests, I went to live in the house of the widow of one of the principal gentry. So many Catholics flocked to see me, bringing their schismatic and even heretic friends for advice, that it was quite impossible to accommodate them in the room that I used as a chapel, spacious though it was. Indeed it often happened that as many as two hundred, mostly of the gentry, would come for a sermon, while on Sundays and ordinary feast-days (not to mention the greater feasts) as many as thirty or forty would receive the sacraments from me, and I never sent them away without nourishing them also with the word of God. Catholics are so numerous that priests can wander through the villages and countryside with the utmost freedom. In the district where I was living the Catholics whenever they met me would go down on their knees, bow their heads and ask my blessing, for there is not a single heretic living in the whole area. On the greater feasts we had to keep the doors shut and admit only a selection. Otherwise we would easily have numbered more than a thousand, and that might have got noised abroad. So I had to go round after these feasts and satisfy all in turn.

Richard Cowling to Claude Aquaviva, 25 September 1600

EDWARD OLDCORNE IN WORCESTERSHIRE

In [the] time of his abode in those parts it is not easy to be believed how many obstinate heretics he converted, how many weak Catholics he confirmed, how many scholars he sent over to the seminaries and religious women to monasteries, how many houses he brought to that degree of devotion that he might and did settle priests in them. Indeed, I may safely say of him, without amplification, that 'in illis partibus totas fere fundavit rexitque ecclesias domesticas.'[1] Yea, to my knowledge, he assisted Fr. Garnet also with yearly provision of money, procured from his own acquaintance, towards his charges and maintenance of others, when the Society grew to be there of greater number. All the chiefest gentlemen and best Catholics of the country where he remained, and the countries adjoining, depended upon his advice and counsel, and he was indefatigable in his journeys. I neither do nor have known any one priest in England that did go so many journeys as he did, especially towards the latter end of his time, when he grew to be acquainted in so many places, that he could never almost stay three days at home but he should be sent for.

Yet was he for many years together of very weak health, proceeding partly from his pains-taking and partly of study, unto which he was very much addicted, and spent in it almost all the time that he had free from needful business. By which means about some eight or nine years ago he did spit blood in great abundance, but being very carefully tended and provided of all helps needful in such a case, he recovered; yet afterwards, with his like labours and earnest manner of preaching (in which he had a very good talent, though his voice were somewhat hoarse and painful unto himself, yet audible unto his hearers), he fell again to spit blood three or four times, which brought him to that weakness that no man thought he could recover. And being much consumed, he grew to have a cancer in his mouth, which afterwards was miraculously cured, as himself did tell me the story in this very manner.

When the physicians did give their judgment that the cancer could not be cured, but that he must have some parts of the roof of his mouth cut out, and some bones also, he resolved first to try what help he could have from St. Winifred, a notable virgin and martyr, who hath in those parts a well famous for many miracles, where she was beheaded. Thither did Fr. Oldcorne resolve to go on pilgrimage before he tried any further physic. And in his journey coming to a Catholic house, where he meant to celebrate, he found upon the altar divers relics, and amongst the rest a little stone of St. Winifred's Well with drops of blood upon it (as many of the stones have that are taken up in that well and in the current that runs from it). This stone Fr. Oldcorne took and went aside into a place by himself, and fell earnestly to his prayers, desiring St. Winifred's help for his health, if so it were best for the service of God. Then he put the stone into his mouth and held it

---

[1] He founded and governed nearly all the domestic churches in those parts.

there for some time, and behold within half an hour his mouth was perfectly well. He went forward to St. Winifred's Well, and there also recovered the strength of his whole body, and returned home so strong and in such sort that all wondered exceedingly. And after this time[1] he was more able to endure pains than he was before; and whereas once a year, commonly about the same time, he did usually grow weak and enter as it were into his consumption together, he used then no other physic but to go to St. Winifred's Well, whence he ever returned with perfect strength and health, which lasted him until that time twelve-month again. All which particulars I set down as himself did recount them unto me.

JOHN GERARD, *Narrative of the Gunpowder Plot*

JOHN CORNELIUS

A poor old man, a Protestant, was lying in a hovel abandoned by all, afflicted with a filthy cutaneous disease beyond hope of recovery, and beset by fleas and all kinds of vermin, by which the poor creature was devoured in every part of his body, for the loathsome sight and stench had prevented any one from approaching him, or bringing him assistance. But Fr. Cornelius, hearing of the miserable destitution of this man, at once hastened to his aid; he searched for him, and, when he had found him, remained with him the whole night, consoling him and rousing him to the hope of a better life. He convinced him of his errors, and, finally, confirming by the Sacrament of Extreme Unction the absolution of his sins in Confession, he promised to bring him the Holy Viaticum on the following day, which however he was prevented from doing, as death released the poor sufferer in the meantime. The Father was so covered with vermin and filth from one night's attendance on the sick man, that he was obliged to lay aside his clothes, which it was impossible for him to wear afterwards, though, considering the service he was able to render to the deceased, he had no cause to regret their loss.

DOROTHY ARUNDELL, *Life of John Cornelius*

ROBERT PERSONS

The fourth manifest calumniation or rather fiction against Fr. Persons is here set down in these words: *Many letters of his have been*

[1] (As himself did constantly affirm unto me). *Erased in original.*

intercepted written by him to his friends in England which do promise invasions of the kingdom by extern soldiers and do dispose the minds of Englishmen to these expectations. But here we would ask these accusers why they have not always alleged some one letter of his to this purpose among so many as they say are intercepted? Nay, why have not those of the Council, or some other heretical writer, published some one letter of his in all this space of 21 years since first he was sent into England and hath dealt ever since in this affair? Divers letters of other men intercepted have been published in print to seek their disgrace as all the world knoweth. And if any one of Fr. Persons had been taken also, among so many as he hath written into England and to other places in this time which might have been published to his disgrace or to the disadvantage of his Order, or English Catholics in this behalf, is it likely it should have been spared? Nay, if the heretics would not have it set forth, these men would have done it, seeing they have not spared to put forth in print and to exaggerate, pervert and exagitate the same by divers peevish commentaries a private letter of his written to one of their own men in friendly sort, for the defence of the doings and proceedings of His Holiness and the two Cardinal Protectors in Rome, towards their two messengers. Wherefore it is easily seen with what spirit these men are governed, seeing that they would gladly make Fr. Persons more odious to the state than already he is, by forging that he hath written letters of invasion and the like, which is a mere malicious invention of their own, to bring him and other good Catholics into disgrace.

ROBERT PERSONS, *An Apology in Defence of Ecclesiastical Subordination*

THE PRIEST'S ARRIVAL

As soon as he [Edward Throckmorton] heard of the arrival of a priest, it seemed to be the most welcome of all news to him. At once he hurried to meet him, and if the servants were not about he himself led his horse to the stable and pulled off the rider's boots—nay, even sometimes he was not ashamed to clean them. And if on any occasion the crowd of gentry and visitors prevented the priest from sitting at table with the rest, he would at once run to his aunt, and beg and implore her to give him leave to wait on him.

Life of Edward Throckmorton

How to Deal with Heretics

When the Father has been conducted to the house of a heretic his companion must say that he is a friend of his and that he has begged for his company to his house in order not to go alone, and in this way the companion must put them on friendly terms with one another, and then make an opportunity for conversation suited to the occasion, when they are seated at table or when there are a number of people assembled, on the subject of history or such-like pleasant topics, so as to show that he is well-informed, and at times even about religion or some point of faith, according as the company seems inclined for it and is well disposed, otherwise he will arouse discord and will reveal himself to be a Catholic too soon; and this will prevent his gaining the fruit expected and will lessen his influence with them. . . . If he were to speak abruptly, he would cause such annoyance that the man would no longer give him a hearing, and therefore it is necessary to proceed very cautiously and not to weary him over much, but to make use of certain methods and of times that are propitious—as for instance, if he should see him in a fit of melancholy or desolation of soul, he will then be able, under the pretext of consoling him, to speak about human misery, how full this life is of it, telling him that we shall have no rest until we are united with God in heaven; that the soul of man is often in desolation because, sharing as it does in the divine nature, it cannot be contented and find rest in these things below; telling him of the glories of heaven and the joy which the saints have there; for how short a time they will endure these petty trials, and thereby gain the enjoyment of eternal glory; of the love which God has for a soul, as is evident from the Incarnation and Passion of Our Lord; of the care which He has for us, giving us angels as our guides and saints as protectors, to defend us from the snares of the devil and the dangers of the world, from hell and the pains of the damned; of the causes which have led souls to damnation. Compassion also can be shown for the unhappy state of Turks, infidels and sinners (not mentioning heretics, for fear of giving offence before he begins to submit), and discoursing of other such things as God will inspire. He should seize also any opportunity from the weather, which renders a man more apt to devotion—as, for instance, when the weather is fine to speak of elevation of spirit, in bad or rainy weather of graver things; on feast days he should tell the story of the saint of the day, or what Our Lord did on that day; on Sunday how it was sanctified after God had created all things; and on all occasions he should cheerfully apply parables and lessons to our own case. If it is Lent or the Ember days or a vigil, he should point out how they have been instituted by the authority of the Church, the consent of mankind, and for the public benefit and advantage, etc. The evening, after the Ave Maria, is the time most apt to make a man receptive and adopt a reflective mood, because then there is a quietness everywhere and repose; the world appears to be deserted and lonely; men, beasts, birds and all else have withdrawn themselves, the adornments and pleasures of the daytime are in abeyance, and the sun has fled to other regions, and the earth has been clothed in darkness, the image of death and the end of the world.

These things will have great influence on him. The place also is to be taken into consideration: for instance, if the man happens to be in a city one can walk in the park or in a garden, if at his country house one can saunter through the fields and woods, or preferably in the neighbourhood of some stream. God will suggest a thousand other means to the man who is tireless in his efforts to gain souls which cannot be written down in detail. One must also take account of circumstances in dealing with a heretic and not touch him too much on the raw, especially in presence of others, nor unmask his faults, nor be too hasty in showing awareness of his imperfections, but treat him gently and use indirect methods. Likewise one can talk with some other person behind his back but so that he can hear, but without letting it appear that it is done with that intention. The Father's companion can assist him much in this conversion of souls by facilitating his approach, for being on terms of intimacy, he has more liberty of action and can say things which the Father cannot say at first. The companion too, who is experienced, and is aware of the natural dispositions of the persons, should at first inform the Father of the imperfections and sins to which they are more liable, of their passions, of their lack of good dispositions, of their virtues and good points, and of all matters that call for amendment; so that the Father, with knowledge of all the particulars, can frame his private discourses and his public sermons more to the point, whether in blame or for correction or in praise. The preacher should be exceedingly discreet in this matter and mask the particular in general terms, and so mix honey with gall that each of his hearers may feel himself intimately touched, and nevertheless feel that none of those present perceives or notices it but himself. In the case of heretics more fruit is gained from sermons giving advice for the direction of one's life, for the saving of one's soul and from other such-like meditations, than from those on subjects of dispute and controversy, which are more likely to stir up contention than bring about amendment of life and conversion. And so, before beginning the discussion of religion with a heretic, the best means towards his conversion (if, that is to say, one can trust him not to give the priest and his congregation away) will be to bring him in to listen to the sermon.

This will be, as it were, a preparation for his conversion, and I know of no other ground why God opens the intellect and moves the will more freely at a sermon when matters of controversy and the faith are not discussed than He did before when these used to be the subjects of discussion and conference between them, if it be not that God, in reward of that act of coming to hear his sermon, inspires him with the humility to receive instruction by it, or gives him the grace to be receptive of truth; but it is found by experience that more are converted by sermons than by any other way. Before the sermon takes place it will help very much if the companion speaks highly of the learning, wisdom, and virtue of the Father or priest. This will increase his influence and reputation with them and will make them hold him in greater esteem and listen to him with more reverence.

Caution also is necessary lest the priest do anything (even though it be with the object of concealing who he is) which could, when he becomes known for a priest, give disedification or appear scandalous; for heretics are very prone to take scandal from another, especially from a priest, and to condone anything done by themselves or their sect of heretics; but his conversation should be chaste and holy, especially in presence of women; he should avoid excessive levity and laughter, abstain from dancing and playing for high stakes but play only for trifles or to pass the time, and that rarely, and at some commendable and lawful game, and always in respectable company and only at their request; and he should refrain from excess in eating and drinking. He should not be over scrupulous or strict in matters that are trifling and of no consequence, but have regard to the good that may come of them or the possible conversion of a soul. This would cause the heretic to think that the Catholic religion is an intolerable yoke and too austere, and thus he would lose courage and draw back before he had tasted of spiritual sweetness: and therefore he should always show a certain restrained cheefulness, so as to give the impression that it derives from the purity and sweetness of his religion, which renders men so contented and full of consolation. In addition to this, pamphlets should be written—of small compass, otherwise they will not be read or bear fruit—pointing out the abuses brought about by the heretics and their evil lives, especially by Luther, Calvin, etc.: and how they have deceived the people, misinterpreting the Holy Scriptures and the Doctors of the Church, and telling lies about the Catholics and the holy faith: they should then declare what are the points of controversy, and how they themselves conform to the true interpretation of Scripture and the opinion of the Doctors; and they should also invite them to public disputations, with unbiased umpires appointed, where they will write a treatise on, or expound, some passage of Scripture in public, one after another; and in this way they should have everything printed, or buy a press and keep it secretly for their needs.

Memorandum of George Gilbert, 1583

BAREFOOT FRIARS

During the time of this Lent we have been every day occupied with seminary priests, Mass-mongers, libellers and such like. It fell out that in the first week of Lent, that there was a book cast abroad, a commending of Campion and of his fellows and of their death. I pursued the matter so near that I found the press, the letters, the figures, and a number of the books, and, being in this search, one Osborne, a seminary priest came dropping into a chamber where Mr. Topcliffe of the Court and I were. Him we examined, and it appeared that he was a seminary priest and had dwelt in the hospital at Rome three years, and after he was professed into the house of Franciscans, being barefoot friars that lived by begging, and laboured as he saith by cutting of wood and bearing of it upon their backs. They lie upon no beds, but tumble in the straw like swine; they use no shirts; they have no more garments but such as they daily wear, the which are slender, thin, and extreme cold; their diet is most slender, and they eat but once a day; and continually they drink water. They may touch no money.

The Recorder of London to Lord Burghley, 2 May 1582

A REPORT BY TOPCLIFFE

About twenty seminary priests of reputation and best learning are now in London. . . . They walk audaciously disguised in the streets of London. Their wonted fears and timorousness is turned into mirth and solace among themselves, as though the day of their expectation were not past, or, at the farthest, coming towards. My instruments have learned out sundry places of countenance where sometimes these men meet and confer together in the day time, and where they lodge a-nights.

Richard Topcliffe to the Lords of the Council, June 1584

HARBOURS IN THE STONY ROCKS

And when any search is made in Yorkshire, [the] Bishopric,[1] Northumberland, Cumberland, Westmorland and Lancashire for any papist priest, then either they are conveyed into caves in the ground or secret places not possible to find them. And, further, some fleeth into Derbyshire into the High Peak, and there is one Robert Eyre, a Justice of Peace only for that county, and he . . . gives warning when any search is pretended, and so makes them flee into the mountains of the Peak country, where the papists have harbours in the stony rocks, and then are relieved by shepherds, so that that country is a sanctuary for all wicked men.

Anthony Atkinson to Sir Robert Cecil, 24 October 1593

PRIESTS IN LANCASHIRE, 1583

They are so plentifully maintained and lie at ease and are kept in a weak house where all that be evil disposed may confer with them at the windows, and receive both exhortations and absolutions at their pleasure.

William Chaderton, Bishop of Chester, to Sir Francis Walsingham,
28 November 1583

HILARY'S CONFESSION

This seminary [priest] talked with the said Hilary under a hedge and there shrived him.

Recorded statement of Hilary Dakins, January 1595

THOMAS HOLFORD, PRIEST

The said Holford is a tall, black, fat, strong man, the crown of his head bald, his beard marquezated,[2] his apparel was a black cloak with

---

[1] Durham.   [2] All shaven except the mustachios.

murrey lace,[1] open at the shoulders, a straw-coloured fustian doublet
laid on with red lace, the buttons red, cut and laid under with red
taffeta, ash-coloured hose, laid on with byllmit[2] lace, cut and laid under
with black taffeta. A little black hat lined with velvet in the brims, a
falling band,[3] and yellow knitted stocks.

Enclosure in letter from William Chaderton, Bishop of Chester to the
Earl of Derby, 23 May 1585

JOHN GERARD

i. Gerard's discovery may the better be by observing this description
of him and his habit. To be of stature tall, high shouldered, especially
when his cope is on his back, black haired, and of complexion swarth,
hawk nosed, high templed, and for the most part attired costly and
defencibly, in buff leather, garnished with gold or silver lace, satin
doublet, and velvet hose of all colours, with cloaks correspondent, and
rapiers and daggers gilt or silvered.

William Byrd (spy) on John Gerard

ii. John Gerard the Jesuit is about thirty years old. Of a good stature,
somewhat higher than Sir Thomas Layton, and upright in his pace and
countenance, somewhat staring in his look or eyes, curled haired by
nature and blackish, and not apt to have much hair of his beard. I
think his nose somewhat wide and turning up; blubbered lips turning
outwards, especially the over lips most upwards towards the nose.
Curious in speech, if he do now continue his custom. And in his speech
he flowereth and smiles much and a faltering or lisping, or doubling of
his tongue in his speech.

Richard Topcliffe on John Gerard, 1597

THE LEAVEN OF THE DECEIVER

Thomas Langdale, formerly of our Society, and now, I think, an
apostate, causes great disturbance, and seduces crowds in Yorkshire.
But I speedily sent men to deal with the Catholics in the same locality,
and to warn them in my name against the leaven of this deceiver.
Yet his discourse spreads abroad like a cancer, and he has so influenced

[1] Of mulberry colour.
[2] This word is an abbreviation of 'habiliment' and signifies 'that which is worn on
clothes', 'trimming'.
[3] A collar of cambric falling on the shoulders, as opposed to a ruff, which stood out.

many as to cause himself to be regarded as the most famous and learned man in Europe. But I doubt not that this cloud will quickly disperse. He went first of all, of his own accord, to the Privy Council and the [Bishop] of Durham, from whom he received a cordial reception, and was sent by them to propagate his seed under the garb of a Jesuit, and, as they hoped, with greater damage to the Catholic religion than could be effected by the adversaries by means of tortures and the gallows. He works with zeal, but so absurdly and mendaciously, that he begins already to incur disgrace with prudent men. At one time he asserts that he was a Professor in the Schools of the Lutherans of Wittenberg, then he styles himself a Doctor of Theology of the Society of Jesus, another time a Penitentiary of the Holy See. . . and that as such he has been sent into England, as well to reform the errors of the seminary priests sent over, as to reassure the consciences of Catholics entangled by us to their former liberty; and, finally, that he may return. to report to the Sovereign Pontiff the state of the entire kingdom. He declares that he will cause us (in fact, that he has already done so) who have preceded him in England, to repent greatly of what we have done. He has never met me, but writes begging specially for an interview after all that has happened, and to confer with me, vowing before God and the whole court of Heaven that he will plot nothing against me if I will not damage his former authority either here or in foreign parts, nor interpose any obstacle to his proceedings. But I shall keep at a distance from the sight of the man. I write in haste, but will do so more fully later on. Farewell, and pray for me.

Jasper Heywood to William Allen, 16 April 1583

WILLIAM WATSON

Now if you did not know this fellow before, you may take a scantling of him. . . . For in his body and outward feature (if you know him) [he is] so wrong-shapen, and of so bad and blinking aspect as he looketh nine ways at once, as scarcely he can discern anything that toucheth not his eyes.

His coming out of England and manner thereof we know not in particular, nor greatly doth it import, only we know that he came to the English seminary of Rheims in France a poor little begging boy. Where being taken of charity, his first allowance was for a good time potage only and licking the dishes which other men had emptied before him: after this he was admitted to serve at the table and carry away dishes; after that again he was admitted to make beds, sweep chambers and other like offices belonging thereunto, in which kind he served specially one Mr. Boast, a good priest and a holy martyr since, which if he had known then or suspected that squint eyed boy (for so he called him) would have proved so wicked a man he should never have come (no doubt) within his chamber door. And yet further you must note that all this while William Watson, besides his poor estate, was the most contemptible and ridiculous thing in all that house for many years, for that his grace was in tumbling and making sport to others, for which his body (if you know him) was perfectly made, and so he passed by the name Wil Wat or Wat Tumbler all that time.

But at length after divers years pretending much humility and devotion, he was upon compassion and favour made a priest and sent into England, where for a time he used himself not evil, but by little and little falling to liberty and sensuality, and not having either sufficient wit or learning (but especially grace) needful for the government of such a charge, he fell into divers great disorders and absurdities, whereof one was his soulfall by going to the Protestants' Church and thereupon also the discovery of many Catholics to the persecutors.

ROBERT PERSONS, A Manifestation of Great Folly

16

The English Nuns

THE DEPARTURE OF THE DOMINICAN NUNS

The nuns of the Order of St. Dominic crossed over in charge of the excellent Father Richard, the Dominican, though some of them had attained the age of eighty years, among whom is the sister of the venerable Bishop of Rochester, herself a woman worthy of respect. The illustrious Count of Feria, a Spaniard, ambassador of King Philip in England, obtained leave for all these to quit the kingdom.

Dr. Nicolas Sander's Report to Cardinal Morone, May 1561

THE VOCATION OF FRANCES BURROWS

Being now come to years of discretion and some ripeness of judgment, conversing daily with priests and hearing many good things (and sometimes her cousin talked of a sister of hers, called Elizabeth, who was a nun at Rouen in France of St. Clare's Order), she got thereupon a great love unto that kind of life, although she could not imagine what it was to be a nun. Being ashamed to ask, she contented herself that surely it was a fine thing, but wavering in her mind, sometimes she would be a nun, sometimes not; thus she continued working with her mind some ten years. Once in an evening, about twilight, having left her company and being alone with thoughts of being a nun, she felt in her soul great and strong inspirations from God in which she took very much delight, yet understood not what she felt, but resolutely resolved to remain a virgin all her life. In the summer after this, being in a Catholic gentleman's house where for some time she remained, it happened on a Sunday after dinner, as she was alone in a little garden with great comfort of mind, thinking of being a nun, she suddenly heard one to knock at the back door of the said garden, where none could come except those of the house, and knowing that the servants were at dinner, she thought it might be some of the children. She went and opened the door, and saw there a man clothed in woollen cloth, all in white. His garments were very long, but neatly tucked up, and such as she had never seen before. He looked cheerfully on her, and spoke unto her, but she understood him not, and so she told him. Then he made signs to her, as she thought, for to have something to eat. Wherefore presently she runs to the butler to ask something for a poor man. He gave her a good piece of bread and meat, and whilst that he went to fetch her also a pot of strong beer, she cut a piece of pie that was there, and conveyed it out at the window that the butler might not see it, and so went with haste to the man, fearing he might be departed, but he was not gone. She gave it to him, who took it graciously, ate the bread and meat, and drank the beer to her seeming, but the pie he took up in the tuck of his garment. She perceiving him about to do it, said to him 'Oh! you will spoil your white coat,' at which he smiled, but yet put it in. All this while she stood, as it were forgetful of herself, earnestly viewing and beholding him, never having seen any man in the like attire before; who, when he had eaten, and drunk, lifting up his hand, with his two forefingers gave her a long blessing and went away. But she forgetting still herself, would not so leave him, but followed him a good way, till coming to a stile, remembering where she was and that alone, forthwith ran back in all haste home, and told the gentleman of the house and the priest who was there what she had seen. They went presently with all speed to fetch him but never could see or spy him. She made inquiry of the neighbours, who all said they had seen no such man, and they never would hear more of him. Neither could she imagine what he might be until, three years after, coming to Louvain to be a religious, and visiting the church of Augustine Friars before she entered (who serve the church in white) she saw theirs to be the same habit which the man wore whom she had seen before, and it was now a great motive to settle her in her vocation; counting this as a means wherewith Almighty God had called her. She was sent over by Fr. Garnet the elder, martyr, who was Superior of the Jesuits in England, being about nineteen years of age, and was professed on the 13th of July [1597], two years after, having been one year scholar and one year novice.

Chronicle of St. Monica's

NEWSLETTER TO A NUN

My very good Sister in our Saviour—All your friends are well and salute you; though besides the general affliction we find ourselves now betrayed in both our places of abode and are forced to wander up and down until we get a fit place, yet we impute to the great providence of God that our persons have escaped through your prayers and others. We kept Corpus Christi day with great solemnity and music, and the day of the Octave made a solemn procession about a great garden, the house being watched, which we knew not till the next day when we departed twenty-five in the sight of all in several parties, leaving half a dozen servants behind and all is well, *et evasimus manus eorum in nomine Domini.*

And so you see I have thus many years rubbed out, not being worthy to suffer anything for His sake in Whose affairs I am employed. God grant that we may all one day meet together before His face to enjoy Him for ever, and the time cannot be long. *Modica passio gloria infinita,* as St. Francis said. To your Reverend Superior and all the rest I humbly commend myself this Midsummer-day, 1605.

Yours always,

H. G.

Fr. Henry Garnet to Sister Elizabeth Shirley

THE ENGLISH BENEDICTINES AT BRUSSELS

1597. The persecution being then great against the Roman Catholics in England, the Lady Mary Percy, daughter of the great Earl of Northumberland, with many other persons of quality, leaving their own country retired into Flanders, living there at Brussels in much retreat and devotion. They began to think of leading a religious life and erecting a monastery. And conferring these their good desires with very Reverend Father Holt of the Society of Jesus, by his advice they soon resolved upon the great work and to undertake St. Benedict his Rule and holy order, which of all others had heretofore most flourished in that now heretical kingdom, confiding it might happily in future times be again a fit reception for them.

1598. Very Reverend Fr. Holt wrote to Rome to the very Reverend Fr. Robert Persons of the same Society of Jesus, to procure such permissions and briefs from His Holiness as were thought requisite. In the meantime Fr. Holt himself procured all other grants from the Bishop,

Archduke and Duchess with necessary approbation, for my Lady Jean Bartley to come from the great monastery of St. Peter's in the city of Rheims in France, with Mother Noelle and two or three other French religious of that house, to come to assist and settle that new establishment at Brussels in Brabant; and Fr. Holt said their first Mass upon the Assumption of Our Blessed Lady in the great hall designed to be their church in the house Fr. Holt had taken.

1599. On the 14th November my Lady Jean Bartley was blessed Abbess by my lord Archbishop of Mechlin, and eight young English ladies offered themselves to be her subjects. On the 21st November the same month and year, being the feast of the presentation of the ever glorious Virgin Mary, these eight ladies, of which number my Lady Mary Percy was the first and chief, received the holy habit at the hands of my lord Mathias Hovius, Archbishop of Mechlin, in the presence of their Highnesses the Archduke Albertus and his Duchess, the Lady Isabella Clara Eugenia, the Infanta of Spain, and all the chief of the town of Brussels.

1601. Rev. Fr. Holt was sent to Rome, and in his place very Rev. Fr. William Baldwin of the same Society came to Brussels, a person of great virtue and veneration, who had been prisoner long in the Tower of London and was there put to the rack for not discovering the confessions he had heard of some of those that were put to death for the gunpowder treason plot.

1603. Under the spiritual conduct of this holy man the first house of our Congregation advanced much in virtue, living in great esteem and veneration, nor was he less of advantage to them in order to their temporals.

ABBESS NEVILLE, *Annals*

ST. MONICA'S, LOUVAIN

For although the House was very poor in temporal maintenance, yet the Order was strictly observed, and the English, having been brought up, most of them, tenderly and daintily in their parents' or friends' houses, nevertheless for the love of Christ unto whom they were espoused, did willingly accommodate themselves to the hard fare and simple diet of the cloister, dressed after the Dutch manner, which indeed was so very mean as to deserve to be recorded to posterity, that we might know with what fervour our elders began to serve God in holy religion.

Their bread was of coarse rye, their beer exceeding small. Their ordinary fare was a mess of porridge made of herbs called *warremus*, sodden together with water only, and thereunto they added at dinner a little piece of black beef, about the greatness of two fingers, and at night for supper they had only a dish of some three or four little pieces of mutton, sodden with broth, which was to pass a table of ten nuns, to this was added bread and butter; nothing else. In Lent also, when they fasted, the fare was very hard, for they had only a mess of porridge of the Dutch fashion, half a herring or suchlike thing each one, and some little portion of peas dressed with lamp oil. Only, one day in the week, the Lord Mayor's wife of the town gave the religious a dinner, of charity, and then they had a portion of salt-fish about the bigness of three fingers, with a little spoonful of salad oil, which was accounted great cheer. For their collation at night, nothing else but a piece of the foresaid black rye bread and small beer. Only, one day in the week, each had a portion of common gingerbread, of one finger's thickness.

The Mother herein assisted the English with the alms and relief which their friends sent them, for they had each a little loaf of wheat bread allowed them every week, because some were sickly and could very hardly pass with the rye bread. Also they had some oatmeal porridge made for them, and the sick were assisted with what the house could afford, which was very little. Besides this, their labours in exterior works were hard for gentlewomen to undergo, as washing of linsey-woolsey clothes, which were to be beaten (as the manner is) in such sort that some of the nuns were sore after the wash-day in all their limbs as if they had been disjointed, besides the washing of linen in lye, which fetched the skin off their fingers; also they helped to mould the great loaves of rye bread, weeded the ways of the paved courts within the cloister, and swept the house, every one as they were able and appointed to do by obedience. Moreover, one or two of them were put into a warehouse, (where) they had to weave linen in looms, which was indeed a man's work, and very hard for tender, weak women. All this notwithstanding, they passed with alacrity of mind for the love of God, and would be as merry with each other as if they had been in the world amidst all dainties and pleasures; also they assisted one the other in their necessities with great love, so that what poverty took away, charity supplied and made up. The English nuns also, being young, helped the old Dutch religious in their cells to go to bed, and, when they needed it, made daily their beds with joy and humility for God's sake, such as might in the world have been their chambermaids.

JUBILEE OF MOTHER MARGARET CLEMENT, 1606

When this worthy Prioress, Mother Margaret Clement, had now laudably governed the Monastery of St. Ursula's thirty-eight years, she was to keep her jubilee of fifty years' profession. Wherefore she procured of her nephew, Dr. Clement, ten pounds sterling, to make the feast and solemnity withal. There were at that present living in the cloister some twenty-two English religious, and six were dead, viz., two scholars, three nuns, and one white sister, professed on her death-bed: for she had received about thirty in all, besides English gentlemen's children, to be brought up for awhile there.

There was great joy and feast all the week, for she was very well beloved of the religious, as her virtue deserved, and they lived very peacefully under her government, although they were of different nations, qualities and conditions, as gentlewomen and persons of mean degree; notwithstanding, there was such grace and virtue among them that it plainly appeared God was there.

Ibid.

THE LAST YEARS OF MOTHER MARGARET CLEMENT

She said, when she first went blind, that a Superior that could do nothing was not fit to be a Superior any longer. Therefore she would not be kept on at any entreaty of the convent, that made great moan therefore. She did often go into the houses of office, as the bakehouse, brewhouse, washhouse and milkhouse, and there she did see all the faults, and sometimes she would go into the vestry (wardrobe and sewing room), and sit among them and work, for she could never be idle; yes, when she was stark blind, she would be winding thread, or something she would make herself work. . . .

After the time that Almighty God had stricken her with blindness, and that she had with much ado and great entreaty procured of the head Superiors to be absolved of her office of government, to her great contentment, but to the great grief and sorrow of all her convent; she wholly gave herself to prayer and meditation, so that I have admired to see a woman of her years to kneel so long, with her hands folded together, without any stay to her feeble body. She frequented the Blessed Sacrament every day with great devotion; and the nun that led her to the place where she was to receive, would often say she found such inward consolation in kneeling by her, as she could not express. . . . It pleased God for her comfort to send her two of her nieces[1] to be religious in the same house with her, in whom she greatly joyed and would often say, 'It is time that I now go to my home, for I have here two pawns to leave in my place.' As so it seemed that Almighty God had ordained; for they were no sooner professed, but, within ten days after, He called her out of this world, for she always prayed to God that she might see those two children settled in religion before her death, and it happened to her accordingly.

Chronicle of St. Monica's

[1] Mary and Helen Copley.

17

Exiles

The better part of the clergy followed in the footsteps of their prelates; very many of them, high dignitaries in the Church, were either thrown into prison or banished the realm, while heretics usurped their dignities and filled their places. Very many religious also, of divers orders, fled the country. Three monasteries[1] of men and women departed, leaving not a single member behind. Many persons too of high rank, of both sexes, followed their example, even to bonds and the loss of their possessions. The very flower of the two universities, Oxford and Cambridge, was carried away, as it were, by a storm, and scattered in foreign lands. Some three hundred persons, of all conditions, went away at once into different parts of Europe, but especially to the Belgian universities, where a most abundant harvest is gathered, to be sown again in the barren lands of England, there to grow at last, so we hope, to be the salvation of all its people.

Some of these wrote books both in Latin and in English, wherein they clearly and vigorously defended many doctrines of the Catholic religion against the heretics. Among these a distinguished place is occupied by Nicholas Harpsfield (who in prison wrote, among other works, an admirable book against the centuriators of Magdeburg, publishing it, however, in the name of Cope), Nicolas Sander, and (they are still living) William Allen and Thomas Stapleton, by whose labours their countrymen who had been deceived are returning daily in unnumbered crowds, by the grace of God, into the bosom of the Church.

NICOLAS SANDER, *Anglican Schism*

[1] The Friars Observant from Greenwich, the Carthusians from Richmond, and the Bridgettine nuns from Sion.

John Tipper in Rome

Now also began the persecution to be more sharp in England. . . . And among other cruelties one John Tipper, a very towardly and discreet youth, was whipped by the Recorder of London, Fleetwood, and Norton, chiefest persecutor in those days, and his ears bored through with a hot iron for confession of the faith, which youth coming afterwards to Rome and studying both Philosophy and Divinity, became a learned priest and so fervent in virtue as he entered the austere Order of the Carthusians and there behaved himself so well as after some years they made him Provincial General of their Order and in that office he died in Rome.[1]

ROBERT PERSONS, *First Entry of the Fathers of the Society*

Robert Peckham

Here lies Robert Peckham, Englishman and Catholic, who, after England's break with the Church, left England because he could not live in his country without the Faith and, having come to Rome, died there because he could not live apart from his country.

English draft of Latin inscription in S. Gregorio

Lord Burghley to Sir Thomas Copley

And now, Mr. Copley, wherein make you the difference so great in matters of religion. . . . that you will for that lose the sweet benefit of your native soil, your friends, your kindred, yea, incur the infamy that wilful exile doth bring, to be accompted, if not a traitor, yet a companion of traitors and conspirators, a man subject to the curses and imprecations of zealous good subjects, your native countrymen, yea, subject to lack of living by your own and thereby compelled to follow strangers for maintenance of livelihood and food? The cause must needs be of great force to induce you thereto.

Lord Burghley to Sir Thomas Copley, 28 December 1574

Sir Thomas Copley's Reply

Your Lordship toucheth divers plausible arguments to move me to like of the religion . . . allowed by Parliament better than the old and

[1] John Tipper died 24 August 1593

universal which I profess. .... Your Lordship, being so wise and learned, cannot be ignorant of the grounds that we Catholics stand on for our faith, to wit, antiquity, universality, unity; the confirmation by miracles and the blood of most holy and approved martyrs; the continual assistance of the Holy Ghost *usque ad consummationem saeculi*; the conquest in time of all other sects and heresies that have sprung up in any age; apostolical succession of the pastors, not by intrusion but by ordinary vocation; assuredness by the promises of Our Saviour that hell-gates shall not prevail against it, and divers other such-like marks and evidence which no sect can with any reason or truth show for itself.

Sir Thomas Copley to Lord Burgley, 25 February 1575

GREGORY MARTIN TO HIS SISTERS

It pleased my parents to bring me up in learning. As you know, as I was not the best, so I was at all times not counted the worst among my fellows and companions. Some small estimation I had in Oxford above my desert, more afterwards when it pleased the duke[1] to make me though unworthy, tutor to the earl his son. As long as his grace did prosper, I lived in his house to my conscience without trouble. When he was in the Tower, and other men ruled his house, I was willed to receive the communion, or to depart: if I would have yielded, I had very large offers, which I need not tell. It pleased God to stay me so with his grace, that I chose rather to forsake all, than do against my belief, against my knowledge, against my conscience, against the law of almighty God. For a time I lay secretly in England, afterwards I came beyond the seas into these Catholic countries, out of schism and heresy, for the which I do thank almighty God much more, than for all the estimation that I had or might have had in England. Whatsoever my estate is here, I do more esteem it, than all the riches of England as it now standeth.

Letter of Gregory Martin to his sisters

ALLEN'S REASONS FOR LEAVING ENGLAND

The universal lack then of the sovereign sacrifice and sacraments catholicly ministered, without which the soul of man dieth, as the

[1] Thomas Howard, 4th Duke of Norfolk.

body doth without corporal food: this constraint to the contrary services, whereby men perish everlastingly: this intolerable oath, repugnant to God, the Church, her Majesty's honour, and all men's consciences: and the daily dangers, disgraces, vexations, fears, imprisonments, impoverishments, despites, which they must suffer: and the railings and blasphemies against God's sacraments, saints, ministers, and all holies, which they are forced to hear in our country: are the only causes, most dear sirs, or (if we may be so bold and if Our Lord permit this declaration to come to her Majesty's reading) most gracious Sovereign, why so many of us are departed out of our natural country, and do absent ourselves so long from that place where we had our being, birth, and bringing up through God, and which we desire to serve with all the offices of our life and death: only craving correspondence of the same, as true and natural children of their parents.

WILLIAM ALLEN, *An Apologie of the English Seminaries* (*1581*)

THE BANISHMENT OF PRIESTS, 1585

The day came at last, though often changed, but for what purpose I do not know; and those persons who had been charged to see us transported, went from prison to prison demanding of the keepers thereof those who had been singled out for transportation. We were all brought to the ship moored in the Thames, near the gate of the Tower, and ordered to go on board. Thereupon some of us, especially the reverend Father Jasper Heywood, made a public complaint in the name of all, that we ought not to be driven out of our country without cause, having committed no crime, without a legal trial and clearly not convicted. . . .

When we had been two days at sea, and had gone far away from land, the reverend Father Jasper Heywood and others once more pressed the queen's servants with great earnestness to allow them to see and read the sentence of our banishment. The men were persuaded, and showed the warrant, in which was read as follows: 'The aforesaid persons, by the confession of themselves and others, found guilty of sedition and of plotting against her majesty and the state, all of them either legally convicted of those same offences, or for the like offences kept in prison, though deserving the last penalties of the law, are, under this warrant, ordered by her majesty, who in her goodness wills to deal more gently with them for this once, to be transported beyond the limits of the realm.'

When they read this they all cried out in one mournful protestation, that a most false accusation had been brought against them, and that they were most grievously wronged, seeing that not one of them, or of their fellow-Catholics, had ever uttered one word that could be construed into a confession of rebellion or conspiracy against the queen or the country, and that one certainly of those whom they were taking away at the time, had been publicly acquitted, after a trial, of that most false charge. Father Heywood then spoke much to the same purpose, again and again imploring those who were in charge to take them back to England that they might be put on their trial publicly, or at least that they might be put to death for Christ, and in defence of their innocence, rather than be sent to a strange land accused of offences which they had certainly never committed. To this the answer was, that it was not within their power to do that which was asked of them, and that they must obey the orders of the queen.

We went on, consoling one another as well as we could, and rejoicing that we could bear patiently this reproach for the name of Jesus. At last, by the help of God, we landed at Boulogne, and having said farewell to those who brought us thither, we departed for different towns in France, each one according to his means. At last we all came to Rheims, finding our brethren or our superiors in great distress about us in every place to which we came. They had heard the lying stories which the heretics, or those who wished us ill, had spread abroad, namely, that frightened by the dangers that were around us in England, we had of our own accord taken measures to bring about our banishment, that we had abandoned our work, or—and that was still worse— had come to some agreement with the heretics in matters of religion. But they rejoiced in our Lord, when they heard the story fully related, and when many of us moreover declared their readiness to return, whenever our superiors bade us, without counting the cost. But our enemies everywhere without any restraint speak of us whom they did not put to death, but banished, as instances and evidences of the queen's kindness. They persist in this, and urge it with so much shamelessness, that they will have it that the more they banish, the more must the great kindness of the queen be remarked, and the more it must commend itself to foreign nations, The same fraud and cruelty were lately practised upon two-and-twenty prisoners taken out of the jails of York and Hull, and carried over to France; all except one being priests, and even he was a deacon. These, for the most part, were worn out not only by bonds and imprisonment, but by old age. Some of them were sixty, others seventy years old, others were still older, and one of them was eighty years of age.

Some of these, though they were very old men, had spent a great part of their life in prison; and there were those among them who for six-and-twenty years had most patiently and bravely borne all those miseries which the wickedness of so many years, and of such heretics, is wont to inflict upon prisoners.

Soon afterwards, on the 24th of September, thirty priests and two laymen, brought together out of different prisons, were with the same intention driven out of the country. This is the way they think they can obtain a reputation for humanity and mercy. But it is very foolish, and nothing else but the kindness of thieves, who are wont to boast that they have given their lives to those from whom they have not taken it. It is more probable that they act thus for the purpose of burdening the seminaries, which they know to be poor, for the maintenance of so many priests. But there is no counsel against God: 'The earth is our Lord's and the fullness thereof.'

NICOLAS SANDER, *Anglican Schism*

THE ROAD TO EXILE, 1585

James Steile, [a] priest, after having been twice taken and cast into prison, first at York and then at Manchester, was put on board a ship to be carried into perpetual banishment. He suffered much on ship-board, but little in comparison with the treatment he afterwards met with; for being cast upon the Irish shore, and stripped of all his clothes, even to his very shirt, he was carried to the next town, where a poor woman gave him a piece of a shift to cover his nakedness; and in that manner he was presented to the sheriff of the county, who sent him, naked as he was, upon a horse, without saddle or bridle, to the city of Cork, conducted by certain wicked wretches, who sported themselves with whipping him frequently, during the whole journey, which was no less than twenty miles. When he arrived at his journey's end, he was put into irons, and kept in the common gaol amongst the thieves, till, by the orders of the Earl of Derby and the Bishop of Cork, he was again shipped off, and sent into banishment.

R. CHALLONER, *Memoirs of Missionary Priests*

SIR TOBIE MATHEW AT NAPLES

Every day under my windows [at Naples] and sometimes oftener, there passed a procession of children, singing the litanies of our Blessed Lady, and I know not by what chance, or rather providence of Almighty God, the tone of that sweet verse, *Sancta Maria, ora pro nobis*, came so often into my ears and did so extraordinarily delight me, that at last my tongue took it up, not as a prayer (such was my misfortune, for it is a misery to have been, at any time, any other than our Lady's humble servant), but as a song, whose ditty fell sweetly to the ear; and so, when I found myself alone, my ordinary entertainment was to sing, *Sancta Maria, ora pro nobis*, in the tune of those babes and sucklings who showed forth her praise.

The Life of Sir Tobie Mathew

18

Controversy

THE DOING AND DEALING OF BOTH PARTIES

But here will I now make an end, desiring thee (gentle reader) with such indifferency to weigh the doing and dealing of both parties, as the importance of the cause, the love of truth, the necessary care of thine own salvation, and thy duty towards God and his Church requireth. There is none of all those points, which the unfaithful contention of our miserable age hath made doubtful, in which thou mayest better behold how upright the ways of truth and virtue be, and how pernicious, double, and deceitful the dealing of heresy is. The one is upholden by the evident testimony of holy scripture, the other maintaineth her train by bold denial of scriptures: the one seeketh with humility the meaning at their mouths, whom God hath undoubtedly blessed with the gift of understanding and interpretation, the other by singular pride foundeth her unfaithfulness upon the phantasies of light and lewd persons that are puffed to and fro with every blast of doctrine. The one resteth upon the practice of all nations, the usage of all ages, and the holy works both of God and man, the other holdeth wholly by contempt of our elders, flattery of the present days and unhappy waste of all works of virtue, religion and devotion: the one followeth the governors and appointed pastors of our souls, whose names be blessed in heaven and earth, the other joineth to such, as for other horrible heresies and wicked life, are condemned both alive and dead, of the virtuous, and can not for shame be named of their own scholars. The one hath the warrant of God's whole Church, the other standeth on curse and excommunication by the gravest authority that ever was under God in earth. To be short, truth is the Church's darling, heresy must have her maintenance abroad. This one, holy, Catholic and Apostolic Church is it, whereunto we owe all duty and obedience both by God's commandment and by the bond of our first faith and profession. There is no force of argument, no probability of reason, no subtlety of wit, no deep compass of worldly wisdom, no eloquence of man nor angel, nor any other motion which can be wrought in the world, that should make a man doubt of any article approved by her authority. And if thou yet fear to give over thy whole sense and thine own self to so careful a mother, in whom thou wast begotten in thy better birth, compare our Church with theirs, compare her authority and theirs, her majesty and theirs.

Ours is that Church that hath borne down heathen princes, that hath destroyed idolatry, that hath converted all nations to Christ's faith, that hath waded in blood, that hath lived in wealth, that hath been assaulted by hell, by evil life, by heresy, and yet she standeth. Take away all this, compare her constancy in doctrine, with their inconstant mutability: compare the noble army of Martyrs, the holy company of Confessors, the glorious train of so many blessed, wise and learned Doctors, of many thousand saints that ever accompany her majesty: compare (I say) all these with the rascal soldiers of the contrary camp: *Ubicunque fuerit corpus, illic congregabuntur et aquilae.* I warrant thee, gentle reader, fear nothing, for wheresoever so honourable a personage is, there is the kingly company of eagles. Behold her grace of miracles, her works, and her wonders, her authority in discipline, her wisdom in government, her equability in all estates: and I am sure thou shalt confess *Quod dominus est in loco isto, et ego nesciebam,* Our Lord surely is in this place, and I was not aware thereof. For Christ's love, if thou hast followed, or yet have any phantasy to the severed company, grope without flattery of thyself, the depth of thine own conscience: feel whether God hath not suffered thee to fall for some sin. Come into this Church, and at the same time thou shalt be healed to thy eternal rejoicing. Touch once the hem of Christ's garment adore his footstool, cleave unto the altar, and if thou find not comfort of conscience, ease of heart, and light of truth, never credit me more. Prove once what is *In horto concluso, et fonte signato,* in the garden enclosed, and the wellspring so surely sealed up. Join with the saints in heaven, with the souls in purgatory, with the fathers of thy faith in earth, with all holy men both alive and dead. And thou shalt think thyself already in heaven, to match with that happy and blessed fellowship, out of which there is neither light, life, nor any hope of salvation.

WILLIAM ALLEN, *A Defense and Declaration of the Catholic Church's Doctrine*

THE MARIAN MARTYRS

The Libeller[1] by sophistical reasons and popular persuasion going about to make men think the English persecution to be nothing so violent as is divulged, nor anything comparable to the justice exercised towards the Protestants in the reign of the late Queen Mary, telleth of hundreds for our scores, as also of the qualities of them that suffered, of their innocency in all matters of state and treason and such like.

To which we say briefly, clearly and to the purpose: that we measure not the matter by the number nor by the severity of the punishment only or specially, but by the laws of God and all Christian nations. . . .

The difference is in these points: you profess to put none to death for religion; you have no laws to put away any man to death for his faith; you have purposely repealed by a special statute made in the first year and parliament of this Queen's reign all former laws of the realm for burning heretics, which smelleth of something which I would not here express; you have provided at the same time that nothing shall be deemed or adjudged heresy but by your Parliament and Convocation: you have not yet set down by any new law what is heresy and who is an heretic; therefore you can neither adjudge of one doctrine as of heresy nor of us as of heretics; nor have you any law left whereby to execute us; and so, to put away any of us to death for religion is against justice, law and your own profession and doctrine.

But nevertheless you do torment and punish us both otherwise intolerably and also by death most cruel; and that (as we have proved) for *Agnus Dei's*, for ministering the holy Sacraments, for persuading our friends to the Catholic faith, for our priesthood, for studying in the Society at Colleges beyond the seas, and such like which you have ridiculously made treason; but afterward (being ashamed of the foul absurdity) acknowledge them to be matters of religion and such as none shall die for. And therefore we most justly make our complaint to God and man that you do us plain violence and persecute us without equity and order.

On the other side Queen Mary against the Protestants executed only the old laws of our country and of all Christendom made for the punishment of heretics, by the canons and determination of all Popes, Councils, Churches and Ecclesiastical tribunals of the world; allowed also and authorised by the civil and imperial laws, and received by all

---

[1] Lord Burghley in *The Execution of Justice in England*.

kingdoms Christian besides; and who then hath any cause justly to be grieved? Why should any man complain or think strange for executing the laws which are as ancient, as general and as godly against heretics, as they are for the punishment of traitors, murderers or thieves?

Secondly, we complain justly of persecution, for that our cause for which we suffer is the faith of all our forefathers, the faith of our persecutors' own ancestors, the faith into which our country was converted and by which we are called Christian; the faith of the Catholic Churches and Kingdoms round about us; the faith that we promised in our regeneration, and therefore cannot be forced from it nor punished for it by any law of God, nature or nations. . . .

Thirdly, we say we have just cause to complain of this present persecution, for that the manner of it is such and the proceeding so conformable to the old pagan, heretical and apostolical fashion and dealing against God's Church and children that nothing can be more like.

They hated all Catholics and compted them traitors; so do you. They specially persecuted Bishops, priests and religious; so do you. They killed them indeed for their belief, but they pretended other crimes more odious, and specially matters of conspiracy and rebellion against the civil magistrate; so do you. They drove the innocent by captious interrogatories into dangers of laws that never offended the laws; so do you. They pressed men by torments to deny their faith under colour of trying their secret intents against the Prince; so do you.

It is not only the slaughter of many, and them specially the priests of God, which is most proper to heretical persecution, but the other infinite spoil of Catholic men's goods, honours and liberty, by robbing them for receiving priests, hearing Mass, retaining Catholic school-masters, keeping Catholic servants, mulcting them by twenty pounds a month (which by their cruel accompt they make thirteen score a year) for not repairing to their damnable schismatical service. By which a number of ancient gentlemen fall to extremity, either of conscience, if for fear they obey, or of undoing in the world, if they refuse. The taking of their dear children from them by force and placing them for their seduction with heretics (which violence cannot be done by the laws of God to Jews themselves), the burning of our priests in their ears, the whipping and cutting off the ears of others, carrying some in their sacred vestments through the streets, putting our chaste virgins into places appointed for strumpets and other unspeakable villanies, not inferior to any of the said heathens' persecutions. They have pined

and smothered in their filthy prisons above thirty famous priests,
above forty excellent learned men; of nobles, gentlemen and matrons
a number; whose martyrdom is before God as glorious as if they had
by a speedy violent death been despatched: every dungeon and filthy
prison in England [is] full of our priests and brethren, all provinces
and princes Christian [are] witnesses.

WILLIAM ALLEN, *A True and Sincere Defence*

FR. PERSONS' ANIMADVERSIONS ON FOXE

I have had occasion these months past to peruse a great part of his
last edition of *Acts and Monuments*, printed the fifth time in the year
1596 and do find it so stuffed with all kind of falsehood and deceitful
manner of telling tales, as I could never (truly) have believed it, if I
had not found it by my own experience. And I do persuade myself
fully . . . that there is scarce one whole story in that huge volume, told
by himself, except when he relateth other men's words out of records
and thereby is bound to the formality thereof, but that it is falsified
and perverted one way or other, either in the beginning, middle or
end, by adding, cutting off, concealing, false translating, wrong citing,
or cunning juggling and falsification, which I do not speak for any
tooth against the man, that is dead, and whom I never knew, but in
respect of truth only, and of so many deceived souls as are in danger to
perish by his deluding them. Nor when I speak of Master Fox his
falsehoods, do I make account of any errors or oversights (though
never so gross) that are found in him, as to reckon some for martyrs
that were alive at the making of the book: (for this he excuseth in his
later edition, in that he was deceived by false informations) nor do I
urge that others are made Calendar-martyrs by him, whom he cannot
gainsay that they were malefactors and some of them either mad or
denied Christ himself, and yet he placeth them in his Calendar for
saints. . . . The points that I for the present accuse him of are wilful
corruptions and falsifications that cannot be excused, as among other
things (for example's sake) when he reciteth any point in controversy
of the Catholic doctrine, he putteth it down commonly in plain
contrary words and sense to that which he must needs know they hold
and teach, for so much as their public books are extant in every man's
hands to testify the same.

ROBERT PERSONS, *A Declaration of the Trial*

COUNT YOUR CARDS BETTER

The Libel[1] . . . maketh a glorious muster of Archbishops; for indeed there was but one,[2] and he a notorious, perjured and often relapsed Apostate, recanting, swearing, and forswearing at every turn; and at the very day and hour of his death sacrilegiously joined in pretended marriage to a woman notwithstanding his vow and order. Other bishops and clergymen there were none of all the pack that was burned . . . but they were of the basest, for the most part, worst and contemptible of both sexes.

Now for these we yield unto the Libeller first fourteen noble and most worthy Bishops at one time, such as himself upon evil intent commended even now so highly (and indeed they were inferior in virtue and learning to none in Europe) who were all deprived of their honours and high callings, and most of them imprisoned and spitefully used in all respects; besides the famous confessor Archbishop of Armagh, Primate of Ireland, and a number of bishops of that country. Next we yield you in banishment two worthy English prelates of the same dignity, the one dead, the other yet alive in Rome; three elected Bishops all now departed this life; we name the honourable Abbot of Westminster; four priors or superiors of religious convents; with three whole convents put out of their possessions either into prison or out of the realm.

In the same case were a dozen of famous learned Deans, which next to the Bishops do hold the chief dignities in the English cathedral churches; fourteen archdeacons; above three score canons of cathedral churches; not so few as a hundred priests of good preferment in Queen Mary's time, besides many more made in our banishment and since martyred; fifteen heads or rectors of Colleges in Oxford and Cambridge; men of great importance in those universities and the commonwealth. And with them, and rather by their good example and provocation, not many years after, many of the chief professors of all the sciences; and above twenty doctors of divers faculties for conscience sake fled the realm or were in the realm imprisoned. And both at the first, and in divers years since then, many of the very flower of the universities came over both into the Society, Seminaries and other places famous for learning, where through God's goodness

[1] Lord Burghley, *The Execution of Justice in England* (1583).

[2] Thomas Cranmer, Archbishop of Canterbury, burned at Oxford 21 March, 1556.

they have passed long banishment in honest poverty, and some in worshipful calling and rooms in universities, with as much grace and favour as to foreigners could be yielded; in no place (thanks be to God) impeached of crimes and disorder. . . .

Count your cards therefore better and look not only [at] so many famous clergymen and the daily increase of them against your violent laws (Sir Libeller) but count, if you dare for shame, among your beggars and bankrupts in Queen Mary's time (as you dishonestly term us now) so many nobles and valiant earls, barons, knights, esquires and gentlemen that have either suffered prison, or, as their conscience led them, stood in arms for the defence of their faith and Christian knighthood, not against their Prince and country, but against such as abused her weak sex and former years of her youth to the establishing of themselves and their heresy; or have forsaken their honourable callings, offices and livelihoods in their countries for defence of the Christian faith, of which I could name you a-noble number of all degrees, able and ready to defend by sword (excepting the respect they have to their Prince and dear country) their religion and honourable actions against all the heretics in the world that defame them.

WILLIAM ALLEN, A True and Sincere Defence

ERGO, THOU HAST NO NOSE

The Fathers speak much of the spiritual altars of our heart, and of mere spiritual sacrifices: *Ergo*, they deny that there be any material altars and that thereon the real and external sacrifice of Christ's body and blood is offered. . . .

As well might one prove there is none other heaven, besides our hearts, because St. Augustine saith, in a sermon, *Corda fidelium coelum sunt*. The hearts of the faithful be heaven. *Ergo*, heaven that is said to be out of this world, is but a tale. As well one might say, Christ is not the Son of God, because he is the son of man. And in a matter of less weight, as well, and by like logic, one shrewd boy might say to another, Jack, I will prove thou hast no nose. Thou hast great lolling ears, *ergo*, thou hast no nose. Of such arguments we have great store in Mr. Jewel's writings, and in manner none other. For which cause to any grave and learned man he seemeth rather worthy of contempt than of answer. Whosoever considereth, not the number of his words, but the weight of his sentences, not the multitude of his patched and pieced allegations, but the force of the matter by the same avouched, shall judge no less. God be thanked, that heresy hath so weak a defence.

THOMAS HARDING, *Rejoinder*

WHO IS THE NODDY?

Where I say that before this alteration of religion by Luther there was unity among Catholics, to wit one God adored throughout all Christendom, one faith and belief, one form of service, one number of Sacraments, one tongue in celebrating, one sacrifice, one head of the Church, etc. and that now all is divided, he (Sir Francis Hastings) answered first, 'that to speak truly the most part of Christians in those days lived without all knowledge of God or of Christ Jesus, having nothing of Christianity but the very name and the outward Sacrament of Baptism.' So that he yieldeth not to them the inward virtue of Baptism nor the true belief of any one article of the Creed before Luther rose. . . .

What will you say to this man that maketh all his ancestors for so many hundred years together, and the ancestors also of her Majesty—her father, grandfather and the rest—mere infidels, and Christians only in name, and that they understood no one article of Christian faith? Were not this fellow worthier to be cudgeled than disputed withal? And his tongue rather be put out than his pen answered by writing? And he goeth forward saying that I do ridiculously distinguish faith from belief, in that I do say, there was then one faith and belief in Christendom before Luther, as though the conjunction *and* did distinguish and not conjoin together. Who is here ridiculous or who is the noddy, or who is the ridiculous noddy, let the reader judge.

ROBERT PERSONS, *The Warn-Word to Sir Francis Hasting's Ward-Word*

A CATHOLIC COMMENT

The Manichees for that their heresies were manifestly confuted by the Gospel of St. Matthew and by the Acts of the Apostles, as they could coin no answer nor other shift, they denied them to be Scripture. . . . Luther rejected the Epistle of St. James, because it was so plain against the doctrine of only faith. His offspring refused the books of Tobias, of Ecclesiasticus, of the Machabees and of some others, because in them is plainly taught the doctrine of the custody of the angels, of free-will, of prayer for the faithful souls departed, and of prayer to saints, all which they deny and therefore must they needs deny those parts of the Holy Bible. For heretics ever framed the Bible to their opinions, changing, wresting, paring and sometimes flatly rejecting all which made overplainly against such doctrine as they devised, and so do mostly impudently the Protestants now. Whereas the Catholics ever squared their doctrine by the line and the level of the word of her Spouse and therefore never had cause to reject the least jot of the holy Bible, and, at one word, the Catholics follow the Bible, but the Protestants force the Bible to follow them.

THOMAS HILL, *A Quatron of Reasons*

BISHOP JEWEL'S COMPLAINT

The popish exiles are disturbing us and giving us all the trouble in their power; and in their published books, I know not whether through any ill luck (shall I say?) or desert of mine, aim at me alone; and this too, three of them have done at once, and with most outrageous clamour: as I alone have to answer them all, you must not imagine that I have nothing to do.

Bishop Jewel to Henry Bullinger, 1 March 1565

THE LOUVAIN WRITERS

There be two other things in my opinion which hinder religion here very much. The Scottish priests that are fled out of Scotland for their wickedness and here be hired in parishes on the borders because they take less than others, and do more harm than others would or could in dissuading the people. . . . The other thing is the great number of scholars born hereabout now living in Louvain without license, and sending in books and letters which cause many times evil rumours to be spread and disquiet the people.

James Pilkington, Bishop of Durham, to the Privy Council,
22 November 1564

BRISTOW'S 'MOTIVES'

About this year [1574] R. Bristow, of the English college at Douai, set forth his *Motives* unto the Catholic faith, to the number of forty-eight: a book of great vogue with the papists, which Dr. Fulk, of Cambridge, now answered in a treatise called *The Retentive*. In the year 1599 it was printed again at Antwerp. And again, the next year, 1600, one Dr.

Hill put it forth at Antwerp, entitled then, *Reasons for the Catholic Religion*, in number twenty-five, as a new book of his own, but containing much of the form and manner, and all the matter for the ground thereof, taken out of Bristow: which was fully and learnedly answered by George Abbot, D.D. master of University college, Oxon, afterwards archbishop of Canterbury.

JOHN STRYPE, *Annals*

'THE MONARCHY OF THE CHURCH'

One thing I had almost forgotten to mention. There came out last summer an immense volume by one Nicolas Saunders, who is, they say, a countryman of ours; the title of which is 'The Monarchy of the Church.' He appears to have been a mercenary employed by certain cardinals, aided by the assistance of others, and decked out like Aesop's jack-daw. The tempest is violent, and would seem to demolish all our pretensions at one blast. It takes away from christian magistrates the right of deciding in matters of religion, and claims it entirely for the pope and his officers as the supreme governor of the church.

Richard Cox, Bishop of Ely, to Rudolph Gualter,
4 February 1573

A BEARER OF BASKETS

I thought it to appertain to me, who am (I trust) a member of Christ his Catholic Church, to do as much as in me lieth, that the broken and battered walls of it may be re-edified. And whereas it passed my strength to bring any principal beams, any corner stones, by writing new works of mine own invention, rather than . . . be an idle looker-on, I thought it my part to be an inferior labourer, to bring mortar, to carry sand, and as it were bear baskets, by translating some worthy work of some other writer.

Richard Shacklock, Preface to his translation of
Osorius' letter to Queen Elizabeth

AQUINAS AT CAMBRIDGE, 1578

Duns and Thomas of Aquin with the whole rabblement of schoolmen . . . were expelled the University.

Letter-book of Gabriel Harvey

AYLMER ON A FALSE ARGUMENT

He compared a false argument to ... 'a painted madam's face, which, so long as nobody blows upon it, nor sweat riseth in it, is gay glistering: but any of these means maketh the wrinkles soon appear. So is a false argument decked with fair words: it seemeth good, but turn it naked, and you shall soon see the botches.'

JOHN STRYPE, *The Life of Bishop Aylmer*

A COUNCILLOR'S CONFESSION

One of the chief members of the queen's council saw and read this book as soon as it came forth, and in speaking of it[1] to one of his friends whom he knew to be well disposed towards the Catholic faith, is reported to have said this: 'I am astonished at the Papists, even the more prudent among them, why do they so earnestly, openly, and plainly make known, answer and protest against the doings and the legislation of the queen and her ministers! Let us admit that they convict us of being in the wrong both as to religion and government, they ought to consider that, now we have gone so far, we cannot draw back with safety and honour, and that so powerful a queen cannot give way before any proofs or clamours of these poor men.' These were his words.

NICOLAS SANDER, *Anglican Schism*

[1] Allen's reply to Burghley's *Execution of Justice in England*.

19

Exhortation and Complaint

'I AM WITH YOU...'

Peter's ship is as safe as ever. She may be tossed by the waves but never can she become a wreck. Buffeted and beaten by the surge, she is never broken. Hell can open wide its jaws, belch forth fire, shroud her in clouds of black smoke, but God's promise stands unaltered. . . . From the day the storm first struck her the Church has gathered great increase. Wherever she is brought to the test, she conquers. When persecution strikes her she is there all the firmer for it. Violently oppressed, she reigns in glory. . . . Prisons are full of priests, but God's word is not in chains. In the midst of tribulation, sorrow and weariness our mother Jerusalem is not sterile, and ceases not to bear her children. One day she shall see peace.

William Weston to Robert Persons, 10 May 1587

ALL THIS BUT ONE DEATH

One death is no more than another and as well the easiest as the hardest taketh our life. Which point a glorious martyr of our days executed for the Catholic faith in Wales, having well understood, when the sentence of his condemnation was read, that he should be drawn upon a hurdle to the place of execution, then hanged till he was half dead, afterwards unbowelled, his head cut off, his body quartered, his quarters boiled and set up in such and such places, he turned unto the people, and with a smiling countenance, said, 'And all this is but one death.'

ROBERT SOUTHWELL, *An Epistle of Comfort*

THE CROCODILE

In this, affliction resembleth a crocodile; fly, it pursueth and frights; followed, it flieth and feareth: a shame to the constant, a tyrant to the timorous. Soft minds that think only upon delights admit no other consideration; but in soothing things become so effeminate as that they are apt to bleed with every sharp impression. But he that useth his thoughts with expectation of troubles, making their travel through all hazards, and opposing his resolution against the sharpest encounters, findeth in the proof facility of patience, and easeth the load of most heavy cumbers.

ROBERT SOUTHWELL, *The Triumphs over Death*

EDMUND CAMPION TO THE BISHOP OF GLOUCESTER

Do you remember the sober and solemn answer which you gave me, when three years ago we met in the house of Thomas Dutton at Shireburn, where we were to dine? We were talking of St. Cyprian. I objected to you, in order to discover your real opinions, that synod of Carthage which erred about the baptism of infants. You answered truly, that the Holy Spirit was not promised to one province, but to the Church; that the universal Church is represented in a full council; and that no doctrine can be pointed out, about which such a council ever erred. Acknowledge your own weapons which you used against the adversaries of the mystery of the Eucharist. You cry up the Christian world, the assemblies of bishops, the guardians of the deposit, that is, the ancient faith; these you commend to the people as the interpreters of Scripture; most rightly do you ridicule and refute the impudent figment of certain thieves and robbers. Now what do you say? Here you have the most celebrated fathers and patriarchs, and apostolic men, collected at Trent, who have all united to contend for the ancient faith of the fathers. Legates, prelates, cardinals, bishops, deputies, doctors, of diverse nations, of mature age, rare wisdom, princely dignity, wonderful learning. There were collected Italians, Frenchmen, Spaniards, Portuguese, Greeks, Poles, Hungarians, Flemings, Illyrians, many Germans, some Irish, Croats, Moravians,—even England was not unrepresented. All these, whilst you are living as you are living, anathematise you, hiss you out, excommunicate you, abjure you.

What reason can you urge? Especially now you have declared war against your colleagues, why do you not make full submission, without any exceptions, to the discipline of these fathers? See you aught in the Lord's Supper that they saw not, discussed not, resolved not? Dare you equal yourself by even the hundredth part with the lowest theologians of this council? I have confidence in your discretion and modesty; you dare not. You are surpassed, then, by your judges in number, value, weight, and in the serious and clear testimony of the whole world. Once more consult your own heart, my poor old friend; give me back your old beauty, and those excellent gifts which have been hitherto smothered in the mud of dishonesty. Give yourself to your mother, who begot you to Christ, nourished you, consecrated you; acknowledge how cruel and undutiful you have been; let confession be the salve of your sin. You have one foot in the grave, you must die, perhaps directly, certainly in very short time, and stand before that tribunal, where you will hear, *Give an account of thy stewardship;* and unless while you are on the way you make it up quickly and exactly with the adversary of sin, it shall be required to the last farthing, and you shall be driven miserably from the land of the living by Him whom you will never be able to pay. Then those hands which have conferred spurious orders on so many wretched youths shall for very pain scratch and tear your sulphurous body; that impure mouth, defiled with falsehood and schism, shall be filled with fire and worms and the breath of tempests. That high pomp of your flesh, your episcopal throne, your yearly revenues, spacious palace, honourable greetings, band of servants, elegant furniture,—that affluence for which the poor ignorant people esteem you so happy, shall be exchanged for fearful wailings, gnashing of teeth, stink, filth, dirt, and chains. There shall the spirits of Calvin and Zwinglius, whom you now oppose, afflict you for ever, with Arius, Sabellius, Nestorius, Wiclif, Luther,—with the devil and his angels you shall suffer the pains of darkness, and belch out blasphemies. Spare yourself, be merciful to your soul, spare my grief. Your ship is wrecked, your merchandise lost; nevertheless, seize the plank of penance, and come even naked to the port of the Church. Fear not but that Christ will preserve you with His hand, run to meet you, kiss you, and put on you the white garment; saints and angels will sing for joy. Take no thought for your life; He will take thought for you who gives the beasts their food, and feeds the young ravens that call upon Him. If you but made trial of our banishment, if you but clear your conscience, and came to behold and consider the living examples of piety which are shown here by bishops, priests, friars, masters of colleges, rulers of provinces, lay people of every age, rank, and sex, I believe that you would give up six hundred Englands for the opportunity of redeeming the residue of your time by tears and sorrow. But if for divers reasons you are hindered from going freely whither you would, at least free your mind from its grievous chains; and whether you remain, or whether you flee, set your body any task rather than let its grossness oppress you, and banish you to the depths of hell. God knows those that are His, and is near to all that call upon Him in truth. Pardon me, my venerated old friend, for these just reproaches, and for the heat of my love. Suffer me to hate that deadly disease, let me ward off the imminent danger of so noble a man, and so dear a friend, with any dose, however bitter.

And now, if Christ gives me grace, and if you do not refuse, my hopes of you are equal to my love; and I love you as passing excellent in nature, in learning, in gentleness, in goodness, and as doubly dear to me for your many kindnesses and courtesies. If you recover your health, you make me happy for ever; if you despise me, this letter is my witness; God judge between you and me, your blood be on yourself. Farewell.—From him that most desires your salvation.

Edmund Campion to Richard Cheney, Bishop of Gloucester, 1572

WELL-TRIED WHEAT

To you our fathers, friends, and brethren in Christ, being either in the furnace of God's probation, or in the burden and broil of that hot harvest of Our Lord, or by sure treading, threshing, and winnowing, laid up for well tried wheat in the barn-floor of Christ's Church, to you we say: Be humble, wise, meek, peaceable, patient and constant, in all your cogitations, words, answers, doings, and sufferings: that Christ Jesus whom you serve, may bless and prosper your endeavours, move her Majesty's heart to have compassion, open her grave counsellors' eyes to see your innocency, alter the enemies and ill-informers' malice and malediction, unto love and good affection towards you, stir up the minds of all men, inwardly and in conscience to consider the cause of your afflictions, and give them such sense, reason, and religion, that they may acknowledge your undeserved calamities.

WILLIAM ALLEN, *An Apologie of the English Seminaries*

Needful Shadows

No picture can be all drawn of the brightest colours nor a harmony consorted only of trebles; shadows are needful in expressing of proportions, and the bass is a principal part in perfect music; the condition of our exile here alloweth no unmeddled joy, our whole life is temperate between sweet and sour and we must all look for a mixture of both: the wise so wish.

ROBERT SOUTHWELL, *The Triumphs over Death*

Life's Burden

If men should lay all the evils together, to be afterwards by equal portions divided among them, most men would rather take that they brought rather than stand to the division.

Ibid.

The Divine Paperer

So God permitted our flesh by you to be mangled to make it more glorious in the second casting. . . . And as the paperer of old rotten shreds, oftentimes gathered out of unclean dunghills, by his industry maketh so fine, white and clean paper that it is apt to receive any curious drawing, painting or limning: so our scattered parts by you cast into dunghills, he will restore to such purity of perfection that they shall be more capable of his glorious ornaments than they were before.

ROBERT SOUTHWELL, *An Epistle of Comfort*

With the Holy Ghost for Your Gale

You are now launched out of the port of worldly prosperity, . . . in God's cause and therefore it behoveth you to uncumber yourselves of all earthly cares. You must display the sail of your soul upon the mast of Christ's cross, betake you to the tackling of virtue, keep your hand upon the stern of good order and discipline, and being aparted from earth, lift up your eyes towards heaven. You must direct your course by the motion of the stars and planets, that is, by the example of former saints, that so having Christ for your pilot, the inspirations of the holy Ghost for your gale, you may go through the storms of persecution, overcome the surges of worldly pleasure, pass the shelves of alluring occasions, avoid the shipwreck of deadly offence and finally safely arrive to the port of life and perfect repose.

ROBERT SOUTHWELL, *An Epistle of Comfort*

WHERE THE DEALINGS OF ALL SHALL BE DISCUSSED

Our days of affliction cannot be long . . . both sides shall shortly have their doom, where the dealings of us all shall truly be discussed and the just shall stand in great constancy against them that vexed them. . . . In joyful expectation of that day, we will continue still this work of God to our own and our country's salvation.

WILLIAM ALLEN, *A True and Sincere Defence*

NO MORE THAN THE OLD HEATHEN

Against [their] holy ashes and memories you can struggle no more than the old heathen and heretical persecutors did, to defame those glorious men of the primitive Church whom they executed in pretence of like treasonable practices; who yet . . . by Christ and his Church's judgment have gotten the victory over their adversaries, and so remain as glorious in heaven and earth as their persecutors be infamous throughout the world.

Ibid.

WITHOUT HOPE OF REMEDY

We are made the common theme of every railing disclaimer, abused without means or hope of remedy by every wretch with most infamous names. No tongue is so forsworn but it is of credit against us: none so true but it is thought false in our defence. Our slanders are common work for idle presses. . . . If any displeasing accident fall out, whereof the authors are either unknown or ashamed, Catholics are made common fathers of such infamous orphans, as though none were so fit sluices as they to let out of every man's sink these unsavoury reproaches.

ROBERT SOUTHWELL, *An Humble Supplication*

THE NAME OF ENGLAND

I could not make up my mind whether or not to write to you, my

Father, about the slaughter which has just occurred. Would it not be better to weep alone for the woes of my motherland than to let the misery of one island spread abroad to other nations? I know that the story of our sorrows cannot fail to stir their pity; but I am very much afraid that the tyranny of our persecutors will excite more loathing for the name of England than the bravery of our martyrs will win for her honour.

Robert Southwell to Claude Aquaviva, 31 August 1588

A CATHOLIC LAMENT

The time hath been we had one faith,
And strode aright one ancient path,
The time is now that each man may
See new religions coined each day.
    Sweet Jesu, with thy mother mild,
    Sweet Virgin mother with thy child,
    Angels and saints of each degree,
    Redress our country's misery.

The time hath been the prelate's door
Was seldom shut against the poor,
The time is now, go wives so fine,
They take not thought the beggar kyne.
    Sweet Jesu, etc.

The time hath been priests' women were
Accounted strumpets everywhere,
The time is now that wed such will,
And every Jack will have his Jill.
    Sweet Jesu, etc.

The time hath been men did believe
God's sacraments his grace did give,
The time is now men say they are
Uncertain signs and tokens bare.
    Sweet Jesu, etc.

The time hath been fear made us quake
To sin, lest God should us forsake,

The time is now the lewdest knave
Is sure (he'll say) God will him save.
  Sweet Jesu, etc.

The time hath been to fast and pray,
And do almsdeeds was thought the way,
The time is now, men say indeed,
Such stuff with God hath little meed.
   Sweet Jesu, etc.

Verses among the Blundell papers

COMPLAINT OF THE PERSECUTED

Our souls to spill they think full soon
Or else our bodies to enthrall
Or, at the least, to wantful state
Through hard pursuits to bring us all;
Come quickly, therefore, Lord Jesus,
And judge this cause between them and us.

Give judgment, Lord, betwixt them and us,
The balance yet let pity hold:
Let mercy measure their offence,
And grace reduce them to the fold,
That we, all children of thy spouse,
May live as brethren in thy house.

A Cry for Relief (c. 1592)

20

Practice and Belief

WATCHFUL IN ACTION

Secondly, I must always stand upon my guard, and be very watchful in every action, seeing that whatsoever I do, they will seek to pervert it, and make it offensive to God, even my very best endeavours.

ROBERT SOUTHWELL, *Short Rules of Good Life*

AN ORDER HOW TO SPEND EVERY DAY

In time of health, hours of going to bed and rising, may be either nine and five, or ten and six, or according to the strength or weakness of every man's body, so they be certain. After I am up, for a good pretty space it is good not to talk, but at the least for half a quarter of an hour to busy my mind in prayer and meditation, and then afterwards to talk if need require, because my business with God being greater than with any man, it is fit that he should be first talked with of matters concerning my soul, and then others of worldly things. I must procure to go neatly and handsome in my attire, agreeable to my calling, and to avoid all kind of indecency, which breedeth dislike and contempt, and doth rather offend than please God.

When I am ready, I must go to my prayers appointed. . . . In prayer I must consider the presence of God, not speaking unto him carelessly or negligently, but think a few prayers well said better and more acceptable than many hastily shuffled over: and I must not omit to remember the joys of heaven, the pains of hell, mine own death, and the death of Christ for me. After prayer I must go about some exercise of work agreeable to my faculty and vocation, such as may be of some profit, having an especial respect above all things to sequester idleness, the parent of all vice. When I go to dinner, I must think and consider for what end I am to eat, which is to help and strengthen nature and to make myself able to serve my Creator and feeder, not to content mine own appetite. I must learn my little children (if I have any) to say some godly grace, or at the least perform that duty of thanksgiving myself. When I am set, before I lay hand to my trencher, I may pause awhile, and desire God to give me temperance and mindfulness of his presence.

At meals I must be neither too curious or doubtful of what I eat, neither precise in the quantity, fineness or coarseness of the meat, but of that which God hath sent take a competent meal, measurable to my need, and not hurtful to my health. After dinner I must thank God for his gifts, remembering the end why he hath fed me is that I should be the better able to serve him. I must also think that many have wanted that sufficiency which I have had, and would be glad to accept of my leavings, and therefore I ought to have care and regard to the poor, procuring something for them, and sometimes seeing them served myself, considering Christ in their persons. If I have strangers, I may keep them company, and talk friendly and merrily with them as occasion shall serve, directing my behaviour agreeable to virtuous conversation: and having the intention in my talk that amity and love may be maintained and all breach and unkindness avoided. I must, if time and place will permit me, be always doing some profitable thing, to avoid sloth, directing mine intention in all mine exercises to this end, that I may avoid idleness and temptations, bestowing my time in good sort to God's glory. After dinner I must call to mind whether I have any promise to perform, or any other business to do that is not ordinary, that I neither forget the thing nor time appointed for it. It is good for me sometimes to go about the rooms of the house to see that they be kept clean and handsome, thinking that God is delighted with cleanness both bodily and ghostly, and detesteth sluttishness as a thing which he permitteth for a punishment of sin and one of the scourges of hell. A little before supper it will be good to read part of some godly book, procuring to take some benefit by it, and continuing in one book till I have read it over, and then begin a new. I must by watchfulness avoid all offence to God, leaving him in one exercise to serve him in another, as he appointeth me occasions. When I sit down to supper, I must remember what my intention ought to be, and to take the same course which is prescribed for dinner. After supper I may talk as occasion shall serve, or employ my time in reading of a godly book.

Towards the hour of my going to bed, I must examine myself, first whether my promises and appointments concerning extraordinary business be performed, or if I have forgotten any necessary thing I must take order to remember it, that I forget it not the second time. This done, I must examine my conscience concerning the thoughts, words, and deeds of that day, and especially touching the purposes that I have made in the morning, and how I have observed my godly determination and what faults I have committed of any moment. After I have examined my conscience, and said my prayers, it is good to abstain from talk that night (unless some just occasion require the contrary) that my mind may be free from idle thoughts when I go to sleep.

ROBERT SOUTHWELL, *Short Rules of Good Life*

THE PRACTICES OF PHILIP HOWARD

In the beginning when he was first committed to the Tower, he spent two hours or thereabouts every morning at his prayers. One hour and a half in the afternoons, and one quarter before he went to bed in the examination of his conscience, and recommendation of himself to Almighty God. And after some time he adjoined to his other devotions the saying of the priestly office, and thereby was of force something longer at prayer than before, which pious custom he continued until the physicians by reason of his weakness some small time before his death compelled him to leave it off. But after his condemnation he spent betwixt four and five hours every morning in prayer and meditation and betwixt three and four, in the afternoon. The rest of his time excepting that little he spent in walking or some other corporal exercise appointed by the physicians, he bestowed either in writing or translating books of piety. One book of Lanspergius containing an Epistle of Jesus Christ to the Faithful Soul he translated out of Latin into English, and caused it to be printed for the furtherance of devotion. He writ also three treatises of the excellency and utility of virtue which never came to light by reason he was forced to send them away upon fear of a search before they were fully perfected and polished. He used to read the spiritual books of Fr. Louis de Granada very frequently; and at other times the works of St. Jerome and other ancient fathers; as also old historiographers, particularly Eusebius, in which, as he signified unto Fr. Southwell, he found exceeding comfort for the confirmation of his faith by beholding there how the Church was in her infancy. Upon Sundays and feasts he used to read some part of the holy scriptures with special reverence and humility.

In the year 1588 soon after his second commitment to close prison, he began to fast three days every week, Mondays, Wednesdays and Fridays, and in them [ate] neither flesh nor fish. But finding by experience that his body was not able to endure so much, he altered it in this manner. That his one meal on Mondays was of flesh: on Wednesdays of fish: on Fridays of neither flesh nor fish, and abstaining also from all whitemeats and wine. And this manner he observed constantly both before and after his arraignment (excepting only the Wednesday immediately following it, wherein he did eat some small thing for supper having then some special need thereof) until he was prescribed by his physicians to alter that course, which was not long before his death. Many time he used also the same abstinence upon Thursdays as upon Mondays with only one meal of flesh. And upon some special days he abstained wholly from all kinds of sustenance either meat or drink. These were the vigils of the feasts of Corpus Christi, of the Ascension of our Saviour, of All Saints, as also the eves of the feasts of the Blessed Virgin, to whom he was particularly devout. Yet he carried it in such manner that none ever had any knowledge thereof, excepting one gentleman his servant, from whom I had it, whose help he used therein. For upon those days as soon as his dinner was brought in, the rest both of his own and the Lieutenant's servants being sent out, and the door fast shut, he made him eat and drink the same quantity that himself usually did on other fasting days, which being done, and the door open again, the other servants came in to take away as at other times without ever perceiving any thing at all, by reason they saw his trenchers and napkin folded, and as much meat eaten as on other days.

His hour of rising in the morning was constantly at five of the clock having to that end a larum in his chamber, and was very careful that it should be set overnight. Immediately as soon as he was risen out of bed, he fell down upon his bare knees, and breathed forth in secret his first devotions to Almighty God, his eyes and hands lifted up to heaven with his kneeling in that manner then and at other times, his knees were grown very hard and black. While he made himself ready (wherein he spent but little time) he used some vocal prayers wherein he was so unwilling to be interrupted, that if it happened any of his servants to have spoken but a word unto him in that time, he would make no answer at all, till he had ended, and then would tell them how great a displeasure therein they did unto him, warning them withal to do the like no more. All the following hours of the day were very orderly distributed by him into a certain and set manner, some to one exercise, some to another; but the most, as I said before, to prayer and practice of devotion. And always at night, except upon some extraordinary occasion, after the examination of his conscience, he betook himself to his rest. In those times which were allotted to walking or other recreation, his discourse and conversation either with his keeper, or the Lieutenant, or his own servants was either tending to piety, or some profitable discourse, as of the lives and examples of holy men, of the sufferances and constancy of the martyrs of ancient times, from which he would usually deduce some good document or other: as of the facility of a virtuous life after a man had once overcome his sensuality; of the happiness of those that suffered anything for our Saviour's sake with such like: to which purpose he had writ with his own hand upon the wall of his chamber this Latin sentence: *Quanto plus afflictionis pro Christo in hoc saeculo, tanto plus gloriae cum Christo in futuro*. (The more affliction we endure for Christ in this world, the more glory we shall obtain with Christ in the next.) The which he used often to show to his servants as well to animate himself to suffer all his afflictions with patience and alacrity, as to incite them also to do the same.

The Life and Death of Philip Howard

VAUX'S CATECHISM

i. *What is Man?*

Man is a reasonable creature of God, which God hath made marvellously of a body and a soul. As concerning the body, he is mortal like unto beasts. But as concerning the soul, he is immortal like unto angels, made after the likeness and image of God, that is to say, with power of knowledge and love, apt to receive felicity, and true blessedness, which consisteth in the clear knowledge and fruition of God.

LAWRENCE VAUX, *Catechism*

ii. *What is the Church?*

The Church is a visible company of people, first gathered together of Christ and his disciples, continued unto this day in a perpetual succession, in one Apostolic faith, living under Christ the head: and in earth, under his Vicar, Pastor and chief Bishop.

Ibid.

iii. *Who be alienated and utterly separated from the Church of Christ?*

The Jews, and all Infidels, and they that by apostasy forsake their faith. And heretics which although they be christened, yet obstinately defend error against the Catholic faith. Moreover Schismatics, which separate themselves from peace and Catholic unity; also they that be lawfully excommunicated. All these manner of people are excluded from the Communion of Saints, the participation of Sacraments, and suffrages of the Church.

LAWRENCE VAUX, *Catechism*

iv. *What Ceremonies be used in Confirmation?*

First, he or she that cometh to be confirmed, must have one god-father or one godmother (that is already confirmed) to hold them up to the Bishop.

Secondly, they that receive confirmation, have a blow on the cheek given to them of the bishop, in remembrance that they must suffer patiently and gladly rebukes and tribulation for the name of Christ and righteousness sake.

Thirdly, they that receive confirmation, for the space of three days ought to have and bear about with them, a band, in signification that Christ lay three days in his sepulchre, and upon the third day they that be confirmed, must be brought to the Priest, and then in the holy place the Priest washeth off that chrism with salt and water, and burneth the band, casting the ashes in the churchyard.

In some countries they use to tie the band upon the forehead of them that be confirmed, where the bishop made the sign of the Cross with holy Chrism.

In England they use to tie the band about the child's neck, and upon the third day the Priest looseth the band, and therewith washeth off the holy Chrism with holy water.

Ibid.

v. *Why are bells hallowed?*

To the end nothing may be profane, which serveth for God his religion, because he is infinitely holy, whom we serve. And thereby the devils also are the more vexed and driven the farther off, because they know them to be the signs, and as it were the trumpets calling faithful soldiers to hear God's word, and to make common prayer.

Ibid.

vi. *What may we learn by holy candles?*

First, that God is a consuming fire, whereof the very burning candle doth warn us.

Secondly, that as the candle being one kind of creature consisteth of fire, wax and wick: so Christ consisteth of the Godhead, soul, and flesh, all being in one person. Therefore on Candlemas day by carrying a holy candle, we do well represent Our Lady carrying Christ to the Temple in her arms.

Thirdly, we ought always to have the fire of charity in our hearts as the wise Virgins had.

Last of all, by the torches which are lighted at the singing of the gospel, it is signified, that the word of God is the light of our soul.

LAWRENCE VAUX, *Catechism*

HOLY WATER

The use of holy water is to make us mindful of our regeneration by the water of baptism; as holy bread of our feeding on the Blessed Body of Christ Jesus; . . . and the framing of the sign of the Cross, of our triumph over death and hell by Christ's holy Passion. They are therefore grateful memorials, because they are a kind of real protestation of our mindful gratuity.

HENRY FITZSIMON, *Justification of the Masse*

PILGRIMAGES

Blessed Hilarion going in pilgrimage to St. Anthony's hermitage, rejoiced in his spirit at every little memory of that holy man, when it was told him—here he was wont to sing, here to pray, in this place he did work, and there he rested himself, these vines and little stocks were of his planting, that alley he made with his own hands, this pool cost him much labour and pains to water the garden, this mattock he had many years to dig and delve withal. All these things . . . scoffing heretics will jest at, and no marvel. The prophecy of Jude the Apostle cannot be false: 'In the later time there shall come mockers, walking in their pleasure in all ungodliness.'

GREGORY MARTIN, *A Treatise of Christian Peregrination, 1583*

CLANDESTINE MARRIAGE

Webster confessed that he was married in the Marshalsea about three or four years past by George Beesley the priest, a notorious executed traitor, and that he gave the said Beesley for his pains 2s. 6d. And he saith that about a year or two after, Beesley came to this examinate to see him; and his wife did make the said Beesley a caudle, and when he had eaten it he went his way.

Richard Young to the Lord Keeper, 23 December 1592

SIN

The Catholic religion teaches differences of sins, some to be more grievous than others, some mortal, some venial, and that concupiscence or natural inclination to lust, of itself is no sin, whereupon Catholics are taught to strive against this motion, knowing it to be no offence except they yield unto it, and also they manfully fight against greater sins, although they cannot easily avoid lesser or venial offences: but the Protestant teaching that every sin, be it never so small, doth deserve damnation, and concupiscence be a sin which no man can avoid, maketh people to leave all to God his mercy, but never to resist sin, nor motion thereunto, for that in his opinion it is but lost labour to do so.

THOMAS HILL, *A Quatron of Reasons*

RITES OF BURIAL

Some use the Popish Rites of Burial towards the dead corpse at home, as it were burying it before it come to the Church. After that they set forth the corpse in their houses all garnished with crosses, and sit round about with tapers and candles burning night and day, till it be carried to the Church. All which time the neighbours . . . visit the corpse, and there every one to say a *Pater Noster* or *De Profundis* for the soul: the bells all the while being rung many a solemn peal. After which they are made partakers of the dead man's dole or banquet of charity.

Thus all things being accomplished in right Popish order at home, at length they carry the corpse towards the Church all garnished with crosses,[1] which they set down by the way at every Cross, and there all of them devoutly on their knees make prayer for the dead. And when in this superstitious sort they have brought the corpse to the Church, some with haste prevent the Minister and bury the corpse themselves, because they will not be partakers of the service said at the burial; some overtreat the Minister to omit the service and sometimes obtain their purpose; and when the Minister is ready to accomplish the order of service appointed for burial, many of these that come with the corpses will depart: for Recusants refuse not to bring it to the Church, though they will not partake the service of the Church.

Then concerning those that remain with the corpse till it be buried, when they have set down the corpse in the Church they bend themselves to their private prayer with crossing and knocking themselves, all kneeling round about the corpse, neglecting the public service then in hand. And when the corpse is ready to be put into the grave, some by kissing the dead corpse, other by wailing the dead with more than heathenish outcries, others with open invocations for the dead, and another sort with jangling the bells, so disturb the whole action that the Minister is often compelled to let pass that part of the service appointed for the burial of the dead and to withdraw himself from their tumultuous assembly. After which burial, at their banquet in the ale house, they oftentimes have a *Pater Noster* for the dead.

All the day and night after the burial they use to have excessive ringing for the dead as also at the twelvemonth's day after, which they call a minning[2] day. All which time of ringing their use is to have their private devotions at home for the soul of the dead.

The State Civil and Ecclesiastical of the Co. of Lancaster

SIXTEENTH-CENTURY CAROL

> CHORUS: This other night I saw a sight,
> A Star as bright as day,
> And ever among a Maiden sung:
> 'By by, Baby, lullaby.'
> This Virgin clear, withouten peer,
> Unto her Son 'gan say:

---

[1] At this time the corpse was wrapped in a shroud and carried uncoffined to burial, usually the day after death.

[2] *Minning:* a word still used in South Lancashire today for 'reminding'.

MOTHER: 'My Son, my Lord, my Father dear,
   Why liest Thou in hay?
   Methinks be right, that King and Knight
   Should lie in rich array;
   Yet, nevertheless, I will not cess
   To sing, "By by, lullaby".'
   This Babe full pain answered again,
   And thus methought He said:

SON: 'I am a King, above all thing,
   In hay if I be laid:
   For, ye shall see that Kinges three
   Shall come on twelve-day;
   For this behest give Me your breast,
   And sing, "By, Baby, lullaby".'

MOTHER: 'In fay I say, withouten nay,
   Thou art my darling dear;
   I shall Thee keep while Thou dost sleep,
   And make Thee goode cheer:
   And all Thy Will I will fulfil,
   Thou wottest it well, in fay;
   Yet more than this, I will Thee kiss
   And sing "By, Baby, lullaby".'

         Royal MSS., British Museum

EPITAPH

Sancta Trinitas unus Deus, miserere nobis,
Et ancilla, tuis sperantibus in te,
O mater dei, memento mei.
Jesu mercy, Lady help.
     Wherefore Jesu, that of Mary sprung,
     Set their souls the saints among,
     Though it be undeserved on their side,
Yet, good Lord, let them evermore thy mercy abide,
     And of your charity
For their souls say a Pater noster and an Ave.[1]

       JOHN WEEVER, *Funeral Monuments*

[1] Robert Trappes and his two wives were buried at St. Leonards, Foster Lane, London and over them was a gravestone with the above inscription in brass, the first four lines of which were on labels from their mouths.

21

At Prayer

DEVOTIONS OF MARGARET CLITHEROW

When she had leisure, she most delighted to read the New Testament of Rheims Translation, Kempis of the *Following of Christ*, Peryn's *Exercise*, and such like spiritual books. I have heard her say, 'if that it pleased God so to dispose, and set her at liberty from the world, she would with all her heart take upon her some religious habit, whereby she might ever serve God under obedience'. And to this end (not knowing what God would do with her) she learned our Lady's Matins in Latin.

JOHN MUSH, *Life of Margaret Clitherow*

MOST MIGHTIFUL AND LOVING LORD

Most mightiful and most loving Lord Jesus, all things that I have and am, and all things in this world, in heaven and in earth, are thine. Wherefore, most gracious, good Lord, I here offer and yield up to thy blessed will and pleasure, my soul and my body, with all my substance that I am or that I have, and all the creatures that ever were or shall be created, most truly and frankly, for this time and for evermore to abide at thy pleasure all adversity ghostly and bodily, all pain and grief of heart and body, and unto all things whatsoever thou wilt send or suffer to come unto me. . . . And I desire that thou might so have me at thy pleasure as thou hadst me before thou createdst me to thy honour and glory.

WILLIAM PERYN, *Spiritual Exercises*

PRAYER FOR PERSEVERANCE

Grant, good Lord, that I may for thy sake and love forgo all things, be they never so great, I may do all good things, be they never so hard, I may suffer all pains, be they never so painful, and that for thy only love and for thy sake, to persevere herein till the end.

WILLIAM PERYN, *Spiritual Exercises*

TAKE FROM ME MY UNKIND HEART

O mightiful Lord Jesu, take from me my unkind heart and give me for it thy sweet heart, or a heart like unto thy loving heart that ever may love, laud and praise Thee.

Mortify in me, good Lord, my wicked will and grant me to have no other will than thine.

O most loving Lord, fix my mind steadfastly on Thee, that I may mind nothing but Thee or nothing so oft as Thee.

My dear and sweet Saviour, grant me grace to come to the perfect knowledge of Thee though I be ignorant of all other knowledge.

Ibid.

QUIETNESS OF CONSCIENCE

A pure and clean heart is known by three signs or marks. The first is the quick and pregnant knowledge of our own defects. For as a small spot is soon espied in a very white linen cloth, so a pure heart quickly perceiveth a small fault in itself. The second is quietness of conscience in all troubles and adversities. For a pure good wine in a clean glass changeth not his colour and clearness be it ever so much troubled: even so a pure heart and clean conscience is well settled and resteth ever in one estate what adversity soever happeneth. The third mark is increase of courage in time of affliction even as a pure fresh wine sprinkleth and leapeth when it is with any force poured into a cup.

JOHN BUCKE, *On the use of Beads*

A PRAYER IN THE MORNING WHEN YE AWAKE

Lighten mine eyes, O Lord, lest at any time I oversleep in sin and lest my enemies do say, I have prevailed against him.

A Manual of Prayers

THE NATURE OF LOVE

i.　Love is but the infancy of true charity.

ROBERT SOUTHWELL, *Mary Magdalen's Funeral Tears*

ii. *Life's death, Love's life*

Who lives in love, loves least to live,
　And long delays doth rue.
If him he love by whom he lives,
　To whom all love is due.

Who for our love did choose to live,
　And was content to die;
Who loved our love more than his life,
　And love with life did buy.

Let us in life, yea with our life
　Requite his living love,
For best we live, when least we live,
　If love our life remove.

Where love is hot, life hateful is,
　Their grounds do not agree,
Love where it loves, life where it lives,
　Desireth most to be.

And sith loves is not where it lives,
　Not liveth where it loves,
Love hateth life, that hold it back,
　And death it best approves.

For seldom is he won in life,
　Whom love doth most desire:
If won by love, yet not enjoyed,
　Till mortal life expire.

Life out of earth, hath not abode,
　In earth love hath no place,
Love settled hath her joys in heav'n,
　In earth life all her grace.

Mourne therefore no true lover's death,
  Life only him annoys,
And when he taken leave of life,
  Then love begins his joys.

ROBERT SOUTHWELL, *Works*

ON CREATURES AND THE CREATOR

Certain differences between love towards God and love towards creatures, and what love God hath and will have to those that will perfectly love and serve him.

1. If I love a creature, it cannot know how much nor in what manner my love is: but if I love God, he knoweth better the love of my heart than myself.

2. If I love a creature, oftentimes I receive no reward or recompense: but if I love God, he rewardeth a hundredfold.

3. If I love a creature, I find it not at all times, nor so often as I would, and I cannot speak to it so often as I desire, and as need requireth, neither doth it hearken to my words as I wish: but if I love God, I have him at all times with me: I may speak with him as often as I please, and at all times he hearkeneth to my words, yea and to the desires of my heart.

4. If I love a creature, oftentimes it putteth me to trouble, and is a hindrance to me in my prayers, for that I think of it: but if I love God, he bringeth peace into my heart and conscience, and if I think on him as I ought in my prayers, he giveth me himself, which is sovereign sanctity.

5. If I love a creature, oftentimes I have care of it: but if I love God, he hath care over me.

6. If I love creatures, I know not their secrets: but if I love God, he openeth often to me the truth of all hidden and secret things.

7. If I love a creature, it yieldeth not my heart's desire: but if I love God he will give me wholly all my desires.

8. If I love a creature, it is out of me: but if I love God, he dwelleth in me and I in him.

9. If I love a creature it knoweth not all my affairs nor the things to me appertaining: but if I love God, he knoweth them better than I do myself.

10. If I love a creature, sometimes it deceiveth me: but if I love God, he will truly assure me.

11. If I love a creature, oftentimes it moveth me to heaviness and grief: but if I love God he giveth me joy and consolation.

12. If I love a creature, often it departeth from me, and for that cause I have short joy and pleasure of it: but if I love God, he remaineth with me. . . .

13. If I love a creature, it perisheth or decayeth: but if I love God, he dwelleth with me everlastingly.

A Manual of Prayers

To Christ Crucified

O cruel death, O wounds most deep,
　O guiltless blood, O bitter pain,
Alas, who can forbear to weep
　To see God's son so cruelly slain?

．　　．　　．　　．　　．

O Angels, look, is this your king?
　O Queen of Heaven, is this thy child?
Is this the maker of each thing?
　Alas, who hath him thus defiled?

．　　．　　．　　．　　．

My pride of heart hath pierced his brain,
　My garments gay hath stripped him so,
My envy opened all his veins,
　My sins, alas, did him this woe.

．　　．　　．　　．　　．

O Saviour sweet, hear my request,
　Make me partaker of thy pain;
In solace let me never rest
　Sith thou in sorrow dost remain.

And if it be thy glorious will
　That I shall taste of this thy cup,
Lo, here thy pleasure to fulfil
　My self I wholly offer up.

SWITHIN WELLS

On Death

And to say a word or two of our death's-head, or dead man's skull, . . . true it is, that it seemeth an ugly and loathsome sight to such as now flourish in flesh, and have not yet their bones discovered, and dried up, nor their fair faces disfigured, as that skull hath: but to spiritual wise-men it seemeth a more pleasant sight than the other, and a much more true and necessary spectacle; for that much more sincerely it maketh us to see what we are, and what we shall be shortly. For which cause many devout people, yea, some Princes also, do use to keep the same by them in their chambers, near about, where often they may be admonished, thereby to hold continually in their mind and meditations, the mystery which it representeth, especially by help of these words which commonly are written about the said skull: *Sum quod eris, fueramque quod es* (I am that which thou shalt be, and have been that which thou art now,) that is to say, I have been as lusty, jocund and frolic, as thou art at this present; I have been as proud and vain of my stature, beauty, hair, skin, agility and nimbleness, and of other qualities, and deckings up of my body, as thou ever hast been, that now lookest upon me with disdain and contempt, and shortly thou shalt be that which I am now, that is to say, a dried skull, bones without flesh, mouth without tongue, ear-holes without hearing, eye-pits without sight, brows without brains, and head without sense or feeling. The soul that was wont to quicken me, and give life to all, hath long ago abandoned me, and left me to the food of worms; and so shalt thou be shortly also, notwithstanding all thy care and diligence now in dressing, decking, and preserving thyself: neither do thou think that the time will be long, for it flyeth with the wind, nor stayeth for any occasion whatsoever.

ROBERT PERSONS, *A Christian Directory*

On Heaven

What joy and jubilee will thy soul receive at that day (dear brother) when she shall be presented by her good angel, in the presence of all these princely states, before the seat and majesty of the blessed Trinity, with recital and declaration of all thy good works done, and travails suffered for the love and service of Almighty God: when (I say) these blessed spirits shall lay down in that honourable Consistory all thy virtuous acts, with their particularities; all thy alms-deeds; all thy prayers; all thy fastings; all thy innocency of life, all thy patience in bearing injuries; all thy constancy in adversities; all thy temperance in meats and drinks; all the virtues of thy whole life, when all (I say) shall be recounted there, all commended, all rewarded, shalt thou not see now the value and profit of virtuous living? Shalt thou not confess now from the bottom of thy heart, that gainful and honourable is the service of God? Shalt thou not now be most joyful, and bless the hour ten thousand times, wherein first thou resolvedst thy self to leave the slavery of this miserable world, to serve only so bountiful a Lord? Shalt thou not think thyself now beholden most deeply to him, or her, that persuaded thee first to make this resolution? Yes verily. . . .

There is no more need now of fear, of watch, of labour, or of care. Thou mayest now lay down all armour, as the children of Israel did, when they came to the land of Promise; for there is no more enemy to assail thee; there is no more wily serpent to beguile thee: all is peace, all is security. Good St. Paul hath no more need now to fast, to watch, or to punish his body: good old Jerome may now cease to afflict himself both night and day for the conquering of his spiritual enemy. Thy only exercise must be now to rejoice and triumph, and to sing Alleluja to the Lamb, which hath brought thee to this felicity, and will continue thee therein for everlasting eternity.

O dear Christian, and most loving brother, what excessive joy and comfort will it be at that day, to see the holy Lamb sitting in majesty upon his seat of state. If the three wise men of the East came so far off, and so rejoiced to see him lying in a manger, what will it be to see him now triumphing in his glory? If St. John Baptist did leap at his approaching towards him in his mother's womb; what shall his presence do in this his royal and eternal kingdom? *It passeth all other joy and glory that saints have in heaven* (saith blessed St. Augustine) *to be admitted to the inestimable sight of Christ's face, and to receive the beams of glory from the splendour of his Majesty. And if we were to suffer torments every day, yea, to tolerate the very pains of hell for a time, thereby to gain the sight of Christ in heaven, and to be joined in glory to the number of his saints: it were nothing in respect of the worthiness of the reward.* O that we made such account of this matter as this holy and learned man did! We would not live as we do, nor lose the same for such vain trifles as most men in the world do lose it daily.

ROBERT PERSONS, *A Christian Directory*

PENITENTIAL SONNET

My sins in multitude to Christ are gone,
Against my soul indictment for to make,
That they his lingering vengeance may awake
Upon my just deserts. Then run, O run
Out of mine eyes tears of compunction,
One after other run for my soul's sake,
And strive you one the other to overtake,
Until you come before his heavenly throne.
There beg of Christ grace for me to repent,
And if he answer that my sins are great,
Then let my second tears the suit repeat,
And if he say I have his grace misspent,
Then let my third and fourth and fifth intreat,
Until that his excuses all be spent.

WILLIAM ALABASTER

HOW TO BEHAVE OURSELVES IN TIME OF TEMPTATION

In the time of my desolation and disquiet of mind, I must not enter into any deliberation, or go about to alter anything concerning the state of my soul or purposed course of life, but persevere in my former resolutions made in time of my good and quiet estate, wherein I was free from passion, and better able to judge of things convenient for my good: yet may I, and ought to resolve upon such helps as are fit to resist and repel my discontented thoughts (so they be not prejudicial to my former purposes) as prayer, repentance, and confession of my sins, with suchlike remedies. In temptations and troubles of mind, I must remember that aforetime I have had the like, and they have in the end passed, leaving me very glad and joyful when I have resisted them, and sorrowful when I have yielded too much unto them, and therefore I must think that these also must pass after a while, and shall feel the like joy in having resisted and overcome them, and in the meantime I must with patience endure the cumber and trouble of them, assuring myself that God therewith is highly pleased, and the enemy most effectually subdued. Neither the multitude, continuance, nor badness of any thought must breed any scruple or disquiet in me: for not to have them is not in my power, but only not to consent unto them: and so long as with deliberation I have not consented, nor willingly, or with delight stayed in them, I have not sinned any more than if I had only had them in a dream. If before I had evil thoughts I had a resolute mind never to yield to any mortal sin, and afterward when I remember myself, and mark that I was in a bad thought, I still find the same resolution, it is a sign that in the time of my distraction and bad imagination, I did not willingly consent or offend in them; neither is it like but my mind being so well affected, I should have easily remembered directly and without doubt, if I had yielded, farther than I ought. Desolations are permitted of God for three causes: first for a punishment of our sins, remissness and coldness in God's service. Secondly, to try whether we be true servants of God, or only hirelings that are willing to labour no longer than they receive the hire and stipend of present comfort. Thirdly, to ascertain us, that it passeth the reach and compass of our ability, either to attain to or maintain in us the fervour of devotion, the intensive love of God, the abundance of godly tears, and other spiritual graces and comforts, which we must acknowledge to proceed from God's mere liberality, not of our own force or desert. It is good while I feel the sweetness of God's visitation and presence, to fortify myself against the desolations that will ensue, and remembering those that are past, to think that all troubles will as well pass as comforts, and that our whole life is but a continual succession and mixture of sorrow and joy, the one always overtaking the other, and neither of them continuing long together, and therefore I must settle my mind in a kind of indifferency unto them both, as it shall please God to send them.

First, to know it is a thing coming from my mortal enemy, and tendeth to my eternal destruction. To look for temptations beforehand, and not to think them novelties but necessary sequels of our hostility with the devil, with whom we must never be friends.

To resist them stoutly at the first, and to crush the serpent in the head, for nothing maketh the devil to become so furious and violent or to redouble his suggestions, as to perceive the soul dismayed with his temptations, or not expecting (by the confidence in God's help and mercy) an assured victory. To bear patiently the multitude and continuance of them, assuring myself that they will have an end ere long.

To think on the joy I shall have for not consenting unto them, and the crown of glory that I shall enjoy. To remember how often I have been as grievously annoyed with the like, and yet by God's help have given the devil the foil. Not to strive with unclean temptations, but to turn my mind to think of other matters, and to change place or work, or to find some way to put me out of those fantasies. To resist vices by practising and doing acts of the contrary virtues. To arm myself beforehand by getting those virtues that are opposite to such vices as I am most inclined unto, for in those doth the devil always seek his advantage to overthrow me.

In my extremest troubles to humble myself in the sight of Almighty God, acknowledging mine own weakness; and wholly relying upon his help most earnestly in word and heart call for his assistance, firmly trusting in his mercy, yea and offering myself (so as he forsake me not) to suffer these and all other whatsoever it shall please God to permit, even so long as he shall think good to inflict them, for of all other things this most overcometh the devil, when he seeth we turn his evil motions and troubles to so glorious and great a victory.

ROBERT SOUTHWELL, *Short Rules of Good Life*

HOW TO KNOW TEMPTATIONS AND GOOD MOTIONS

It is always a spiritual desolation original and proceeding from the devil, when it darkeneth and disquieteth the mind, awaketh and stirreth up our passions, when it draweth to external and earthly solaces, leaving in the mind a tediousness and unwillingness to prayer and other works of devotion. Also when it diminisheth our affiance and trust in God, and driveth to a despair in God's mercy, or persevering in His service, making it seem an irksome and impossible thing, and moving us to forsake it: and when I find myself troubled in this sort, I must assure myself without all doubt that I am then tempted by the devil, and therefore arm myself to resist him by doing that which those temptations dissuade me from. On the other side, comfort which is caused by God's Spirit is known by these signs: it incenseth the mind by a quiet and calm motion to the love of God, without any inclination to any creature's love more than for God's only glory, and it breedeth a kind of inward light and brightness, whereby for the time the mind seeth after a most effectual sort the necessity, profit, and true comfort that is in God's service, conceiving a contempt and dislike of worldly delights, and tasting that which is the greatest felicity in this life, that is, so assured contentment in being in God's grace, and seeking to please him, that it then judgeth no contentment in the world like or comparable unto it, as in truth there is none. Also true spiritual comfort bringeth a delight and desire to think of the benefits of God, the joys of heaven, the comfort of meditation, and talking with God.

Finally, it confirmeth our faith, quickeneth our hope, and increaseth charity, furnishing the mind with a sweet taste of joy, quiet and free from all cumbers. Sometimes the devil transformeth himself into an angel of light, and at the first when he knoweth our good desires and purposes, he seemeth to soothe us in them, and to set us forward towards the performance thereof, but in the end he seemeth to draw us to his bias, and by corrupting our intention, or by perverting the manner, time, or other circumstance of the due execution, maketh the whole action worthless and faulty, though otherwise virtuous in itself.

There must be great heed taken in the beginning, middle and end of our thoughts: for when either at the first or at the last it tendeth to apparent sin, or withdraweth from the greater good, or tendeth to courses of less piety, or more danger than we are in, or if it disquiet the mind, bereaving it of the wonted calm and love of virtue, it is a sign that the devil was beginner of it, whose property is to hinder good, and withdraw us to evil. When in any suggestion I find the serpent by his sting, that is, Satan by the wicked end he moveth me unto, it is good to untwist and reverse his motion, and to look backward even unto the beginning, and to mark what plausible colour he first pretended, that the next time I may the better spy his cunning and subtle dealings and drifts.

ROBERT SOUTHWELL, *Short Rules of Good Life*

A STUDENT'S PRAYER

In the name of the Most Blessed Trinity I . . . protest in thy presence, O holy angel of God, that I have an absolute desire of dying in the Catholic, Apostolic and Roman Church, wherein all the saints have died who have been to this present time, and out of which there is no salvation. . . . O my dear Angel . . . fight strongly against the enemies of my salvation. In that moment receive my soul at her separation from my body, and make my Jesus favourable to me after my departure.

Prayer of Edward Throgmorton, student at the
English College, Rome

LIVING LORD OF LORDS

O ever living Lord of Lords,
　O mighty King of Kings,
O solace of the sorrowful,
　O glass, who gladness brings:
O puissant prince, O passing power,
　O regent of all rule,
My guide, my guard, expel from me
　All foolish fear and dule:

. . . . .

Let not my sins me cause, O Lord,
　To wander from the rock,
But grant I may be found in fold
　Of thine afflicted flock.

. . . . .

As is thy holy ghost, O Lord,
　I pray that thou wouldst spare
The workers of my web of woe,
　The causers of my care:
I humbly thee beseech, O Lord,
　Even by thy blessed blood,
Forgive their guilt, forgive their ill,
　And send them all much good:
Turn not, O Lord, thy face from me,
　Although a wretched wight,
But let me joy in thee all day,
　Rejoice in thee all night:

. . . . .

That after stirring storms are stayed,
　And surging seas do cease,
I may with mirth cast anchor in
　The pleasant port of peace.

FRANCIS TREGIAN

FROM 'THE GOLDEN LITANY'

By the creation of heaven and earth and all things that in them are, have mercy upon us.

By the frail nature of ours that it pleased thee to take for our sin, not abhorring the same, have mercy upon us.

By the ineffable joy which thy Mother had in thy birth, have mercy upon us.

By the cold crib, in the which with vile clothes thou was wrapped and laid, and with maiden's milk nourished, have mercy upon us.

By the joy of the shepherds which honoured thee in the crib, have mercy upon us.

By thy meek obedience and pains, have mercy upon us.

By the sorrow of thy heart, labour and weariness, have mercy upon us.

By thy meek washing of thy disciples' feet and Judas the traitor's feet, have mercy upon us.

By thy profound love, in that thou suffered thy disciple Saint John to rest upon thy breast at thy last supper, have mercy upon us.

By thy passing great heaviness that thou hadst when thou didst pray to thy Father in the garden near to the mount of Olivet, have mercy upon us.

By thy immutable goodness that thou refuseth not to take the kiss of Judas, have mercy upon us.

By the labours that thou sufferedst in going from one judge to another, have mercy upon us.

By thy great patience and stillness, have mercy upon us.

By the hard step that thou hadst, bearing the Cross, when thou wentest to thy death, have mercy upon us.

By thy being naked, full of wounds, laden with sorrows, enduring the cold of the wind till the Cross was made ready, have mercy upon us.

By the lifting up of thy most holy body on the Cross and by the violent pains where withal thy holy members were ruefully pained, have mercy upon us.

By the heaviness of thy heart and all the strength of thy soul, save me, defend me and have mercy upon us.

By the reproaches and words full of confusion that thou heardst hanging on the Cross, have mercy upon us.

By the care thou hadst of thy Mother in thy torment, commending her to thy beloved disciple, have mercy upon us.

By the inclining of thy holy head upon thy breast, incline sweet Jesus unto us and have mercy upon us.

By the precious blood and water that ran out of thy holy heart, wash and make us clean in the same holy water and blood from all our sins and have mercy upon us.

By the merits and prayers of all thy holy chosen saints that are, were and be for to come in heaven and earth, have mercy upon us.

Succour us, sweet Jesu, in the trembling and strait day of judgment, and grant us in this exile and transitory life, those things that be necessary to the health of our body and soul, and after this life to live in joy with thee everlastingly without end. Amen.

Pray we

Lord, give to the quick grace, to the dead rest, in especial to them that I am bounden, *N.*, and to the Church holiness, grace and concord, and that thou wilt vouchsafe to take this prayer to the honour and glory of thy holy name, and that without end, sweet Jesu, Amen.

A Manual of Prayers

To Obtain a Fervent Love Towards Our Enemies

Grant me, O Lord, to love my enemies most perfectly, not in word and show only, but in deed and truth. Take from me all bitterness of mind, wrath, evil anger, rancour, disdain, suspicion, envy and whatsoever is against or contrary to pure and sincere charity: so that in all simplicity of heart, I may have a good opinion of all men; that I may judge no man rashly but may love everyone in thee with most holy and hearty affection and that I may show them both in words and works all sweetness, clemency and love. Amen.

Ibid.

The Jesus Psalter

i. Jesu, make me constant and stable in faith, hope, and charity with continuance in virtue, and will not to offend thee.

Make me oft to remember thy Passion and bitter pains, which thou suffered for me.

Make my soul to holy doctrine obedient, and to things pertaining to my ghostly weal for the love of thee.

To the hour of my death, my five wits Jesu keep I beseech thee.

From excess in speaking, in feeding and working, preserve my frailty.

Have mercy on all sinners, Jesu I beseech thee: turn their vices into virtues, and make them true observers of thy law, and lovers of thee: bring them to bliss in everlasting glory.

Have mercy also on the souls in purgatory for thy bitter Passion, I beseech thee, and for thy glorious name, Jesu.

The holy Trinity, one very God have mercy on me.

Jesus Psalter

ii. Jesu grant me grace and specially in the time of temptation, to call for help to thee, and then with faithful mind to remember thy Passion which thou suffered for me: then most merciful lord, keep my soul from consent of sin for very true love of thee: then let sin appear stinking and abominable to me.

In my temptations, Lord, I beseech thee, help me, for the tender love that thou didst show to thy mother, and she to thee.

Repel [the] power of my adversaries, which intend the damnation of me.

Inhabit my soul, O Saviour, which with all humble subjection desireth the blessed presence of thee.

Make me pure in spirit, meek in speaking, patient in suffering, hungry of righteous working, and merciful to all them that be in misery.

Make me peaceable in conversation, clean in heart with holy meditation, and joyful to suffer persecution in the cause of thee.

Let all my powers and desires be ruled according to the will of thee: and all my petitions order to thy wisdom, and to the everlasting profit of me.

Have mercy on all sinners . . . [*as before*].

Ibid.

THE BURNING BABE

As I in hoary Winter's night stood shivering in the snow,
Surpris'd I was with sudden heat, which made my heart to glow;
And lifting up a fearful eye to view what fire was near,
A pretty Babe all burning bright, did in the air appear,
Who scorchèd with excessive heat, such floods of tears did shed,
As though His floods should quench His flames which with His tears
    were fed;

Alas! quoth He, but newly born, in fiery heats I fry,
Yet none approach to warm their hearts or feel my fire but I!
My faultless breast the furnace is, the fuel wounding thorns,
Love is the fire, and sighs the smoke, the ashes shame and scorns;
The fuel Justice layeth on, and Mercy blows the coals,
The metal in this furnace wrought are men's defilèd souls,
For which, as now on fire I am, to work them to their good,
So will I melt into a bath to wash them in My blood:
With this He vanisht out of sight, and swiftly shrunk away,
And straight I callèd unto mind that it was Christmas-day.

ROBERT SOUTHWELL, *Poems*

22

Layfolk

DAMNABLE TRAITORS

We do protest before the living God that all and every Priest and Priests, who have at any time conversed with us, have recognised your Majesty their undoubted and lawful Queen *Tam de jure quam de facto*. They speak reverently of you, they daily pray for you, they zealously exhort your subjects to obey you, they religiously instruct us to suffer patiently what authority shall impose on us, yea they precisely admonish us, that it is an heresy condemned by general council for any subject to lift up his hand against his anointed. This is their doctrine: thus they speak, thus they exhort. And if we knew or shall know in any of them one point of treason or treacherous device or any undecent speech, or any thought injurious to your royal person, we do bind ourselves by oath irrevocable to be the first apprehenders and accusers of such. If now, most gracious Lady, those Priests who have not at any time been detected, accused, or charged with any act or devise of treason, should offer to continue and live within this your realm, and (for so doing) shall be adjudged traitors, . . . then consequently we your faithful loving subjects are like to be capitally touched with the same treason. And we know by no possible means how to clear and keep ourselves free from it. For when the prophets and anointed priests of God, moved by zeal to gain souls, do repair hither . . . and coming to our gates do crave natural sustenance for their hungry and persecuted bodies, proffering us also ghostly food, what shall we now do? . . . O God and heavens, earth and men witness with us and plead our cause. . . . If we receive them (by whom we know no evil at all) it shall be deemed treason in us: if we shut our doors, and deny our temporal relief to our Catholic pastors in respect of their function, then are we already judged most damnable traitors to almighty God and his holy members, and are most guilty of that curse threatened to light upon such as refuse to comfort and harbour the Apostles and disciples of Christ, saying, *And whosoever shall not receive you nor hear your words: truly it shall be easier for them in the land of Sodom and Gomorrah in the day of judgment.*

Petition of Loyal Catholics to the Queen, 1585

MARGARET CLITHEROW

i. 'If God's priests dare venture themselves to my house, I will never refuse them.' These and such like words I have heard from her mouth many times, when talk hath been moved of the dangers wherein all Catholics do live under the ravenous heretics.

JOHN MUSH, *Life of Margaret Clitherow*

ii. The body of Mrs. Clitherow being by her tormentors buried in a filthy place the same night she was martyred, six weeks after a Catholic by diligent search found it, and taking it up he found it whole without any putrefaction, and so carried it a great journey where he buried it again more decently eight weeks after her martyrdom, leaving then her body so pure and uncorrupted as though the blessed soul had departed from the body the day before, albeit it was so pressed and bruised, as in the order of her death is set down.

An Ancient Editor's Note Book

iii. Mrs. Clitherow's body was buried besides a dunghill in the town where it lay full six weeks without putrefaction, at which time it was secretly taken up by Catholics and carried a long journey to a place where it rested six days, unbowelled before necessary preservatives could be gotten, all which time it still remained without corruption or evil savour, and after was laid up as a worthy treasure, till God free us from this persecution.

GRENE, *Collections*

THE HUMBLE SUBMISSION OF MARGARET NEVILLE

Most humbly, with tears . . . your Majesty's most desolate, poor subject, Margaret Neville, one of the daughters of the unfortunate late Earl of Westmorland, [beseecheth your Highness] to take princely pity upon my lamentable estate. With great grief I do confess, most gracious Sovereign, that sithence the death of my dear mother, having no part of that allowance which it pleased her Majesty graciously to bestow upon me, nor any other maintenance, I was even forced by reason of great want to receive relief of Papists, by whose subtilty my needy simplicity was allured from mine obedience and loyalty to their superstition and errors; and so, being drawn into the company of a seminary priest, I was condemned at the assizes the last summer. Being destitute of help, it pleased the good Bishop of Durham, at the motion of my Lord Treasurer and the judges, to take me into his house, where he only hath and doth yet wholly relieve, and by his godly and sound earnest instructions he hath, I most humbly praise God, fully reformed me in religion; which by God's grace I shall, with all obedience unto your Highness, constantly profess while I live. And now, alas! this pitiful Bishop, my only help, is very shortly to leave this country, and I know not how or where to be relieved. I commend my case and woeful state unto God and your Majesty; most humbly beseeching your Highness, of your princely and most gracious wonted compassion, to be merciful unto me, a most distressed poor maiden, and to vouchsafe me your most comfortable pardon for my life, and somewhat also for my relief; which if I still want, my life will be no life, but only misery. So shall the enemies of true religion have no cause to rejoice at my woe; the repenting converts, by my example, will be comforted; and I, as most bound, shall never cease with them to pray for your Majesty's most happy reign in all wished felicity, and long to endure.

> Your Majesty's most woeful poor prisoner,
> MARGARET NEVILLE.

14 Feb. 1594.

> *The Correspondence of Dr. Matthew Hutton*

SIR JOHN SOUTHWORTH

i. This day, being the 14th day of July 1568, I have had Sir John Southworth here with me according to your Lordships' order, I offered him the form of submission prescribed by your honours. He refused to submit himself to any such subscription, his conscience cannot serve him in most points of that order, he offereth to promise not to receive or to sustain any such disordered persons as heretofore he hath sustained and helped. He further seemeth to desire that he may be suffered to live according unto his conscience, and desireth much to have license to go oversea. The consideration of all such suits I refer to your honorable wisdoms, which I beseech God to assist to do what may please him and may be safety to the Queen's highness and to the state of the realm.

Matthew Parker, Archbishop of Canterbury,
to the Privy Council (1568)

ii. I, Sir John Southworth, Knight, forgetting my duty towards God and the Queen's Majesty in not considering my due obedience for the observation of the ecclesiastical laws and orders of this realm, have received into my house and company and there relieved certain priests, who have not only refused the ministry but also in my hearing have spoken against the present state of religion, established by Her Majesty and the state of her realm in Parliament, and have also otherwise misbehaved myself in not resorting to my parish church at evening prayer, nor receiving the holy communion so often times as I ought to have done, I do now by these presents most humbly and unfeignedly submit myself to Her Majesty and am heartily sorry for mine offences in this behalf both towards God and Her Majesty. And do further promise to her Majesty from henceforth to obey all Her Majesty's laws and ordinances set forth by Her Majesty's authority in all matters of religion and orders ecclesiastical, and to behave myself therein as becometh a good humble and obedient subject, and shall not impugn any of the said laws and ordinances by any open speech or by writing or act of mine own nor willing to suffer any other in my company to offend therein whom I may reasonably let or disallow, nor shall assist, maintain, relieve or comfort any person living either out of this realm without the Queen's Majesty's license, or within the realm being come and known to be an offender against the said laws and orders now established for godly religion as is aforesaid. And in this doing I firmly trust to have Her Majesty my gracious good Lady as hitherto I and all other her subjects have marvellously tasted of her mercy and goodness.

Form of submission offered to Sir John Southworth and
rejected by him

iii. Sir,—I have sent inclosed letters to certify my lords and you of the council, that I can do no good with Sir John Southworth for altering his opinion in religion. . . . The man is altogether unlearned, carried with a blind zeal without knowledge. His principal grounds are: 'he will follow the faith of his fathers: he will die in the faith wherein he was baptized, etc.'

Edmund Grindal, Bishop of London, to Sir William Cecil,
3 August 1569

THE WISBECH BOY

My examination and usage first before the Mayor of Rye in the beginning of June 1595 and afterwards at Lambeth before the Bishop of Canterbury and the rest of the Commissioners, and my answers to them as follows. The Mayor of Rye caused me to be searched, so they found thirty shillings sewed in my doublet, which the Mayor took from me. Within two days the principal women of the town did entreat for me to him that he would set me at liberty, but he would not in any wise grant it, except I would go to church, and then he said I should have my money again and he would give me some more to make me recompense for the two days he had kept me in prison. And then I said unto him that if he had more right to it than I, much good may it do him, for to their church I would not go. Within three weeks after, the mayor riding up to London caused two footmen to bring me after. Then was I brought to Lambeth before the bishop and the rest of the Commissioners, which, hearing that I was a boy of Wisbech, three or four of them at once were very earnest at me why I would not go to church; and I told them I could not answer so many at once, and therefore I desired the Bishop of Canterbury and the rest of the Commissioners to let me go back again and tomorrow I would give them my answer in writing, for I would not answer to anything by word of mouth. Whereupon they sent me back to the Gatehouse from whence I was brought to see them again the next day, to whom then I delivered in writing this answer following, which before my coming from Wisbech I had learned by heart to have it always in readiness in any such time of need.

My answer why I will not go to church.
First, because I think it not good and godly to go to it. Secondly, if you could prove it good and godly to go to it, then you would and

ought to go to Wisbech Castle and consult the priests there, but if any few come out there they so confound them that they dare not come there any more. Thirdly, if it were good and godly to go to it, I am sure the Catholics in Wisbech Castle and in other prisons would not leave their lands and lie in prison for flying from it as they do. Fourthly, if I should go to your church I should sin against God and the peace and unity of the whole Catholic church, exclude myself from all holy sacraments and be in danger to die in my sins like a heathen. But although I am but a poor lad I am not so far to obey you, having a soul to save as well as any other Catholic. Fifthly, I hear say that England hath been a Catholic Christian country a thousand years afore this Queen's reign and her father's. If that were the old high way to heaven then why should I forsake it? I have no goods to leave, I pray you give me leave to save my soul. My soul doth hunger after my maker, God made man, under the form of bread, whom none but the priests can give me; while you do keep both them and me from the old mass, I dare not go to your new communion.

This my answer was read from man to man throughout the bench but in secret, only to themselves, whereupon I was presently sent away with a pursuivant to Doctor Stanhope to be committed by him, as I was, to Bridewell, where they kept me eight months in the hemp house work, where every day's task is to bunch five and twenty pounds of hemp or else to have no meat. And then I was chained nine weeks to a block and a month besides with it and five months without it in Little Ease and one of the turrets which is as bad, and five weeks I went in the mill and ten days I stood with both my hands stretched above my head against the wall in the standing stocks, whereof one day, because I would not work on the Assumption of our Blessed Lady, they said I should fast as well as play, and would let me have no food at all. And last of all for my freedom and release from the hemp house work and such like, I had twenty lashes of the whip upon the tross, since which time I have been ever since Ash Wednesday, being the twenty-fifth of February, in commons with the Catholic lay men, eight of us together at the charge of ten groats a man the week, with very slender commons through the dearth there of things, and op-pressions withal upon us, but yet by God and good men other ways so comforted that I would not have missed my time there spent for a great deal more misery. And at last God so wrought that we took our leave of that place the third of November 1596.

Statement by Robert Colton of Wisbech

JANE WISEMAN

After her husband's decease, exercising the works of a holy widow, it pleased our Lord to rank her not only among the troops of holy confessors, but also, as we may say, of valiant martyrs, and of the most famous women that England afforded in this our miserable times of heresy, for she was ever most fervent and zealous in religion, and so devout in prayer, that she was once heard to say by her daughter, our Reverend Mother: 'It seems,' said she, 'that if I were tied to a stake and burned alive for God, I should not feel it, so great is the love to Him which I feel in my soul at this time.' Wherefore, Almighty God to make her love to Him indeed apparent, permitted that Topcliffe, the cruel persecutor, did vehemently set against her, and, at length, only for proving that she had relieved a Catholic priest by giving him a French crown, brought her before the Bar to be condemned to death for felony. But she constantly refused to be condemned by the jury, saying that she would not have twelve men accessory to her innocent death, for she knew, although they could not by rights find her guilty, yet they should be made to do it when her enemies pleased. Hereupon they told her that she was by the law to be pressed to death, if she would not be tried by the jury.

But she stood firm in her resolutions, being well content to undergo so grievous a martyrdom for the love of Christ; yea, when they declared unto her the manner of that death in the hardest terms,[1] as the custom is at their condemnation, the worthy woman, hearing that she must be laid with her arms a cross when the weights were to be put on her, exulted with joy and said: 'Now, blessed be God that I shall die with my arms a cross as my Lord Jesus.' And after this, when her sons lamented with sorrow, she rejoiced and cheered them up. [But] Almighty God accepting of this courageous matron's fervour to martyrdom, would not have her to depart so soon out of this life that she might have a longer time of suffering for Him, as also do more good works for His honour: therefore He ordained that Queen Elizabeth hearing of her condemnation, stayed the execution. For by bribes her son got one to speak a good word unto the Queen in his mother's behalf. Who when she understood how for so small a matter she should have been put to death, rebuked the justices of cruelty and said she should not die. Notwithstanding, she [was] in prison as long as the Queen lived, in which time Topcliffe ceased not often to molest

---

[1] For sentence on Mrs. Wiseman see p. 84.

her with divers vexations, insomuch that she was once made for a good space to lie with a witch in the same room, who was put to prison for her wicked deeds, and it was a strange thing to see that many resorting to the same witch there in prison, to know things of her by art of magic, she never had the power to exercise her necromancy in the room where Mrs. Wiseman was, but was forced to go away into another place.

One thing also we will not omit, which was a miraculous thing. Upon a time her friend Topcliffe passed under her window, being mounted upon a goodly horse going to the Queen, and Mrs. Wiseman espying him thought it would not be amiss to wash him a little with holy water, therefore took some which she had by her, and flung it upon him and his horse as he came under her window. It was a wonderful thing to see; no sooner had the holy water touched the horse, but presently it seems he could not endure his rider, for the horse began so to kick and fling that he never ceased till his master Topcliffe was flung to the ground, who looked up to the window and raged against Mrs. Wiseman calling her an old witch, who, by her charms, had made his horse to lay him on the ground, but she with good reason laughed to see that holy water had given him so fine a fall.

Chronicle of St. Monica's

MRS. THORPE

First I will begin with a gentlewoman known to myself, by name Mrs. Thorpe, a woman of good birth and place, both by herself and her husband allied to the best gentlemen of the country, and in her husband's days one of the best housekeepers in those parts. She, after her husband's death, lost her jointure, house and all she had, and, at the length, came to that misery and want (being now of good years) that she, not having a house to dwell in nor money to relieve her, was forced to come to the manor house (of which she had been before mistress . . .) and there to lie in an out-house, where she had neither bed, meat nor drink, but such as those who had been before her poor tenants brought; and some bringing her bread, some drink, some pottage, and other lending her bed clothes and other necessaries; and amongst the rest a Protestant gentleman in compassion gave her a cow, which she herself milked; and so for a good time remained till, at the length, she was provided of a better house, to wit, York castle, to which she was sent and there for certain years remained.

Relation of the Persecution in the North

EDMUND PLOWDEN REFUSES TO BECOME LORD CHANCELLOR

Hold me, dread Sovereign, excused. Your Majesty well knows I find no reason to swerve from the Catholic faith in which you and I were brought up. I can never, therefore, countenance the persecution of its professors; I should not have in charge your Majesty's conscience one week before I should incur your displeasure, if it be your Majesty's royal intent to continue the system of persecuting the retainers of the Catholic faith.

Edmund Plowden to Queen Elizabeth

DOROTHY VAVASOUR

Knowing her husband's mind for faith and religion, and seeing him somewhat careful for her and his children, before his apprehension did desire him to cast away all care and fear for her and his children, and to do that constantly and nobly in God's cause which his conscience did teach and move him to do. Herewith, he being marvellously encouraged, did take heart and comfort unto him and prepare himself, with God's grace, to suffer what persecution soever God should suffer to fall upon him.

After whose taking, she being troubled, sick, disquieted, and, as some thought, distract for a time, saying Our Lady's Matins with her goodman upon one of Our Lady's days, she was suddenly at the same time restored unto her perfect health both of body and mind. After the which time, she being the chief matron and mother of all the good wives in York, did in a manner addict and give herself wholly unto the service of God. Her house was a house of refuge for all afflicted Catholics, of what state, degree, or calling soever, resorting thither. There God's priests, wandering in uncertain places for fear of imminent danger, had harbour and the best entertainment that she could make them. There gentlemen and poor men too, so that they were honest and Catholics, were well accepted. There women, their times of bearing and bringing forth their children approaching, had good and safe being, both for the time of their delivery, the christening of their children, and the recovery of their health again. There all good Catholics resorting thither had free access, with her good will, unto Divine service and Sacraments. In the which good works this happy woman passing her time, in the year of Our Lord 1578, upon the Assumption day of Our Lady, being the 25th, the 15 day of August,[1]

[1] Old and New Styles.

meaning to serve God, many Catholics being come there for that purpose, but for fear of that which did happen divers of them gone away, her house was environed with watch and ward upon every side, and before that the Mass was entered on, became invaded by Mr. Andrew Trewe, alderman, and Mr. Richardson, the Sheriff of York the same year. The priest and many others were apprehended and put in prison, and she herself left at home, and appointed to appear in the Consistory upon such a day, as Sands their bishop would sit upon such matters.

GRENE, *Collections*

ANNE DACRES, COUNTESS OF ARUNDEL

Another kind of alms besides all these she practised very much, consisting in medicines, salves, plasters and other remedies to all kind of people who either wanting will, or means to go to doctors and chirurgeons, came to her for the curing of their wounds and distempers. And her charity herein was so famous, that not only neighbours, but several out of other shires, twenty, forty, and more miles distant did resort unto her to that end, and scarce a day passed in which many did not come, sometimes more than three score have been counted in one day: and to everyone that came besides advice and medicines if the matter did require it, she usually gave some alms in money if they were poor, as many were. Insomuch that some now and then would feign infirmities to get some money of her. A hundred marks every year she assigned for her private purse, and the greatest part thereof was distributed either by herself, or some of her gentlewomen to such kind of patients or other distressed people. She ordered divers kinds of drugs to be bought every year to make her salves and medicines, and herself in person would ever be present at the making of them to see and be more sure they should be well done and good. Threescore dozen of sheepskins were spent some years merely in making the plasters she gave, and about one hundredweight of one only matter, whereof some of them were made for aches and other accidents. To some of those poor patients who came to her, besides medicines and money she gave also their diet and lodging when coming far off, she thought it necessary for their cure they should stay there any time: and I have known some to whom she has done this charity for more than a quarter of a year together. And others whom she could not cure of their distempers she has furnished with money to

London, and procured that there they might be received into hospitals and cured. Others again I have known who being dismissed from the hospitals as incurable, she out of compassion has taken again into her own house, and in the end has cured them, God especially assisting and blessing her charitable endeavours.

The Life and Death of Philip Howard, Earl of Arundel

LADY MONTAGUE

i. She maintained three priests in her house,[1] and gave entertainment to all that repaired to her, and very seldom dismissed any without the gift of an angel; she redeemed two out of prison at her own cost, and attempted the like for others, and gave money to other Catholics both in common and particular. Her alms, distributed every second day at her gates unto the poor, were plentiful, and such as some of the richer Protestants did calumniate that they augmented the number of beggars and nourished their idleness. When she desisted from her prayers, she accustomed to spend much time in sewing shirts or smocks for poor men and women, in which exercise she seemed to take much pleasure, sometimes also when she had leisure she visited the poor in their own houses, and sent them either medicines or meat or wood or money as she perceived their need, and when she could not perform this herself, she sent her waiting women. Which kind of charity she omitted not in her greatest and last infirmity, but even then enquired how it fared with the poor, and lamented their infirmities, when herself of all other needed most commiseration.

RICHARD SMITH, *The Life of Viscountess Montague*

ii. These priests did minister the word of God and the Sacraments, not only to the Lady Magdalen and her family, but to all Catholics repairing thither. She built a chapel in her house (which in such a persecution was to be admired) and there placed a very fair altar of stone, where she made an ascent with steps and enclosed it with rails; and to have everything conformable, she built a choir for singers, and set up a pulpit for the priests, which perhaps is not to be seen in all England besides. Here almost every week was a sermon made, and on solemn feasts the sacrifice of the Mass was celebrated with singing and musical instruments, and sometimes also with deacon and subdeacon.

[1] At Battle, Sussex.

And such was the concourse and resort of Catholics, that sometimes there were 120 together, and sixty communicants at a time had the benefit of the Blessed Sacrament. And such was the number of Catholics resident in her house, and the multitude and note of such as repaired thither, that even the heretics, to the eternal glory of the name of the Lady Magdalen, gave it the title of *Little Rome*.

RICHARD SMITH, *The Life of Viscountess Montague*

iii. Whilst she was present either at Mass or sermon, she did not conceal herself for fear to be betrayed by some false brother, as it sometimes happeneth in England, but she did serve God publicly in the sight of all, that by her example she might encourage all; and when she walked abroad, by her beads or cross which she used to wear about her neck, she professed herself to be a Catholic, even to whatsoever heretical beholders, and so manifest was her religion, that scarce any in England had heard her name who knew her not also to be a Catholic.

Ibid.

NICHOLAS OWEN

But the man that was most extremely used and with extremities brought unto the last extremity, which is death itself, was one Nicholas Owen, commonly called and most known by the name of Little John. By which name he was so famous and so much esteemed by all Catholics, especially those of the better sort, that few in England, either Priests or others, were of more credit. This man did for seventeen or eighteen years continually attend upon Father Garnet, and assist him in many occasions. But his chief employment was in making of secret places to hide Priests and Church stuff in from the fury of searches; in which kind he was so skilful both to devise and frame the places in the best manner, and his help therein desired in so many places, that I verily think no man can be said to have done more good of all those that laboured in the English vineyard. For, first, he was the immediate occasion of saving the lives of many hundreds of persons, both ecclesiastical and secular, and of the estates also of these seculars, which had been lost and forfeited many times over if the Priests had been taken in their houses; of which some have escaped, not once but many times, in several searches that have come to the same house, and sometimes five or six Priests together at the same time.

One reason that made him so much desired by Catholics of account, who might have had other workmen enough to make conveyances in their houses, was a known and tried care he had of secrecy, not only from such as would of malice be inquisitive, but from all others to whom it belonged not to know; in which he was so careful that you should never hear him speak of any houses or places where he had made such hides, though sometimes he had occasion to discourse of the fashion of them for the making of others. Yea, he did much strive to make them of several fashions in several places, that one being taken might give no light to the discovery of another. Wherein he had no doubt great aid from Almighty God, for his places were exceeding fortunate (if so we may term the providence of God), and no marvel, for he ever began his work with communicating that day he entered upon it, and, as much as his labour would give him leave, did continually pray whilst he was working. But the contriving of his works in the safest manner were also very much assisted by an extraordinary wit and discretion which he had in such measure as I have seldom in my life seen the like in a man of his quality, which is also the opinion of most that did know him well.

Now to come to the manner of his death. It was such as might be expected from so innocent and holy a life; yea, such as the enemy did therefore much malign and to seek to hide, and that with disgrace in all he might. Being taken with Father Garnet, he was first committed to the Marshalsea, and not close prisoner of purpose (as it is thought) to observe who would come into him; but he was too wise to give any advantage. When Father Garnet was committed to the Tower, he also was sent thither, there to be tortured, and that with all extremity, as it was before intended when he was first known to be taken; for even then a chief Councillor said, 'Is he taken that knows all the secret places? I am very glad of that. We will have a trick for him.' And so indeed they tricked him when they had him in the Tower, for they tortured him so long and so often that his bowels gushed out together with his life; which when they did espy, thinking to cover their own cruelty with his slander, they gave it out that he had slain himself with a knife that was lent him to eat his meat withal. And to make this report to go for current amongst the common people, they sent forth a ballad with his picture, ripping out his own bowels with a knife as he lay in bed, his keeper being also in the chamber busy about some other thing.

But this false slander was so improbable that even his enemies did not believe it, much less his friends that were so well acquainted with his innocent life and long-continued practice in virtue, besides his former tried constancy in that kind . . . [Indeed], if he would have yielded to sin to save himself from pain, would he not rather have yielded to their desires and discovered the secret places that he knew, for which he might be well assured not only to escape torments, but to be most highly rewarded, as one that could have done them more service in that kind than any man in England whosoever, and might have brought more priests into their hands and more gentlemen's and noblemen's livings into their possession than any one man could; yea, he might have made it almost an impossible thing for priests to escape, knowing the residences of most priests in England, and of all those of the Society, whom he might have taken as partridges in a net, knowing all their secret places which himself had made, and the like conveyances in most of the chief Catholics' houses in England, and the means and manner how all such places were to be found, though made by others. So that as no one man did more good than he in assisting the labours of all the priests that were workmen in that vineyard, so no ten men could have done so much harm as he alone might if he had been so disposed; by which he well knew he might have made himself great in the world, not only by their rewards for so great and extraordinary service, but also by the spoil of Catholics' goods, being so many and so great, as he might have come to the rifling of, and have had no doubt much thereof for his own share, especially the Church stuff, which he knew to be very rich in some places, and where and how it was laid up.

No; the truth was this: the man had lived a saintly life, and his death was answerable, and he was a glorious martyr of extraordinary merit. God assisted him with so much grace that in all his torments he gave not the least sign of relenting, not any sign of impatience, not any one word by which the least of his acquaintance either did or might come in any trouble, of which three kinds they could not so much as feign any little instance to set forth with their forged slander, but set out the bare lie without any colour or likelihood at all. Indeed, I think they intended not to have killed him by torture, though they meant to give him enough, and more than ever any sustained of whom we can find records. For he hung in the torture seven hours together, and this divers times, though we cannot as yet learn the certain number, but day after day we heard of his being carried to torments.

Now true it is, and well known to many, that the man had a rupture in his belly, taken with excessive pains in his former labours; and a man in that case is so unable to abide torments, that the civil law doth forbid to torture any man that is broken. He, therefore, being not only tortured, but that with so much extremity and so long continuance, it could not otherwise but that his bowels should come out; which, when they perceived, and minding as yet to continue that course with him, they girded his belly with a plate of iron to keep in his bowels, but the extremity of pain (which is most, in that kind of torment, about the breast and belly) did force out his guts, and so the iron did serve but to cut and wound his body, which, perhaps, did afterwards put them in mind to give it out that he had ripped his belly with a knife. Which, besides all the former reasons, is in itself improbable, if not impossible. For first, in that case, knives are not allowed, but only in time of meat, whilst one stands by, and those such as are broad at the point, and will only cut towards the midst. And if one be sore tortured (though much less than he was), he is not able to handle that knife neither for many days, but his keeper must cut his meat for him. But his particular case proceeded yet further, for his weakness was such that when a kinswoman of his (to whom they sent for some relief for him) desired to see by his handwriting what he would have, his keeper answered, 'What would you have him write? He is not able to put on his own cap: no, not to feed himself, but I am forced to feed him.' This man was likely, then, belike, to do such a deed with a knife which he was not able to grasp. But afterwards, the same party, seeking further to know his estate, and coming to the keeper to learn, as desirous to help him with anything that was needful, he secretly wished her to trouble herself no more, for, said he, 'The man is dead, he died in our hands.' This was known presently to divers Catholics, though reported in private, as it was spoken, for fear of further examination and trouble. For after they had published that he had killed himself, and seeing it was not believed, the only argument they had to give it credit was to commit those to prison that spake against it, of which there were divers examples to terrify others. 'Sed Deus revelabit abscondita tenebrarum et manifestabit consilia cordium.'[1]

And of this great and worthy martyr there is no question but many witnesses will one day be produced to the glory of God and His servant, and the safety of their own souls if ever they come to penance. In the meantime I desire my soul may have part with his, and myself

---

[1] 'But God will bring to light the hidden things of darkness, and will make manifest the counsels of the hearts' (I Cor. iv. 5).

may be assisted with his holy prayers. About whose life and death I have been the longer, to show how much the truth of his virtuous life and glorious death is contrary to the published slander. This happy soul suffering all this, only for his conscience and constant practice of charity, not being so much as accused of any other crime.

JOHN GERARD, *Narrative of the Gunpowder Plot*

MR. THOMSON

I will set down here that little I remember of him. He was a gentleman of fair living in Oxfordshire not far from Burford, a widower and a father to many young children. Yet he lived Catholickly at his own house and ever kept one priest at least, besides entertainment he gave to strangers. In the end heat of persecution drove him into the Forest of Dean in the county of Gloucester, where he lived some years in that vast wilderness in a poor house he hired under the name of Mr. Groves with his priest as before. At last he was found out by the pursuivants, Robert Aulfield and others, and committed to Gloucester castle where . . . he was many times searched and spoiled of all he had; but yet he endured and brought up his children as he might, albeit a certain lawyer of Oxfordshire was by favour of the wicked laws crept into his estate and afforded him very small relief thence. At last he died prisoner there in Gloucester.

GRENE, *Collections*

MRS. BARNES

Mrs. Barnes a virtuous gentlewoman died in a very strange manner, with an end answerable to a very rare life. She heard angelical harmony and departed with extraordinary comfort, herself singing with an unwonted but most sweet voice and art more than ever in life she had uttered or learned. After her death in the thick of the feather-bed there appeared so perfect a white cross as if it had of purpose been made by art, to the great admiration of all, and continued a long time.

Ibid.

SIR EVERARD DIGBY

For indeed to do him right, he was as complete a man in all things that deserved estimation or might win affection, as one should see in a kingdom. He was of stature about two yards high, very little lower than Mr. Catesby[1] but of stronger making; of countenance so comely and manlike, that when he was taken and brought up to [trial] some of the chiefest in the Court seeing him out of a window brought in that manner, lamented him much, and said he was the goodliest man in the whole Court. He was skilful in all things that belonged unto a gentleman, very cunning at his weapon, much practised and expert in riding of great horses, of which he kept divers in his stable continually with a skilful rider for them. For other sports of hunting or hawking, which gentlemen in England so much use and delight in, he had the best of both kinds in the country round about. . . . For all manner of games which are also usual for gentlemen in foul weather, when they are forced to keep house, he was not only able therein to keep company with the best; but was so cunning in them all, that those who knew him well, had rather take his part than be against him. He was a good musician and kept diverse good musicians in his house; and himself also could play well of divers instruments. But those who were well acquainted with him do affirm that in gifts of mind he excelled much more than in his natural parts; although in those also it were hard to find so many in one man in such a measure. But of wisdom he had an extraordinary talent, such a judicial wit and so well able to discern and discourse of any matter, as truly I have heard many say they have not seen the like of a young man, and that his carriage and manner of discourse were more like to a grave Councillor of State, than to a gallant of the Court as he was, and a man but of twenty-six years old (which I think was his age or thereabouts). And though his behaviour were courteous to all, and offensive to none, yet was he a man of great courage and of noted valour, which at his end he showed plainly to the world, all men seeing and affirming that he made no account at all of death. He was so studious a follower of virtue, after he became Catholic, that he gave great comfort to those that had the guiding of his soul (as I have heard them seriously affirm more than once or twice), he used his prayers daily both mental and vocal, and daily and diligent examination of his conscience: the Sacraments he frequented devoutly every week, and to that end kept a Priest in his house continually, who for virtue and learning hath not many his betters in England. . . . [I have] written thus much of him, that it may appear what was the cause why he was so much and so generally lamented, and is so much esteemed and praised by all sorts in England, both Catholics and others,

[1] Robert Catesby, Gunpowder Plot conspirator, killed at Holbeach, Staffordshire, 8 November 1605.

although neither side do or can approve this last outrageous and exorbitant attempt against our King and country, wherein a man otherwise so worthy, was so unworthily lost and cast away to the great grief of all that knew him and especially of all that loved him. And truly it was hard to do the one and not the other.

JOHN GERARD, *A Narrative of the Gunpowder Plot*

PERSONS AND A BUCCANEER

One that had been with Drake in the action of St. Domingo, ever an heretic, coming home chanced to read the *Resolution*,[1] with the terror whereof he was so frighted that his hair stood on end, went presently to some Catholic friends, desiring them to help him to a priest. They not trusting him, he persevered in reading of good books with such show of hearty sorrow for his former life that they fulfilled his request. He became Catholic, and continueth very constant, even with danger of being disinherited for it. In all that voyage with Drake, he never had anything of all their spoils.

An Ancient Editor's Note Book

[1] *The Book of Resolution* was the first title of Fr. Persons' *Christian Directory.*

23

Pursuivants

ARREST OF FR. FRANCIS INGLEBY

He was arrested, as I have repeatedly heard, in this manner. On a certain day he left York on foot and in the dress of a poor man without a cloak, and was courteously accompanied beyond the gates by a certain Catholic of that city. The gentleman, though intending to return at once, stayed for a few moments' conversation with the priest on an open spot, which, unknown to the priest, was overlooked by the windows of the Bishop's Palace. It happened that two chaplains of the pseudo-bishop idly talking there espied them, and noticed that the Catholic as he was taking leave, frequently uncovered to Ingleby, and showed him, while saying good-bye, greater marks of respect than were fitting towards a common person meanly dressed. They ran therefore and made inquiries, and finding he was a priest, they apprehended him, and after casting him into prison delivered him to death.

WILLIAM WARFORD, *Relation of Martyrs*

FRANCES BURROWS, AGED ELEVEN

She showed great courage when the pursuivants and other officers came to the house to search for priests, church stuff, or Catholic books, which was there often to do, the rest hiding them in secret places made in the house for that purpose. But she was always let out to go up and down to answer the officers, because her courage was such as she never seemed to be daunted or feared of anything. It happened, when she was but eleven years of age, a priest being at Mass in the chamber above, and another present, a great noise was heard in the house below; and fearing it to be as indeed it was, the priest desired the gentlewoman of the house to go down and the girl with her to see what the matter was. They went, and in the hall found, through negligence of the doorkeeper, the pursuivants and constables, entered with many swords drawn; which the child seeing, cried out, 'Oh! put up your swords, or else my mother will die, for she cannot endure to see a naked sword.' The officers perceiving the gentlewoman's countenance to change, believed her and put up their swords. But Frances runneth back again, pretending to fetch some wine for her mother, shut the doors, gave warning to the priests, helped to hide them, and then came back again to the pursuivants, having frustrated them of their expectation, for they could find no priest. Such was her present will, not disturbed in time of danger.

Another time, a pursuivant thinking with terror to make her disclose the secret places of the house, caught her by the arm, and holding his naked dagger at her breast, threatened that if she would not tell him where the priests were, he would stab her in the heart. She, undaunted, as not apprehending anything of death, bade him if he durst, and with courage said, 'If you do, it shall be the hottest blood that ever thou sheddest in thy life.' The pursuivant, perceiving that death could not fright her, offered her £100 to have her, for to make a present to the Lord Bishop of London, saying it was a pity a maid of her courage should be spoiled with papistry.

Chronicle of St. Monica's

JUSTICE KILLCROSS AND HIS LADY

A justice, riding on Whitsunday to search and molest Catholics, fell from his horse, broke one or both of his legs. The same justice, for his malice towards crosses, is called Justice Killcross. His wife is as malicious as himself, and rather more, for when she finds him not so willing as she would have him, she never leaves biting, pinching, scratching, and brawling with him until she have gotten him from his bed, and seen him out of doors to that purpose; hoping at least that thereby he may get some chalices or such commodity, the better to maintain their beggarly estate.

An Ancient Editor's Note Book

NOTWITHSTANDING ALL OUR TROUBLES

This last week there was the cruellest search at London in the night that ever was, and some days before and after the Court was guarded and the gates of London, and rumours spread abroad that the Jesuits and the King of Scots were about to kill the Queen. One Justice said that for his part he had searched four hundred houses. . . . Notwith-standing all our troubles we sing Mass.

Henry Garnet to Thomas Strange, 30 June 1601

A JUSTICE AT THE BEDSIDE

But one thing must not be omitted, to wit, that coming over, Our Lord would have them make public confession of their faith; for lying at the inn in Southwark, expecting to depart with a widow that went under the Spanish Ambassador's charge, in the meantime there was much ado in London, in searching of houses upon news that the King of France was killed. Wherefore, the innkeeper's wife, having one night disputed with the eldest of these two sisters,[1] and finding she was too hard for her in matters of religion, confounding her even by the Bible, upon which she still harped; whether she had given notice to the officers of them no one knoweth, but one night when they were abed, there comes a justice of peace with many men, and in they would come. They refusing to open the door, being about midnight, they threatened to break it open. Wherefore the two sisters not knowing what might happen, took such Catholic books as they had into the bed with them, as also the money for their voyage (and it was wisely done), leaving only one vain book of Virgil's, that was taken away and they saw it no more. So laying themselves still, they desired their old nurse, who had come out of Spain for their sakes, and was now to come over with them to open the door. Then came into the room many men, and drew open the curtains. They lay still; the justice of the peace sat him down by the bedside, and asked them of what religion they were, and whether they went to church. The eldest answered, That they were well known in Southwark to be recusants, for their father hath one manor, and many houses there. Then he asked if they would go to the church? She answered, No. He asked again, Why? She answered, Because she would not be a dissembler, to be in her mind of one religion and make a show of another. He hearing this, could not tell what to say, but having demanded the cause of their coming to London, finding nothing to make against her but her constant resolu-tion not to go to church, asked of the younger sister if she was also of the same mind, who answered, Yea. Then he willed them to stay in

[1] Helen and Mary Copley.

that inn till they heard further from him, and their man, who lay in another chamber, he took and sent to prison; but in respect of their father being well known there, he did not send them to prison, and so departed. After this they sent their mother word, who lived but fourteen miles off, what had happened; who came speedily up and speaking with the justice got them freed. So that within a few days they came away with the foresaid widow, and the good mother had a new grief at the parting with her children; for having no more daughters but them, according to nature she felt it most heavy to part from both. But for the love of God and their greater good, she overcame herself, and went with them even to the Thames side, though before she wished them to depart without her knowledge, for she could not find in her heart to take leave of them, yet now she saw them take boat with heavy heart. Their man was still detained in prison, until that by means of the Dutch Ambassador they got him released, being a stranger born, of the Dutch nation, who came after and overtook them here at Louvain.

Chronicle of St. Monica's

Pursuivants' Wages

[1592]. Bartram Gofton's charges at Shields, two times making search for James Watson—one time with George Liddell, and the second time with George Still, 7s. 6d.; paid for the charges of three horses two days, and riding to Darneton and Shields to make enquiry for James Watson, commanded by Mr. Mayor, 6s. 6d.; paid for a sleuth-hound and a man which led him, to go make enquiry for James Watson, 5s.; paid for the charges of three men, one sent to Alnwick, the two to Stockton, and the three to Seaton Delaval, with my Lord President's letters to make search for Watson, 5s.

Newcastle Corporation Accounts

Counterfeit Scutcheon

William Newnham, *alias* Claxton, condemned at Nottingham for a robbery committed by him on the highway, brake from his keeper, the gaoler there, took away with him the daughter of one Griffith Aparraye, minister, and now hath gotten a counterfeit pursuivant's scutcheon and warrant, and so under that pretence robbeth and spoileth as others of like quality.

An Ancient Editor's Note Book

HUDDLESTONE'S END

Huddlestone, a great persecutor in the north, the very hour he died, surprised by sudden death, did stink so abominably that nobody could endure to come nigh him.

An Ancient Editor's Note Book

WITH SIX FINGERS AND TOES

These fellows [pursuivants] could get no Justice in Shropshire to aid them, but they met with a monstrous apostate, one Lewis, that had been a schoolmaster and Catholic. He hath six fingers on every hand, and as many toes on either foot, a monster five times over in making and manners. This monster directed them to all the places he knew.

GRENE, *Collections*

24

Prison

IN THE GATEHOUSE

When I was taken to the prison-hall, I found there no small number of prisoners,—nobles, priests, women, gentlemen, and lay people,—all shut up for the Catholic faith. They congratulated me on my arrival. We have soft beds, rooms tidy enough, where we can read our hours, say our prayers, and study. From my room I have a charming prospect, from one window towards the south, and from the other towards the north. Twice a day we all go down to the dining-room, and there sit down together to table. We are very well treated for diet, having many dishes, both boiled and roast. We always have the best white bread, and capital beer and wine. Nothing is heard among us but what is Catholic, pious, and holy. The daily expenses for the table are ten stivers (pence) a-day,—four for dinner, four for supper, and two for our beds. A maid makes the beds and sweeps the rooms. So I remain a prisoner, but well content with my state; we hope for better things at last. The Jesuits prosper. Farewell, and pray for me. In haste, 20 Oct. 1580.

Laurence Vaux to the Prior of St. Martin's

CONDITIONS OF RELEASE

Some of the imprisoned Catholics are allowed to go to their homes, but under such terrible conditions that they prefer to remain in prison. The first is that they should pledge themselves to go to the preachings one a month, under penalty of £20 for each time they fail; second, that they may not go more than three miles from their homes; third, that they are not to converse with any other Catholic, even though he be a relative; fourth, that they are to have no Catholic servant, and they may not even converse with any priest or other person who may have come from Rome, nor may they harbour or associate with anyone who may have given shelter to such a man. All this is to be punished as high treason, but nevertheless God allows the same to happen here as we read of in the early Church, and there are people, even though they be heretics, who are so faithful to the many priests who are here in disguise that, for their sakes, they disregard wives, children, and possessions, saying that they are good people and they will not betray them.

Bernardino de Mendoza to the King of Spain,
4 July 1581

LANCASTER RACES

I hear that the prison at Lancaster is very ill kept; that recusants there have liberty to go when and whither they list; to hunt, hawk, and go to horse races at their pleasure; which notorious abuse of law and justice should speedily be reformed.

Richard Vaughan, Bishop of Chester, to Thomas Hesketh,
29 January 1598

HAMPSHIRE PRISONERS

In Hampshire, three prisons full of Catholics to the number of eighty at least, but most poor men, who pray earnestly to be made worthy to suffer death in God's cause. The gentlemen are removed from their country, lest among their neighbours, tenants, and acquaintance their good life and behaviour should win many unto them, as in truth it did whilst they were there imprisoned.

An Ancient Editor's Note Book

A PRISONER'S PRAYER

O Christ my lord who for my sins
  Didst hang upon a tree;
Grant that thy grace in me, poor wretch,
  May still engrafted be.

Grant that thy naked hanging then
  May kill in me all pride
And care of wealth, since thou didst there
  In such poor state abide.

Grant that thy crown of pricking thorns
　　Which thou for me didst wear
May make me willing for thy sake
　　All shame and pain to bear.

Grant that the scorns and taunts, which thou
　　Didst on the cross endure,
May humble me, and in my heart
　　All patience still procure.

Grant that thy praying for thy foes
　　May plant within my breast
Such charity as, from my heart,
　　I malice may detest.

Grant that thy pierced hands, which did
　　Of nothing all things frame,
May move me to lift up my hands,
　　And ever praise thy name.

Grant that thy wounded feet, whose steps
　　Were perfect evermore,
May learn my feet to tread those paths,
　　Which thou hast gone before.

Grant that the bitter gall, which did
　　Thy empty body fill,
May teach me to subdue my flesh,
　　And to perform thy will.

Grant that thy wounds may cure the sores,
　　Which sin in me hath wrought,
Grant that thy death may save the soul,
　　Which with thy blood was bought.

Grant that those drops of blood, which ran
　　Out from thy heart amain,
May melt my heart into salt tears,
　　To see thy grievous pain.

Grant that thy blessed grave, wherein
  Thy body lay a while,
May bury all such vain delights
  As may my mind defile.

Grant that thy going down to them
  Which did thy sight desire,
May keep my soul, when I am dead,
  Clear from the purging fire.

Grant that thy rising up from death
  May raise my thoughts from sin:
Grant that thy parting from this earth
  From earth my heart may win.

Grant lord that thy ascending then
  May lift my mind to thee.
That there my heart and joy may rest
  Though here in flesh I be.

                    Amen.

Verses by Philip Howard, Earl of Arundel,
written in prison

NUMBERED AMONG THIEVES

The persecution of Catholics here has reached such a pitch that they want to deprive the prisoners of human charity, and have ordered that the gifts sent to them should not be given to them alone, but divided amongst all the prisoners. They are mostly incarcerated with crowds of thieves, and are left to die with hunger amongst them, in order that their torment may be the greater. If anyone goes to ask after one of them he is arrested, and consequently most of the gifts are sent through me, and are distributed amongst them by my own servants, the Catholics alone receiving them. In the same manner I take charge of the money sent by the Catholics who have fled the kingdom, and of the sums given by others for the maintenance of Englishmen in the seminaries of Rheims and Rome, in order to save the donors from the penalties inflicted, the least of which is to punish them as traitors.

Bernardino de Mendoza to the King of Spain,
1 October 1581

CHEESE AND A FEATHER BED

A warrant brought by John Marden from the Lord Bishop of London to have access to James Braybrooke twice, brought the 28th day of October.

Sent to James Braybrooke from his wife the 30th day of October a pheasant hen two geese and two capons two chickens and 14s. in money.

Brought by Thomas Willis whereof he hath given a capon and a goose to the poor prisoners that are of his religion in the house.

A cake sent to James Braybrooke from his sister the 31st day of October, brought by Thomas Willis his servant.

Brought to Polydor Morgan the 5th day of November by Robert Lidgard his brother, a leg of mutton and three pies, a bottle of wine.

Sent to Thomas Edwards from his wife the 10th day of November, a cheese and a feather bed, brought by his son.

Brought to Polydor Morgan by Robert Lidgard the 12th day of November, two mutton pies, one pudding pie, a leg of mutton.

Certificate of Keeper of the Gatehouse, 21 November 1581

YORK CASTLE

The following persons died prisoners in the Castle or suffered martyrdom in the city of York for the Catholic faith in 1583:

Sir William Guet, priest	9 January
Sir John Swall, priest	28 ,,
Mr. Cuthbert Dawning, Esq.	22 April
Anthony Clackson	,, ,,
William Hart, presb. and Richard Thirkill, presb.	29 May
James Robinson, eodem die	,, ,,
Paul Lethame	1 June
Mrs. Frances Webster	13 ,,
John Gille	1 July
Mr. Marmaduke Bowes	13 ,,
Roger Parker	
John Ellerby	21 ,,
William Burton	23 ,,
Sara Jackson	24 ,,
Robert Jebber	25 ,,
John Finglay, priest	8 August

GRENE, *Collections*

Thomas Woodhouse's Interview with Lord Burghley

Then the Treasurer began to dispute with him against the Pope's authority, and the other did defend it and heated the Treasurer a little, yet at last he grew cold again and asked Mr. Woodhouse if he would be his chaplain? and he said yea. 'And wilt thou say Mass in my house?' 'Yea, that I will,' saith Woodhouse. 'And shall I come to it?' saith the Treasurer. 'No,' saith Woodhouse, 'that you shall not, unless you will be reconciled to the Catholic Church.' And so he was sent back again to the Fleet, where he was separate from his companions and put in a chamber by himself. Either then or some few days after a smith was called to lay irons on him, which being done Mr. Woodhouse rewarded him with two shillings; but seven days after, when the smith by order from the Council had taken off his irons, he stood with cap in hand looking to be rewarded much better than before, till he saw Mr. Woodhouse attend to his business and little to mind him, that he thought it necessary to put Mr. Woodhouse in remembrance with the words, 'Sir, this day sennight when I burdened you with irons you rewarded me with two shillings; now I have taken them away for your more ease, I trust your worship will reward me much better.' 'No,' saith Mr. Woodhouse, 'then I gave thee wages for laying irons on me, because I was sure to have my wages for bearing them; now thou must have patience if thou lose thy wages when thou hast with taking away my irons taken also away those wages I was to have for carrying them. But come when thou wilt to load me with irons, and if I have money, thou shalt not go home with an empty purse.

Relation of the sufferings of Mr. Thomas Woodhouse

The Death of the Earl of Arundel

After he had lived divers years in this virtuous and pious manner to the great edification of all, and admiration of such as had known the exceeding liberty wherein he lived while he was a Protestant, it happened that in the month of August of the year 1595, he fell one day sitting at dinner so very ill immediately upon the eating of a roasted teal that he was forced to rise from table, and after some vehement casting he entered into a dysentery which could never be stayed till his very death, which gave occasion unto many to suspect he was poisoned. Whereupon the Countess his wife forthwith sent him some antidotes and all the remedies she could any way procure: but all in vain. For the disease had so possessed him that it could not be removed, but by little and little so consumed his body that he became like an anatomy having nothing left but skin and bone. Some were of opinion that the poison was put by his cook into the sauce of the roasted teal being thereto corrupted by one Nicolas Rainberde who sometime had been the Earl's servant, and after was employed by the Queen against him prosecuting sundry suits in the Exchequer to overthrow his estate, . . . and two things there were which much increased this suspicion. The one that though the Earl had used much endeavour to have the said cook removed, yet could by no means obtain it. The other that the said cook came to the Earl a little before his death and asked him forgiveness though not specifying that thing in particular. But however it was the good Earl did freely forgive him, and all others who had any way perhaps concurred thereunto.

He had a great desire to have the assistance of Fr. Weston at his death by whose means he was first reconciled to the Church: but it would by no means be permitted that either he or any other priest should come to him. He desired moreover to see his brother the Lord William Howard, or his uncle the Lord Henry (made Earl of Northampton afterwards) at least to take his last leave of them before his death; but neither would that be granted, no not so much as to see his brother the Lord Thomas Howard though both then and ever he had been a Protestant. The Queen had made a kind of promise to some of his friends in his behalf that before his death his wife and children should come unto him. Whereupon conceiving that now his time in this world could not be long, he writ humble letters both to her, and some of the Council petitioning the performance of that supposed promise. The Lieutenant of the Tower carried his letters and delivered them with his own hands to the Queen, and brought him this answer from her by word of mouth. That if he would but once go to their Church, his request should not only be granted, but he should moreover be restored to his honour, and estates, with as much favour as she could show. Which message being delivered he gave thanks to the Lieutenant for his pains, and said he could not accept her Majesty's offers upon that condition; adding withal that he was sorry he had but one life to lose for that cause.

Not long after he grew so faint and weak decaying by degrees, that he was not able to rise from his bed. Whereupon by the advice of his physicians he gave over the saying of his breviary and the reading of other books, betaking himself only to his beads and some other devotions whereto by vow he had obliged himself; and these he never omitted till the very last day of his life, having his beads almost always with him in his bed. His physicians coming to visit him some few days before his departure, he desired them not to trouble themselves now any more his case being beyond their skill, and he having then some business, meaning his devotions, which he desired, but feared he should not have time sufficient to dispatch. And they thereupon departing Sir Michael Blount then Lieutenant of the Tower, who had been ever very hard and harsh unto him, took occasion to come and visit him, and kneeling down by his bedside, in humble manner desired his Lordship to forgive him. Whereto the Earl answered in this manner. 'Do you ask forgiveness, Mr. Lieutenant? Why then I forgive you in the same sort as I desire myself to be forgiven at the hands of God.' And then kissing his hand offered it in most charitable and kind manner to him, and holding him fast by the hand said, 'I pray you also to forgive me whatever I have said or done in any thing offensive to you'; and he melting into tears and answering that he forgave him with all his heart.

The last night of his life [the Earl] spent for the most part in prayer, sometimes saying his beads, sometimes such Psalms and prayers as he knew by heart. And oftentimes used these holy aspirations: O Lord into thy hands I commend my spirit. Lord thou art my hope; and the like. Very frequently moreover invocating the holy names of Jesus and Mary. Seeing his servants in the morning stand by his bedside weeping in a mournful manner, he asked them what a clock it was; they answering that it was eight or there about. 'Why then' said he, 'I have almost run out my course, and come to the end of this miserable and mortal life,' desiring them not to weep for him since he did not doubt by the grace of God but all would go well with him. Which being said, he returned to his prayers upon his beads again, though then with a very slow, hollow and fainting voice, and so continued as long as he was able to draw so much breath as was sufficient to sound out the names of Jesus and the glorious Virgin, which were the last words which he was ever heard to speak. The last minute of his last hour being now come, lying on his back, his eyes firmly fixed towards Heaven, and his long lean consumed arms out of the bed, his hand upon his breast laid in cross one upon the other, about twelve o'clock at noon, in which hour he was also born into this world, arraigned, condemned, and adjudged unto death, upon Sunday the 19th October 1595 (after almost eleven years' imprisonment in the Tower) in a most sweet manner without any sign of grief or groan, only turning his head a little aside, as one falling into a pleasing sleep, he surrendered his happy soul into the hands of Almighty God, who to his so great glory had created it.

Some have thought, and perhaps not improbably, that he had some foreknowledge of the day of his death, because about seven or eight days before making certain notes (understood only by himself) in his calendar, what prayers and devotions he intended to say upon every day of the week following, on Monday, Tuesday, etc.: when he came to the Sunday on which he died, he there made a pause saying, 'Hitherto and no farther: this is enough,' and so writ no more, as his servants who then heard his words, and saw him write, have often testified.

The Life and Death of Philip Howard

FROM A CELL WINDOW

Negligent of himself, he was lavish to the poor, and gave them all that came to his hands, committing the care of himself to God's good providence, which he exhorted others to do also, assuring them that necessaries would never fail them whilst they lent to the Lord. Those, who had not anything to give, he advised to relieve their neighbour's wants by reciting the Lord's Prayer. When he was in prison . . . he would look out of the window of his cell, and if he saw any poor of whatever condition he would throw out to them money, or whatever else he might have, depriving himself of what he needed for support.

DOROTHY ARUNDELL, *Life of Fr. John Cornelius*

TWICE CONDEMNED, NOT ONCE DEAD

As for my own part here I live twice condemned, which perhaps may seem strange unto you, and not once dead. I have not wanted, thank God, anything necessary to me except the full service of God for the space of these three years and somewhat more since I was first imprisoned. I thank God I am now cunning in wearing of iron shackles. . . . I have been now twice clogged with them. The first time was from the fifth of September 1591, as well night as day, until the 25 April next following, at which time my keeper . . . was grievously reprehended for showing such favour and commanded to lay irons upon me and Mr. Slade again, with straight charge to keep us one from the other and to see that no access might be to us. But we consider that irons borne for this cause on earth shall surmount gold and precious stones in heaven—that is our mark, that is our desire. In the mean season we are threatened daily and do look still when the hurdle shall be brought to the door. I beseech you for God's sake we want not the good prayers of you all for our strength, our joy and our perseverance to the end.

Letter from John Bodey, in prison,
16 September 1583

Fr. Pattison in Limbo

After condemnation he was put into Limbo with six other prisoners condemned to die for felonies. He persuaded and reconciled five of them, the sixth betrayed it. But the other five died in the Catholic faith, albeit not openly protesting the same, as forbidden by their ghostly father to the end that the like opportunity of saving souls may not be prevented by separating the one from the other.

GRENE, *Collections*

A Thread from Heaven

Fr. Weston told me something of what he suffered in his great isolation. . . . [How] after a few months had passed, he endured fierce assaults from demons, of the kind that the ancient Fathers of the desert experienced: and he observed that there was no greater torment than a solitary confinement extending over a long period of time. To an English priest, who pressed him to speak further, he confided in strict secrecy that in these conflicts, both visible and invisible, the onslaught was unremitting both day and night, and now that the devils had him by himself they threatened to swallow him up and have done with him: they boasted that they would persuade him to hang himself and brought him ropes and knives so that he could do it. And they buffeted him night and day, preventing him from sleeping and taking any rest. To such an extent did he suffer from insomnia that in the course of fifty days he did not get as much as ten hours' sleep.

To combat this solitude and the assaults of the demon he armed himself with prayer, vigils and penance and with constant reading of the Bible, the only book he was permitted. Ordinarily each day he prayed for six hours, more on special days. . . . And in his first year or two in the Tower he dipped all his food in water, in order to destroy its savour and mortify himself. Then one day he observed that this practice was harming his health and he gave it up. Usually he slept on the floor. But once the Lieutenant of the Tower, entering his cell on a visit, was moved by compassion—for it was a very cold and damp place—and ordered a bed to be brought in. That night he slept in it, but when he opened the Bible the next morning the first sentence he read was from Proverbs, chapter 26. *Sicut ostium vertitur in cardine suo, ita piger in lectulo suo* (as the door turns on the hinge so the slothful man turns on his couch). And then the very same day when the servant brought him his food he ordered him to remove the bed. What with his continual lack of sleep he was unable to give his attention to anything, and, besides, at this time he had almost entirely lost his sight and hearing. Distraught by his suffering he wished to die, for living was an unending death, and, in any human reckoning, he could live but little longer. One day in this state of extreme distress —he told the incident to a Father of the Society (who himself was undergoing great torment and persecution from devils and felt abandoned by God) getting him to promise that he would not say a word about it in his lifetime—one day, I say, while he was at prayer calling the attention of God to his afflictions, incapable, it seemed, of enduring them further, he saw with his physical sight a thread descending like a ray of light from the sky, and at the same time heard a voice, 'With this thread you are attached to my good keeping. I am with you and shall not abandon you.' And this consoled him greatly and reconciled him to his sufferings, giving him such peace of mind and sense of oneness with God that his soul was suffused with contentment and nothing henceforth troubled him.

FRANCIS DE PERALTA, *Life of William Weston*

GLUT OF RECUSANTS

We are further to let your honour understand that our gaols do now grow to be over-glutted with recusants, and that the county begins to be shrewdly infected in sundry places by their obstinacies. . . . For now that the common gaols are rented by persons of no credit that live only upon the gain thereof, all justice is subverted, and Papists live at ease and have their conventicles in despite of us, do what we can.

The Justices of Dover to Francis Walsingham,
October 1586

CHESTER CASTLE

Richard Sutton ⎤ Two old priests very wilful and obstinate remain-
John Culpage ⎦ ing in the Castle of Chester.
William Aldersey, linen-draper and his wife. They are but poor and
he lieth bed-ridden as it is said.

A certificate of recusants in the diocese of Chester,
29 November 1577

Trial

Fr. John Bennet

To confess Christ before man is not contumacy, but constancy.

Fr. John Bennet to William Hughes, Bishop of
St. Asaph, 1583

Behaviour before the Bench

The Recusant for the most part behaved himself more civilly before the magistrate than did the Puritan; who was commonly most insolent, and thereby deserved more sharp words and reproofs than the other.

JOHN STRYPE, *Life and Acts of Archbishop Whitgift*

Fr. Edmund Campion

It was not our death that ever we feared. But we knew that we were not lords of our own lives, and therefore for want of answer would not be guilty of our deaths. The only thing that we have now to say is, that if our religion do make us traitors, we are worthy to be condemned; but otherwise are, and have been, as good subjects as ever the Queen had.

In condemning us you condemn all your own ancestors—all the ancient priests, bishops and kings—all that was once the glory of England, the island of saints, and the most devoted child of the See of Peter. For what have we taught, however you may qualify it with the odious name of treason, that they did not uniformly teach? To be condemned with these lights—not of England only, but of the world —by their degenerate descendants, is both gladness and glory to us.

God lives; posterity will live; their judgment is not so liable to corruption as that of those who are now going to sentence us to death.

Edmund Campion to his judges before receiving
sentence of death

A Most Barbarous Inhuman Question

But Mr. Thomas Cottam thus spoke at the bar ... 'Indeed you are searchers of secrets, for you would needs know of me what penance I was enjoined by my ghostly father for my sins committed; and I acknowledge my frailty, that, to avoid the intolerable torment of the rack, I confessed, God forgive me, what they demanded therein; but when they further urged me to utter also what my sins were, for which that penance was enjoined me,—a loathsome and unchristian question, —I then answered that I would not disclose my offences saving to God and to my ghostly father alone; whereupon they sore tormented me, and still pressed me with the same demand, and I persisted that it was a most barbarous inhuman question, and that I would not answer though they tormented me to death.' Thus spake Mr. Cottam at his arraignment, wherewith the enemies being ashamed, the Lieutenant of the Tower there present began to deny the whole; whereto Mr. Cottam replied again thus, 'And is not this true? Here is present Dr. Hammon, with the rest of the commissioners that were at my racking, to whose consciences I appeal. God is my witness that it is most true, and you know that Sir George Carey did ask me these unnatural questions, deny it if you can.'

WILLIAM ALLEN, *A True and Sincere Defence*

Hence the Blame or Merit

'I alone concealed him. And so entirely was it my own act that I did not even name it to my mother; and hence the blame or the merit, whichever of these it is, belongs to me alone. And in doing this I have intended no offence to the Queen, nor to yourselves, nor to any one else, but have obeyed the laws of piety and of nature rather than those of men. Father John has in our house a mother, a poor Irish woman, decrepit, aged, and bed-ridden. You can satisfy your own eyes of this if you please. Now, if it is a crime to afford a mother of such age, and under such circumstances, the extreme consolation of seeing her own child; if there is any generation of savages that would refuse it, then I give up, and will acknowledge that I have done wrong in inviting him to satisfy this duty of piety and to pay this debt of nature. Not because you reprehend me for it as for a crime, will that make it to be one; on the contrary, I esteem it as a meritorious act.'

Dorothy Arundell at the trial of Fr. John Cornelius

MY CAUSE IS GOD'S QUARREL

'You charge me wrongfully. I die not desperately nor willingly procure mine own death: for not being found guilty of such crimes as were laid against me, and yet condemned to die, I could but rejoice; my cause also being God's quarrel. Neither did I fear the terror [of the] sentence of death, but was ashamed on their behalfs to have such shameful words uttered in the audience as to strip me naked, and press me to death among men, which methought for womanhood they might have concealed. As for my husband, know you that I love him next unto God in this world, and I have care over my children as a mother ought to have; I trust I have done my duty to them to bring them up in the fear of God, and so I trust now I am discharged of them. And for this cause I am willing to offer them freely to God that sent them me, rather than I will yield one jot from my faith. I confess death is fearful, and flesh is frail; yet I mind my God's assistance to spend my blood in this faith, as willingly as ever I put my paps to my children's mouths, neither desire I to have my death deferred.'

JOHN MUSH, *Life of Margaret Clitherow*

SIR JOHN SOUTHCOTE

Queen Elizabeth made him a Judge of the Common Pleas, and soon after he had probably been Lord Chief Justice but for a conceit of the Queen's, who said she should govern too like a woman, if she suffered a woman to be Chief Justice of England. The occasion of this reflection was that he, being a good-natured man, had a reputation in the world of being governed by his wife. . . .

Being in his circuit and on the bench at Norwich, a Priest happened to be tried for his life; which being the first time that anything of this kind had come before him, one may easily imagine he had no small conflict within himself; but, to the great glory of God, he behaved himself with so much courage upon this occasion that when he perceived he could not save the man's life by giving a favourable charge to the jury, rather than give the sentence of death against him, he stood up in the open court and pulled off his robes of Judge, declaring that he there resigned his office rather than he would bring upon himself and family the guilt of innocent blood. After which he retired to his house at Merstham in Surrey, where for three years he led a penitential life, and then happily ended his days. His body was brought to Witham, and there deposited in a vault, over which a handsome marble monument was erected by his son John, who was left sole executor to his last will, though his mother was still living.

Sir Edward Southcote to his son, John

Christopher Bales, 1590

He was asked by the judge according to custom . . . when judgment was about to be pronounced, if he had anything to say for himself. He answered, 'This only do I want to know, whether St. Augustine sent hither by St. Gregory was a traitor or not.' They answered that he was not . . . He answered them, 'Why then do you condemn me to death as a traitor? I am sent hither by the same see: and for the same purpose as he was. Nothing is charged against me that could not also be charged against the saint.' But for all that they condemned him.

Grene, *Collections*

Robert Southwell

The Chief Justice asked him how old he was, seeming to scorn his youth. He answered that he was near about the age of our Saviour, Who lived upon the earth thirty-three years; and he himself was as he thought near about thirty-four years. Hereat Topcliffe seemed to make great acclamation, saying he compared himself to Christ. Mr. Southwell answered, 'No; he was a humble worm created by Christ.' 'Yes,' said Topcliffe, 'you are Christ's fellow.'

Henry Garnet, *Account of the Trial of Robert Southwell*

Fr. John Ingram

There is no Christian law in the world that can make the saying and sacrifice of the Mass treason; and as well might the celebrating of the Maundy of Christ's disciples be made treason, as the saying and hearing of Mass.

Fr. John Ingram to his judges

FR. JOHN CORNELIUS

At the bar, amongst other things, he appealed to the law of God, and Judge Anderson answered, 'We come not hither to do the law of God but the law of the Queen.'

Catalogue of Martyrs

FR. JOHN BENNET

Sir George Bromley. 'What say you of the Queen's Majesty?'
Fr. John Bennet. 'That I am her subject; and, as my duty is, I pray to God for her, and have done so this very day before you were out of your bed.'

JOHN BRIDGEWATER, *The Examination of John Bennet*

ROBERT BICKERDICK

Robert Bickerdick at York supposed to be seen in company of a priest drinking a pot of ale and paying for it, was indicted for aiding a priest. A jury empanelled upon him found him not guilty. They indicted him a year after for the same cause. Again the jury found him not guilty. They removed him hereupon from the town gaol to the Castle, there indicting him again, asking him, if the Pope should invade the realm, what part he would take. He answered he could not tell at present what he would do in time to come, more than what God should put into his mind. The judge said that he blew treason out of his mouth and that the other juries had been too favourable and scrupulous. Thereupon he was found guilty of high treason, condemned and executed. Afterwards some gentlemen asked the judge if those words of Bickerdick were treason by any statute or law; which demand the judge took in great dudgeon, saying, you do no less injury to us than the traitor did at the bar: we are not sent hither to scant or dispute the statutes, but to give judgment against offenders.

GRENE, *Collections*

CHRISTOPHER BLACKALL

One Christopher Blackall of the Temple, a young gentleman of seventeen years, of heretical parents and education, and unknown to be a Catholic to his best acquaintance, on a moonshine night this last

month went with his man and took down a quarter of Friar Godfrey
Morris, *alias* Buckley, about Lambeth fields, and by chance was overtaken by a hue and cry about a robbery, and so the next day carried
to the Lord Chief Justice, who asked him how he dare take down a
traitor's quarter. He said he knew not that he was a traitor. 'What!
was he not hanged and quartered?'—'Yes, for I was by and saw it.'—
'Is he not then a traitor?'—'No, for I heard your Lordship say that you
condemned him not for any treason committed, but because he was a
priest: and priesthood alone is no treason: and therefore I, knowing
him in prison, and hearing no evil of him, but loving him, was loth
the crows should eat him.'—'Ah, sir-rah! you are then a Papist and
reconciled.'—'My Lord, I know not what you mean by being reconciled, but I am a Catholic.' He threatened him with torments: he
answered, he had forecast all difficulties. He examined him of his
father, and knowing him to be a hot heretic was more incensed and
threatened his father's displeasure: he professed that neither father nor
mother nor all the world should remove him. So he abideth comforted in prison, in the resolution that when all friends fail he will live
of the common purse.

Henry Garnet to Robert Persons, 21 October 1598

26

Torture

ALLEN'S CHALLENGE

All their confessions both voluntary and forced by torment are extant in the persecutors' hands. Is there any word [that] soundeth or smelleth of conspiracy? They have all sorts and sexes of Catholics in prison for their faith, and divers honourable personages only upon pretence of dealing and conversing with them. Hath any one of all the Realm in durance or at liberty, by fair means or foul, confessed that either priest or Jesuit persuaded them in confession, or otherwise, to forsake the Queen? That ever they were absolved on that condition? That ever they received *Agnus dei* at their hands or other spiritual token for earnest, or pressed to rebel or join with the enemy, as this slanderous libel[1] doth not so much avouch (for that were intolerable) as by guileful art insinuate without all proof or probability.

WILLIAM ALLEN, *A True and Sincere Defence*

PITIFUL EXTREMITIES

We speak nothing of the pitiful extremities you have brought divers unto by horrible fetters, stocks, dungeons, famine; or of the death of well-near twenty happy Catholics at once, infected and pestered in York prison, where they perished by the unmercifulness of the Protestants, of whom by no pitiful complaints they could obtain liberty or fresh air for the saving of their lives without condescending to go to their abominable service. We tell you not here again that for the more affliction of Catholics . . . you have profanely made choice of Sundays and great holidays to practice your torments upon them, after the old fashion of the pagans, rather than upon weekdays; that

[1] Lord Burghley's *Execution of Justice in England.*

you bring other Catholic prisoners near to the place of torture, to hear their brethren's sorrowful cries; and eftsoons lead some newly taken from the rack under their fellow prisoners' windows that by hearing their pitiful complaints, sighs and groans proceeding of infinite pains, they may relent in religion.

WILLIAM ALLEN, *A True and Sincere Defence*

THE WORKS OF ANTICHRIST

The priests they succeed in capturing are treated with a variety of terrible tortures; amongst others is one torment that people in Spain imagine to be that which will be worked by Antichrist as the most dreadfully cruel of them all. This is to drive iron spikes between the nails and the quick; and two priests in the Tower have been tortured in this way, one of them being Campion of the Society of Jesus, who, with the other, was recently captured. I am assured that when they would not confess under this torture, the nails of their fingers and toes were turned back; all of which they suffered with great patience.

Bernardino de Mendoza to the King of Spain, 12 August 1581

THE CAUSE OF CONFIDENCE

Notwithstanding the torture by which they sought to extract from the martyrs declarations of the persons with whom they were in communication, they were unable to obtain them, and I cannot exaggerate the beneficial effect that this has had, and the confidence that it has inspired in all sorts of people.

Bernardino de Mendoza to the King of Spain, 11 December 1581

METHODS OF FRENCH PROTESTANTS

I have found by experience that the Protestant preachers expect and desire great applause of their hearers as Paulus Samosatenus did of his followers; they overthrow altars, abuse the Blessed Sacrament, handle despitefully holy chrism, as the Donatists did. . . . The same Donatists did torment most cruelly Catholic priests, plucking out the eyes of some, and of one Bishop they cut out the tongue and hand, and murdered many. And the Protestants of late in France did the like to

Catholic priests, and besides tying halters about their necks, they drew them dispiteously after their horses; that done, they cut off their ears [and] noses; they wore their ears in their hats instead of brooches, and finally they either hanged up their carcases or shot them through with pistols. Of others they hacked and mangled their faces; of other some, to try force and strength, they did cleave in two at one stroke their heads. . . . At S. Macharius they buried the Catholics quick, they cut infants in two, they ripped the bellies of priests and drew out their entrails by little and little, winding them about a stick or tree. At Patte, some six leagues from Orleans, they burned Catholics and threw infants into the fire there to perish with the rest. And many other like outrages they committed which who so desireth to know may find them set down by Claudius de Saintes[1] in his book noted before.

THOMAS HILL, *A Quatron of Reasons*

FOR, LO, THE DRUMS

Sir, I presume somewhat rashly to address unto you as to a patron of orphans in these miserable days, imparting my present calamity which surely, without temporal comfort, I am very hardly able long to endure, the time of the year and the hard handling of my torture masters . . . growing so fast towards their extremity. This bearer, Mr. N., I think, can partly relate unto you mine estate from the mouth of one in prison. (He was) my dearest friend in bonds, for he hath spared of himself to relieve me with victuals and with other such necessaries as he could by that means do; whom I did never see in my life, but through a hole. Nothing was too dear unto him that he could convey unto me, for whom, as I am bound, so will I daily pray while I live.

I have been a close prisoner since the 18th day of September, whereof 46 days together I lay upon a little straw in my boots, my hands continually manacled in irons, for one month together never once taken off. After they were twice or thrice taken off to shift me and ease me for a day together—this was all the favour my keeper did show. The morrow after Simon and Jude's day I was hanged at the wall from the ground, my manacles fast locked into a staple as high as I could reach upon a stool: the stool taken away there I hanged from a little after 8 o'clock in the morning till after 4 in the afternoon, without any ease or comfort at all, saving that Topcliffe came in unto me and told me that the Spaniards were come into Southwark by

[1] *Livre du Sacrament des Eglises.*

our means; 'For, lo, do you not hear the drums' (for then the drums played in honour of my Lord Mayor). The next day after also I was hanged an hour or two: such is the malicious minds and practices of our adversaries. For my clothes I have no other than my summer weed, wherein I was taken. And then I was rifled of all my hose that cost but then seven pound, of four pound in money, and odd money, with my rings, a silver pix worth 20 shillings and many other things, nothing left me more than on my back.

Fr. White to Fr. Garnet from prison,
23 November 1591

JOHN GERARD

i. Then they produced a warrant for putting me to torture. They had it ready by them and handed it to me to read. (In this prison a special warrant is required for torture.)

I saw that the warrant was properly made out and signed, and then I answered:

'With God's help I shall never do anything that is unjust or act against my conscience or the Catholic faith. You have me in your power. You can do with me what God allows you to do—more you cannot do.'

Then they began to implore me not to force them to take steps they were loath to take. They said they would have to put me to torture every day, as long as my life lasted, until I gave them the information they wanted.

'I trust in God's goodness,' I answered, 'that He will prevent me from ever committing a sin such as this—the sin of accusing innocent people. We are all in God's hands and therefore I have no fear of anything you can do to me.'

This was the sense of my answers, as far as I can recall them now.

We went to the torture-room in a kind of solemn procession, the attendants walking ahead with lighted candles.

The chamber was underground and dark, particularly near the entrance. It was a vast place and every device and instrument of human torture was there. They pointed out some of them to me and said that I would try them all. Then they asked me again whether I would confess.

'I cannot,' I said.

I fell on my knees for a moment's prayer. Then they took me to a big upright pillar, one of the wooden posts which held the roof of this huge underground chamber. Driven in to the top of it were iron staples for supporting heavy weights. They then put my wrists into iron gauntlets and ordered me to climb two or three wicker steps. My arms were then lifted up and an iron bar was passed through the rings of one gauntlet, then through the staple and rings of the second gauntlet. This done, they fastened the bar with a pin to prevent it slipping, and then, removing the wicker steps one by one from under my feet, they left me hanging by my hands and arms fastened above my head. The tips of my toes, however, still touched the ground, and they had to dig away the earth from under them. They had hung me up from the highest staple in the pillar and could not raise me any higher, without driving in another staple.

Hanging like this I began to pray. The gentlemen standing around asked me whether I was willing to confess now.

'I cannot and I will not,' I answered.

But I could hardly utter the words, such a gripping pain came over me. It was worst in my chest and belly, my hands and arms. All the blood in my body seemed to rush up into my arms and hands and I thought that blood was oozing out from the ends of my fingers and the pores of my skin. But it was only a sensation caused by my flesh swelling above the irons holding them. The pain was so intense that I thought I could not possibly endure it, and added to it, I had an interior temptation. Yet I did not feel any inclination or wish to give them the information they wanted. The Lord saw my weakness with the eyes of His mercy, and did not permit me to be tempted beyond by strength. With the temptation He sent me relief. Seeing my agony and the struggle going on in my mind, He gave me this most merciful thought: the utmost and worst they can do to you is to kill you, and you have often wanted to give your life for your Lord God. The Lord God sees all you are enduring—He can do all things. You are in God's keeping. With these thoughts, God in His infinite goodness and mercy gave me the grace of resignation, and, with a desire to die and a hope (I admit) that I would, I offered Him myself to do with me as He wished. From that moment the conflict in my soul ceased, and even the physical pain seemed much more bearable than before, though I am sure it must, in fact, have been greater with the growing strain and weariness of my body.

When the gentlemen present saw that I was not answering their questions, they went off to the Lieutenant's house, and stayed there.

Every now and again they sent to find out how things were going with me.

Three or four robust men remained behind to watch and supervise the torture, and also my warder. He stayed, I think, out of kindness, for every few minutes he took a cloth and wiped the perspiration that ran in drops continuously down my face and whole body. That helped me a little, but he added to my sufferings when he started to talk. He went on and on, begging and imploring me to pity myself and tell the gentlemen what they wanted to know. And he urged so many human reasons for this that I thought that the devil had instigated him to feign this affection or that my torturers had left him behind on purpose to trick me. But I felt all these suggestions of the enemy like blows in the distance: they did not seem to touch my soul or affect me in any way. More than once I interrupted him:

'Stop this talk, for heaven's sake. Do you think I'm going to throw my soul away to save my life? You exasperate me.'

But he went on. And several times the others joined in. 'You will be a cripple all your life if you live. And you are going to be tortured every day until you confess.'

But I prayed in a low voice as well as I could, calling on the names of Jesus and Mary.

Sometime after one o'clock, I think, I fell into a faint. How long I was unconscious I don't know, but I don't think it was long, for the men held my body up or put the wicker steps under my feet until I came to. Then they heard me pray and immediately they let me down again. And they did this every time I fainted—eight or nine times that day—before it struck five.

After four or before five o'clock Wade returned. Coming to me he asked:

'Are you ready now to obey the Queen and her Council?'

I answered:

'You want me to do what is sinful. I will not do it.'

'All you have to say,' said Wade, 'is that you wish to speak to Cecil, Her Majesty's Secretary.'

'I have nothing to say to him,' I said, 'except what I have said to you already. If I asked to speak to him, people would be scandalised. They would think I had given way, that at last I was going to say something that I should not say.'

In a rage he suddenly turned his back on me and strode out of the room, shouting angrily in a loud voice:

'Then hang there until you rot off the pillar.'

He left. And I think all the Commissioners left the Tower then, for at five o'clock the Tower bell is rung, a signal for all to leave unless they want to have the gates locked on them. A little later they took me down. My legs and feet were not damaged, but it was a great effort to stand upright.

JOHN GERARD, *Autobiography*

ii. Of John Gerard, I have already written where he is. He hath twice been hung up by the hands with great cruelty on the part of others, and not less patience on his own. The inquisitors say he is exceeding obstinate, and a great friend of either God or the devil, as they say they cannot extract a word from his lips, save that amidst his torment he ejaculates 'Jesus.'

They lately took him to the rack, and the torturers and examiners stood ready for work, but he when he entered the place straightway threw himself on his knees, and with a loud voice prayed God that as He had given strength to some of His saints to be torn asunder by horses for the sake of Christ, so He would give him strength and courage to be rent in pieces before he should speak a word that would be injurious to any one, or to the Divine glory. And so they did not torture him, seeing him so resolved.

This Father hath indeed been always very courageous, and when he was first taken the gaoler putting heavy irons on his feet he gave him some money. The man, thinking that if he took them off he would get more, removed them next day, and received nothing; accordingly he put them on again and received a gratuity; and taking them off once more got not a farthing. They continued this game for some time, but finally the keeper left the irons perpetually on, so that his legs were in great danger of withering. Thus your Lordship[1] will understand that our times do not lack valiant soldiers of Christ. May God grant him perseverance, and enable those who follow him to imitate his example.

Henry Garnet to Claude Aquaviva, 17 May 1597

NO QUESTION PERTAINING TO FAITH

And the place serveth here to say somewhat of the cause also of their

[1] Fr. Garnet always addresses Fr. Aquaviva, the General of the Society, as 'your Lordship' (*Dominatio vestra*) in order to conceal his identity in the event of his letters falling into the hands of the Council.

racking of Catholics, which they would have strangers believe never
to be done for any point of religion. As, for example, they say, none
is asked by torture what he believeth of the Mass or Transubstantiation
or suchlike. As though (forsooth) there were no question pertaining to
faith or religion but toucheth our inward belief. Whereas indeed it
concerneth religion no less to demand and press us by torture where,
in whose houses, what days and times we say or hear Mass, how many
we have reconciled, what we have heard in confession, who resorteth
to our preachings, who harboureth Catholics and priests, who sus-
taineth, aideth or comforteth them, who they be who have their
children or pupils in the Society or seminaries beyond the seas, where
such a Jesuit or such a priest is to be found, where Catholic books are
printed, and by whom and to whom they be uttered in England?
Which things being demanded of evil intent and to the annoyance
of the Catholic cause, God's priests and innocent men, no man may by
the law of God and nature disclose, though he be expressly commanded
by any prince in the world, for that God must be obeyed more than
men.

Yet these were the interrogatories for which the famous confessor M.
Briant was tormented with needles thrust under his nails, racked also
otherwise in cruel sort and specially punished by two whole days and
nights famine, which they attribute to obstinacy, but indeed (sustained
in Christ's quarrel) it was most honourable constancy. The like
demands were put to the most blessed martyrs Campion, Sherwin and
others upon the torture, . . . M. Thomson, a venerable and learned
priest, was put to torments only to get out of him to what end he kept
certain superaltaries[1] and where he intended to bestow them. The . . .
young man Carter[2] . . . was examined upon the rack, upon what
gentlemen or Catholic ladies he had bestowed or intended to bestow
certain books of prayers or spiritual exercises and meditations which
he had in his custody. Which may suffice to refute the adversary's[3]
asseveration: 'that none have been tormented for other matter than
treason'.

WILLIAM ALLEN, *A True and Sincere Defence*

HIDE ME IN YOUR HOSE

His keeper with compassion giving him warning that he was to be

---

[1] Portable altar stones used by priests in the celebration of Mass.

[2] A Catholic artisan.   [3] Lord Burghley in *The Execution of Justice in England*.

racked again, he was so little moved therewith, as merrily and with a cheerful countenance he said these words, 'I am very little and you are very tall. You may hide me in your great hose and so they shall not find me,' which the keeper did afterwards report to divers, marvelling at his great fortitude and courage.

Account of Thomas Sherwood, martyr, 1578

CAMPION'S FORTUNE

When Campion was executed it was noticed that all his nails had been dragged out in the torture.

Bernardino de Mendoza to the King of Spain,
4 December 1581

LIKE UNTO AN ELEPHANT

He [Edmund Campion] used to fall down at the rackhouse door upon both knees to commend himself to God's mercy, and to crave His grace of patience in his pains. As also being upon the rack he cried continually with much mildness upon God and the holy name of Jesus. And when his body was so cruelly distent and stretched upon the torment that he did hang by his arms and feet only, he most charitably forgave his tormentors and the causers thereof, and thanked one of the rackmen meekly for putting a stone under his backbone. He said to his keeper after his last racking that it was a preface to death. . . .

And being . . . benumbed both of hand and foot, he likened himself to an elephant, which being down could not rise; when he could hold the bread he had to eat betwixt both his hands, he would compare himself to an ape; so merry the man of God was in his mind in all his bodily miseries.

WILLIAM ALLEN, *Father Edmund Campion*

INSTRUMENTS OF TORTURE

Of the means or instruments of torture employed in the Tower there are seven different kinds.

The first is the Pit—a subterraneous cave, twenty feet deep and entirely without light.

The second is a cell or dungeon so small as to be incapable of admitting a person in an erect posture: from its effect on its inmates it has received the name of *Little Ease*.

The third is the rack on which, by means of wooden rollers and other machinery, the limbs of the sufferer are drawn in opposite directions.

The fourth, I believe from the inventor, is called *The Scavenger's Daughter*. It consists of an iron ring, which brings the head, feet and hands together until they form a circle.

The fifth is the iron gauntlet which encloses the hand with the most excruciating pain.

The sixth consists of chains or manacles attached to the arms: and The seventh, of fetters, by which the feet are confined.

EDWARD RISHTON, Tower Journal

THE SCAVENGER'S DAUGHTER

i. 2 February 1584. Robert Nutter, a priest, was taken and two days later was condemned to the Pit, where he remained forty-seven days. He wore fetters during forty-three days; and on each of the two days, the fourth and the sixth, after his apprehension, suffered compression in the Scavenger's Daughter.

10 November 1584. Robert Nutter was again confined in the Pit for two months and fourteen days.

Ibid.

ii. 10 Dec. Thomas Cottam and Luke Kirby, priest, suffered compression in the Scavenger's Daughter for more than an hour. The former bled profusely from the nose.

Ibid.

iii. 1 September 1581. John Gitter (a lay youth) after suffering compression in the Scavenger's Daughter, was confined in the Pit for eight days. He was then led to the rack and cruelly tortured until he nearly fainted; but in the midst of his agony, when ready, as it were, to expire, his countenance brightened with joy: he invoked the name of Jesus and laughed his persecutors to scorn.

Ibid.

THE PIT

23 July 1582. Richard Slack, a priest, was taken and loaded with fetters for twenty-three days and then confined for two months in the Pit.

Ibid.

IN THE DEVIL'S NAME

One Gitter hath been monstrously racked. He showed great patience and courage. In the extremity of torment he never ceased to call upon the name of Jesus, so that Topcliffe in a great fury said, 'What in the Devil's name! Here is such a mumbling of the Jesus Psalter as I never saw.' The tormented still [called] upon Jesus, saying, 'Sweet Jesu, have mercy upon me; with thee is mercy, but I see there is none with men.' . . . The poor man lieth in such misery that he is able to receive nothing into his body but with a quill at the hand of his keeper, who (God knoweth) looketh but slenderly to him. I think notwithstanding this he hath been racked again.

Letter of G. B. from England, 25 October 1582

WHILE MUSING ON THE PASSION

Whether what I am relating be miraculous or no, God knoweth, but true it is, and thereof my conscience is a witness before God. And this I say that in the end of the torture, though my hands and my feet were violently stretched and racked, and my adversaries fulfilled their wicked desire in practising their cruel tyranny upon my body, yet, notwithstanding, I was without sense and feeling well nigh of all grief and pain; and not only so, but as it were comforted, eased, and refreshed of the grief of the past torture. I continued still with perfect and present senses, in quietness of heart and tranquillity of mind. Which thing, when the Commissioners did see, they departed, and in going forth of the door, they gave orders to rack me again the next day following after the same sort. Now, when I heard them say so, it gave me in my mind [courage] by and by, and I did verily believe and trust that with the help of God I should be able to bear and suffer it patiently. In the meantime, as well as I could, I did muse and meditate upon the most bitter Passion of our Saviour, and how full of innumerable pains it was. And whilst I was thus occupied, methought that my left hand was wounded in the palm, and that I felt the blood run out. But in very deed there was no such thing, nor any other pain than that which seemed to be in my hand.

Letter of Alexander Briant

AN ANGEL DID COME

The same Father Horner was so long kept in Limbus and in the common gaol as one of his legs rotted and in the Justice hall was cut off. Afterwards for money he had his liberty, but shortly after they apprehended him again, at which time Mrs. White came unto him, to whom he told that in the night there was a great light in his chamber and that an angel did come and comfort him. He desired that until he were executed she should not utter it to any; neither did she.

GRENE, *Collections*

EDMUND CAMPION AFTER HIS SECOND OR THIRD RACKING

Upon his second or third racking he was so benumbed that he could neither take the cup and lift it to his mouth, nor draw off his cuff at the bar, nor straight after his last torment, nor for many days following had he any feeling or use of his limbs, as he confessed to his keeper asking him how he felt his hands: 'Not evil,' quoth he, 'for I feel them not at all.'

Ibid.

RACK-MASTER NORTON

Upon his death-bed in desperate manner he cried out that he was racked more cruelly than ever he racked any.

Ibid.

27

The Eve of Execution

Fr. Alexander Crowe

This priest and soldier of Jesus Christ was a prisoner in York Castle, where, after much ill treatment, he received sentence of death; whereupon he began to be exceedingly comforted, and to show so great joy in the court that all that were present took notice of it; and returning to the prison (where he was lodged with another Catholic), he could not contain himself all that day, so great was the satisfaction he conceived by thinking that he was to die the next morning. When the night came, and the time of going to bed, he told the other Catholic to take his rest, 'but for my part,' said he, 'for this one night which remains of life, I am willing to watch in prayer with Christ our Lord.' And when the other Catholic insisted that either the Father should come to bed also, or should admit him to bear him company in his watching, he would not consent, but bid him go to bed and leave him alone. The Catholic submitted, and went to bed, and the priest, lighting a taper that was there, and setting it upon the stool, knelt down, and began to enter into very quiet prayer, as his companion took notice, who remained awake to see what passed.

After an hour of silent prayer, the Father began to speak as if he were holding a colloquy, and by little and little to enter into a heat, so that his voice began to change like a man that was disturbed. At length, getting up, he went to the bed where his companion lay, and touching him with his hand, asked him if he was asleep; his companion answered, 'No.' The priest begged of him then that he would recommend him, to the best of his power, to our Lord, because he stood in need of his prayers. So he returned again to his place, and began in the same manner to be troubled as before, giving signs in his exterior of being in great anguish, and, as it were, out of himself, till at length he put out with his own hand, like a man in anger, the taper that was burning by him. With all this his trouble did not cease, but he still continued, as it were, in a conflict and agony, sometimes speaking low, and begging the assistance of our Lord and the Saints, at other times raising his voice as one angry and in a rage; and this lasted for the space of half an hour after he had put out the light, whilst the poor gentleman in bed was not a little terrified at seeing and hearing what passed and begged of our Lord as well as he was able to deliver him from this affliction, for he plainly perceived that he was in a conflict.

At length he saw him coming towards the bed, reciting with much joy the psalm, *Laudate Dominum de Coelis*,[1] etc.—Praise ye the Lord in the heavens, etc., continuing it to the end; and then, as one inebriated with an abundance of consolations, he broke out into other praises of our Lord God, admiring His unspeakable mercies and His divine sweetness towards the children of men. He set himself down on the bed by his companions, not having been able for many days to lift his feet up from the ground for the great weight of the bolts and chains, and remained as one asleep for a quarter of an hour; but at length he broke out again into the praises of God, and asked his companion if he had not been frightened. The gentleman answered, he had, and withal begged of him, that he would tell him what was the meaning of that great noise and of those changes and alterations he had discovered that night. The priest answered, that though as to his own part it would signify little to relate it, yet, as it might be of some comfort to the Catholics to know what had passed, he would tell him the whole matter.

'After a while,' said he, 'that I had been in quiet prayer, my flesh began to creep upon me and my hair to stand on end, and I perceived myself quite changed, and on a sudden I saw before my eyes a most ugly monster which began to terrify me, and when I least looked for it assaulted me with these words: "Thou thinkest to-morrow to be a martyr, and to go straight to heaven; but I assure thee it will not be so, for I know thou art condemned to hell, and that the sentence is passed against thee in God's tribunal, which cannot be recalled. And to-morrow, though thou shalt be drawn to the gallows, thou shalt not be executed, but they will keep thee two years longer in prison with these bolts and chains which thou hast on, and will give thee only two morsels of black bread and a little water every day, and thou shalt be

[1] Psalm 148.

abhorred by all, and shalt lead the most miserable life that ever man led upon earth. Therefore that thou mayest be delivered from so great sufferings it will be better for thee at present to put an end to thy life by a knife or a halter, and not to wait for to-morrow." And though I shook him off,' said the Father, 'many times, answering what God put in my mind, he never left off importuning me, and whatever way I turned my eyes, he placed himself always before me, giving me intolerable trouble with his horrid figure. And when I extinguished the light, it was that I might no longer see so frightful a sight; but he still continued terrifying and molesting me very much, and the conflict went on still increasing, till our merciful Lord, taking pity on my weakness, sent me succour from heaven. And this was, that at the time when I found myself in the greatest straits, I saw a great light come in at the door with two persons, who, as I believe, were our Lady and St. John the Evangelist, who by their presence gave me unspeakable comfort; and then the monster that had troubled me began to draw back and tremble; and one of them said to him, "Begone from hence, thou cursed creature! thou hast no part in this servant of Christ, who will shed his blood to-morrow for his Lord, and will enter into his joy." Immediately the monster disappeared, and they likewise, leaving me so full of consolation that I cannot express it. Upon this, I came with great joy of heart and canticles of praise in my mouth, and sat me down here in the manner that you saw, not being sensible whether I was on the ground or in bed, in heaven or in earth. This one thing I beg of you for Christ's sake, that you do not speak one word of this to any one till you see my race finished, and till I am delivered of the burden of the flesh.' Having said this, they both glorified our Lord, and so continued till the morning, discoursing together with great satisfaction of heavenly things.

DIEGO DE YEPEZ, *History of the Reformation in England*

MR. NICHOLAS HORNER

[He] had been condemned to die for comforting priests, and giving them alms. Before his death, while he was sitting with a lighted candle in his filthy and dark dungeon, he saw the form of a crown on the head of his shadow. Raising his hand to feel what could cause such an appearance, he found nothing. He then changed his place, to see whether it came from some peculiar position of his body; but as he walked, there was the same appearance, which moved when he moved,

and stood when he stood, and so remained visible for a whole hour,
like a diadem upon his head, to foreshadow his future glory. He told
this a little before his martyrdom to a pious woman. Horner was the
man's name.

Robert Southwell to Claude Aquaviva, 8 March 1590

Fr. Robert Sutton

Of this man it is constantly reported that he was seen by his keepers
to pray in the midst of a light, within the prison the night before he
suffered. And when three of his quarters were taken down after they
had hanged a twelvemonth in the air, all being consumed to the bones,
the index and the thumb consecrated for the touch of Christ his body,
were found whole and are so conserved.

JOHN GERARD, *Catalogue of Martyrs*

Fr. Stephen Rowsham

In Gloucestershire was taken Mr. Stephen Rowsham . . . a man of
singular perfection. In prison God the Father, Christ our Saviour, our
Blessed Lady and glorious souls of saints, full often appeared to him,
leaving behind them such odoriferous smells, and sometimes lasting
many hours with him, that for the space of one day and a half he
thought himself in heaven, his joys were so great and strange. This
heavenly company had divers speeches with him in their several
apparitions, which he would not utter, neither did he reveal this but a
little before his martyrdom to a dear friend after long suit to him. . . .
He celebrated daily in prison even on the day he died.

GRENE, *Collection*

Fr. Ralph Sherwin

i. Innocency is my only comfort, against all the forged villainy
which is fathered on my fellow priests and me. Well, when by the
high judge, God himself, this false vizard of treason shall be removed
from true Catholic men's faces, then shall it appear who they be that
carry a well meaning, and who an evil murdering mind. In the mean
season God forgive all injustice; and, if it be His blessed will to convert
our persecutors, that they may become professors of His truth.

Letter of Ralph Sherwin to his uncle, John Woodward
on the eve of his martyrdom, 30 November 1581

ii. My sins are great I confess, but I flee to God's mercy: my negligences are without number I grant, but I appeal to my redeemer's clemency. I have no boldness but in his blood, his bitter passion is my only consolation.

Ralph Sherwin in the Tower to his friend

28

The Gallows

SIX PRIESTS AND EIGHT TEMPORAL MEN

The 26th of August [1587] at the Sessions Hall without Newgate of London, were condemned six persons, for being made priests beyond the seas, and remaining in this realm contrary to the statute thereof made, four temporal men for being reconciled to the Roman Church, and four others for relieving and abetting the others. And on the 28th, W. Deane and H. Webley were hanged at the Miles end, W. Gunter, at the Theatre, Ro. Morton and Hugh Moore, at Lincoln's Inn Fields, T. Acton at Clerkenwell, T. Felton and James Carkson, between Brentford and Hounslow. And on the 30th of August, R. Flower, Ed. Shelley, R. Leigh, R. Martine, I. Roch, and Margaret Ward, Gentlewoman (which Margaret had conveyed a cord to a priest in Bridewell, whereby he let himself down and escaped) were hanged at Tyburn.

JOHN STOW, *Annals*

MARGARET CLITHEROW

The place of execution was the tollbooth, six or seven yards distant from the prison. There were present at her martyrdom the two sheriffs of York, Fawcet and Gibson, Frost, a minister, Fox, Mr. Cheeke's kinsman, with another of his men, the four sergeants, which had hired certain beggars to do the murder, three or four men, and four women.

The martyr coming to the place, kneeled her down, and prayed to herself. The tormentors bade her pray with them, and they would pray with her. The martyr denied, and said, 'I will not pray with you, and you shall not pray with me; neither will I say Amen to your prayers, nor shall you to mine.' Then they willed her to pray for the Queen's majesty. The martyr began in this order. First, in the hearing of them all, she prayed for the Catholic Church, then for the Pope's Holiness, Cardinals, and other Fathers which have charge of souls, and then for all Christian princes. At which words the tormentors interrupted her, and willed her not to put her majesty among that company; yet the martyr proceeded in this order, 'and especially for Elizabeth, Queen of England, that God turn her to the Catholic faith, and that after this mortal life she may receive the blessed joys of heaven. For I wish as much good,' quoth she, 'to her majesty's soul as to mine own.' Sheriff Gibson, abhorring the cruel fact, stood weeping at the door. Then said Fawcet, 'Mrs. Clitherow, you must remember and confess that you die for treason.' The martyr answered, 'No, no, Mr. Sheriff, I die for the love of my Lord Jesu;' which last words she spake with a loud voice.

Then Fawcet commanded her to put off her apparel; 'For you must die,' said he, 'naked, as judgment was given and pronounced against you.'

The martyr with the other women requested him on their knees that she might die in her smock, and that for the honour of womanhood they would not see her naked; but that would not be granted. Then she requested that women might unapparel her, and that they would turn their faces from her for that time.

The women took off her clothes, and put upon her the long habit of linen. Then very quietly she laid her down upon the ground, her face covered with a handkerchief, the linen habit being placed over her as far as it would reach, all the rest of her body being naked. The door was laid upon her, her hands she joined towards her face. Then the sheriff said, 'Nay, you must have your hands bound.' The martyr put forth her hands over the door still joined. Then two sergeants parted them, and with the inkle strings,[1] which she had prepared for that purpose, bound them to two posts, so that her body and her arms made a perfect cross. They willed her again to ask the Queen's Majesty's forgiveness, and to pray for her. The martyr said she had prayed for her. They also willed her to ask her husband's forgiveness. The martyr said, 'If ever I have offended him, but for my conscience, I ask him forgiveness.'

After this they laid weight upon her, which when she first felt, she

[1] *inkle*, inferior tape.

said, 'Jesu! Jesu! have mercy upon me!' which were the last words she
was heard to speak.

She was in dying one quarter of an hour. A sharp stone, as much as
a man's fist, put under her back; upon her was laid to the quantity of
seven or eight hundred-weight at the least, which, breaking her ribs,
caused them to burst forth of the skin.

JOHN MUSH, Life of Margaret Clitherow

FARMER MILLER

One named Miller was condemned with him [Fr. Roger Dicconson],
a poor honest farmer, having a wife and ten children. This man ... had
been an earnest and most diligent furtherer of God's service and helper
of priests. When he was arraigned, the Judge said he was worse than
any Seminary priest, meaning that he did more good to the Catholics.

'Yea,' answered Miller, 'you say most true, my lord; I am far
worse than any of those good men, and am not worthy to be compared to them.'

When Miller, who suffered after Mr. Welby, was going up the
ladder, the Justice said, 'Come down, fool, and look to thy children.'
He thinking he had meant he should live, came down, and then the
Sheriff told him that if he would go to church the Queen would spare
him. He presently goeth up the ladder again, saying that she might
keep that mercy for others, but he said he had not lived so long a
Catholic to go now to heretical service.

When he was on the ladder, his children asked him blessing. He
desired God to bless them and to send them no worse death than their
father, at which all the people laughed; but he thought it a high
blessing to wish them to die martyrs.

GRENE, Collections

MR. RIGBY

In the way towards the place of execution, called St. Thomas
Watering, came riding as was thought two courtiers, but shortly one
of them was known to be the Earl of Rutland and the other was Captain
Whytlock in his company, they coming near the hurdle and viewing
the prisoner, the Captain demanded of him what he was, of what
years, and what might be the cause of his condemnation to this kind of
death? Mr. Rigby looking up, and hearing some name the Earl of

Rutland, supposing the Captain to be the Earl, took off his hat and desired his honour humbly to pardon him in being so undutiful as to have been covered in his presence, for I knew not (said he) of such honourable assembly, and to your questions may it like your honour, my name is John Rigby, a poor gentleman, of the house of Harrock in Lancashire; my age about thirty years, my judgment and condemnation to this death is only and merely for that I answered the judge that I was reconciled, and for that I refused to go unto the church to hear the English service. Whereat the Captain seemed to marvel, and said, sure it is very strange that any man should be put to death for that. Undoubtedly, said the prisoner, it is for no other cause, I do assure you. The Captain wished him to do as the Queen would have him (that is, to go to the Protestants' church), and turning to the Sheriff's deputy, conferred with him about the matter. After a little space the Earl and the Captain rode again to the hurdle, and causing it a little to be stayed, the Captain said, are you a married man, or no? No, sir, said he, I am a bachelor, and (in smiling wise), more than that, I am a maid. That is much, said the Captain, for a man of your years; you have, it seemeth, striven much against your own flesh. Mr. Rigby answered, I would be loth to speak anything contrary to the truth, I am indeed a maid, and that is more than I needed to say. The Captain concluded, Then I see thou hast worthily deserved a virgin's crown. I pray God send thee the kingdom of heaven and that thou mayest do well. I desire thee, pray for me, and so they rid to the place of execution, not speaking any more to him, and when the officers were ready to turn him off the earth, the Earl and the Captain posted away, much astonished at his courage and constancy.

The Captain often related these particulars, and withal added that he had seen many die, but never had nor should see the like to him for modesty, patience, and undoubted resolution in his religion. And that it would not be good for our state to put such men to death.

Now the prisoner being in place, to end this tragedy the officers brought him from the hurdle to the cart, where he knelt down and said the Pater noster, Ave Maria, Credo and Confiteor all aloud, until he came to those words, *the holy Apostles St. Peter and St. Paul*, whereat the ruder sort of the people exclaimed that he prayed to saints, and so he was not permitted to come to the end. The executioner helping him up into the cart, he gave him an angel of gold, saying, here, take this in token that I freely forgive thee and all others that have been accessory to my death. Thou shalt have more, a poor suit of fustian, and a new shirt which I put on this morning. I would it were better for thee. Then taking off his hat, he threw it from him. And making the sign of the Cross, he viewed the multitude (which was very great) round about him. And with cheerful countenance, holding his hands before his breast, with his eyes closed he meditated a little while. And after looking up, seemed to make countenance to some of his friends in the press. The executioner in the meantime untied his garters, himself untrussed his points, and that so nimbly as the beholders marvelled to see a man in such case, so quick and active and nothing dismayed for death so near approaching. Taking also his falling band from his neck, he rolled it on a heap and cast it from him as far as he could. Whereupon some said: that will be taken up for a relic. His clothes being taken off all to his shirt, the hangman offered to put the halter over his head, which he stayed, taking it betwixt both his hands, so kissed it, and gave it to him again saying: Now do your pleasure with it. And presently he put it over his head. Beginning then to speak to the people, More, the under-sheriff's deputy, bade him pray for the Queen, which he did very affectionately, as might appear to come from a charitable and loyal heart. The deputy asked him: What traitors knowest thou in England? If thou knowest any reveal them. God is my witness, said he, I know none. What! saith the deputy again, if he will confess nothing, drive away the cart. Which was done so suddenly that he could neither speak to the people nor recommend his soul again to God, as he was about to do. Again the deputy very shortly commanded the hangman to do his duty, meaning that he should cut the rope and let him fall down, which was so incontinently done, that he stood upright upon his feet, like a man a little amazed, till the butchering fellows clasping about him, by main force threw him on the ground. Where coming again perfectly to himself, he said aloud and distinctly: God forgive you, Jesus receive my soul. And immediately another cruel fellow standing by (who was no officer at all, but a common porter) set his foot upon the martyr's throat and so held him down that he could not speak any more. Whereof the same fellow made great vaunt, and boasted afterwards, until some of the more civil people, reprehending him for his bad mind and hard heart, he began to be ashamed of his fact and denied it to others that charged him therewith. Others held his arms and legs whiles the executioner dismembered and unbowelled him. And when he felt them pulling out his heart, he was yet so strong that he thrust the men from him which held his arms. Finally they cut off his head and divided his quarters, disposing of them in several places about Southwark, as is accustomed. The people going away muttering much at the cruelty used in the execution. And generally all sorts bewailed his death.

THOMAS WORTHINGTON, *A Relation of Sixteen Martyrs*

FR. MUMFORD SCOT

i. Mr. Scot, priest, by means of one Baker, was to be banished by order from the Council, which he obtained for money. When the time of banishment was come, he was committed again to prison by Topcliffe, and afterwards brought to the Sessions, where for want of further matter Topcliffe signified that it was good policy to put him to death and said that his austere life was a means to draw people unto him, for he said that Mr. Scot was accounted a saint. So he was condemned, hanged and quartered in Fleet Street, whose mild behaviour pierced the hearts of the people so much that many of them said it was a pity he should be put to death.[1]

GRENE, *Collections*

ii. Some too noticed, when the hangman held up his quarters, that his knees were hardened as horn by much prayer.

Ibid.

FR. ROBERT SUTTON

He had some special comfort in prison the night before he suffered, for in the morning, being ready to go towards execution, he turned him towards his fellow-prisoners, giving them his blessing, then said these words: 'God comfort you all, for I am comforted,' and so went most cheerfully and boldly towards his end.

When he came to the place he desired he might speak, but they would not permit him. Then he took his handkerchief out of his pocket, lapped it together, made a fine discourse of the candle we receive in baptism and in the hour of death, and in remembrance of what he said, he held up the handkerchief in token he lived and died in the light of the Catholic faith. He was put off the ladder and cut down very lively, for he stood upon his feet, was taken by great violence, dismembered, spoke these words, 'O! thou bloody butcher! God forgive thee.' So calling upon Jesus and Mary, he gave up his spirit.

Ibid.

[1] Executed in Fleet Street, 1 June 1589.

FR. GEORGE BEESLEY

This last [George Beesley] was of a very austere life and passing zealous. At his execution his knees were seen to be so hardened that the people were much edified, and many said they should not see the like in any minister.

A Catalogue of Martyrs

FR. RICHARD SIMON

What he said at his execution I cannot learn, but embracing the ladder, he kissed the steps. When he was in quartering, the people cried: 'A devil! a devil!' because he had on him a shirt of hair.

GRENE, *Collections*

JAMES BIRD

'I beg you, Mr. Sheriff,' said he, 'seeing that I am a native of this city [Winchester], that you would grant me one favour before I die.' 'What favour?' said he. 'Tell me what I am to die for.' 'I know not,' quoth the sheriff. 'You received the death sentence in the presence of the judge. Who can know better than you the reason for which you were condemned?' 'Nay,' said the other, 'I do not understand it at all.' Then said the sheriff, 'Come, now, confess your crime. Promise to go to church, and the Queen's pardon will be begged for you.' 'Right heartily do I thank thee,' quoth Bird. 'If by going to the church I can save my life, surely all the world will see this, that I am executed solely for faith and religion and nothing else. It was just this that I wished to elicit from you. Now I gladly die.' With these words he was thrown from the ladder.

Henry Garnet to Claude Aquaviva, 17 March 1593

FR. WILLIAM DAVIES

After his condemnation he was put in a place in the castle[1] called the black alley, a dark loathsome aisle between two walls, where he gave himself wholly to prayer and meditation and omitted none of his daily wonted exercises until the very morning he was brought forth to

[1] Beaumaris Castle, Anglesey.

be executed. All his friends that came to visit him, he did so replenish with comfort that howsoever they came they returned merrily. Such as were Catholics, he hoped he would meet with them merrily again: for his own father, and such as were not, nor yet would not be, Catholics, he bid them farewell for ever. When any would tell him that he hoped he would be reprieved, he would wax very sad and heavy, as contrariwise, when he were told that he must be executed, he would be most merry and pleasant. A preacher was with him to have him recant and swear to the Supremacy and he should be reprieved, whom he sore checked and bid him get away thence.

There could not be found an executioner in all the country, but at length the sheriff was forced to send to Westchester, 42 miles off, for a poor butcher and a hangman that was in prison for thievery. These two were brought to the country and hired for four or five pounds, and because they could have no lodging in the town, they were hid in a barn and there kept like hungry dogs until the day appointed with stolen scraps and meat secretly conveyed unto them. The deputy sheriff had much ado to provide necessaries for execution. The best man there and the townsmen denied the sheriff of a place to set the gallows upon any of their grounds: he was fain to make a new gallows and to set it within the liberties of the castle, out of the liberties of the town. The word is about the country that the sheriff was fain to send to his own house for a pan, but the truth is that an old covetous woman in the town that would not be known for it, lent her pan and gave a few faggots withal to the deputy sheriff for 8 shillings of money.

That day being St. Pantaleon's day [27 July 1593] wherein he was executed, the blessed father delivered through a crevice of the wall tokens to his children and brethren abroad for a remembrance to persist in the Catholic faith. So having done, he said now, 'Let them come when they will. I am ready for them.' The sheriff's bailiff and servant calling him forth, bound his arms with a cord and set him on a cart, which they themselves were fain to drive the horse to draw forward, whereat being ashamed the deputy sheriff threatened to hang a poor boy that met him on the way unless he would drive the horse. Whereunto the boy answered, 'I am well content to be hanged with this man with all my heart.' Then said Mr. William, 'You shall not need, master sheriff, to trouble you any more, the horse will go of himself.'

Being come to the place he was permitted a good while to pray upon his knees, which he did devoutly until at length a preacher called Burgess had overheard him say *Ave Maris Stella*, or naming Our

Blessed Lady, whereat the preacher fretted and bade despatch him. Here the deputy sheriff (for the sheriff was not there) asked him what he thought of the Queen. 'God give her a long, prosperous reign and grace to die a member of the Catholic Church.' Then caused to climb up the ladder, he said, 'This island (meaning the isle of Anglesey) was called in old times the dark island, the which name it never better deserved than at this present. But I beseech God that the blood which I was brought hither innocently to shed, may give a light unto it of the faith which it hath received about a thousand years agone.' So being interrupted he was not suffered to speak more, but thrice, *In manus tuas, Domine.* The ladder was turned; whereupon he closed his fists hard and so kept them till he died, at which time he opened his hands broad.

GRENE, *Collections*

Fr. John Boast

John Boast, a Jesuit, was executed for high treason at Durham on the 24th. When he was taken from prison towards the place of execution, more than three hundred ladies and women of good position, all with black hoods, set out to follow him, and being asked where they were going, they answered, 'To accompany that gentleman, that servant of God, to his death, as the Maries did Christ.' A minister offered to dispute with them by the way, but a horseman came up and pushed him away, crying, 'Begone, knave, Mr. Boast has shown himself a true gentleman and a true man.'

Ibid.

Fr. Nicholas Garlick

The day following [his trial] he was drawn towards the place of execution [and] met with one of his companions, who told him that they had oft shot together. 'True,' said he, 'but now I am to shoot such a shot as I never shot in all my life.'

Thomas Carey to Richard Green, 4 June 1566

Fr. Oliver Plasden

Oliver Plasden, priest, born by Fleet Bridge, in London, was next put into the cart, who prayed for the Queen and the whole realm, which when Sir Walter Raleigh heard, 'What,' said he, 'dost thou think as thou prayest?'

'Otherwise,' quoth he, 'I expect no salvation at God's hands.'

'Then thou dost acknowledge her for thy lawful Queen?' said Raleigh.

'I do sincerely.'

'Wouldst thou defend her,' quoth Raleigh, 'against all her foreign and domestical enemies, if so thou wert able?'

'I would,' said Plasden, 'to the uttermost of my power, and so I would counsel all men who would be persuaded by me.'

The people hearing this, began to speak one to another: 'There is no cause why this honest man should die. He would never say thus at death, except he thought so in his heart.'

Then Raleigh said: 'How happened it that yesterday before the judges thou wouldst not say thus much? Then thou hadst not come thus far. I know, good people,' said Raleigh, turning himself [towards them], 'her Majesty desireth no more at these men's hands, than that which this man hath now confessed. Mr. Sheriff,' said he, 'I will presently go to the Court, let him be stayed.'

Which when Topcliffe heard, 'I pray you,' saith he, 'suffer me to offer him one question, and anon you shall hear that I will convince him to be a traitor.' Then he said: 'Plasden, in thy conscience, before all this assembly, tell me thy judgment. If the King of Spain or the Pope would come into this country by force for no other end precisely, but by his canonical law,' for so he spake, 'to establish that faith which thou believest and which thou thinkest to be the true Catholic faith as you call it, tell me, wouldst thou resist them?'

'I am a priest,' quoth he, 'and therefore may not fight.'

'Although thou mayst not fight, wouldst thou give counsel to others who would fight to defend her Majesty?'

'I would,' said the priest, 'counsel all men to maintain the right of their prince.'

'He saith marvellous well,' quoth Raleigh. 'No more. I will presently post to the Queen. I know she will be glad of this plain dealing.'

'Then,' said Topcliffe, 'let me say but one word unto him,' which was granted. 'Thou sayest, Plasden,' quoth he, 'that thou wouldst counsel all to defend the Queen's right, but tell me, dost thou think that the Queen hath any right to maintain this religion, and to forbid yours?'

'No,' said the priest.

'Then thou thinkest not,' quoth he, 'to defend the Queen against the Pope, if he would come to establish thy religion; speak, what sayest thou to this? I charge thee before God.'

'I am a Catholic priest,' quoth he, 'therefore I would never fight, nor counsel others to fight against my religion, for that were to deny my faith. O Christ,' saith he, looking up to heaven and kissing the rope, 'I will never deny thee for a thousand lives.'

Then lo! they cried, he was a traitor, and the cart was drawn away, and he, by the word of Raleigh, was suffered to hang until he was dead; then he was drawn and quartered after their custom.

Relation of Fr. James Young

Fr. Christopher Robinson

One Robinson, a seminary priest, was lately . . . hanged at Carlisle. The rope broke twice, and the third time he rebuked the Sheriff of cruelty, saying that though he meant no way to yield, but was glad of his combat, yet flesh and blood was weak, and therefore he showed little humanity to torment a man so long: and when they took order to put two ropes, then saith he, by this means I shall be longer a-dying: but it is no matter, I am very willing to suffer all. This is all the particulars I have yet heard.

Henry Garnet to Robert Persons, 7 April 1598

Fr. Christopher Wharton

There [at the gallows] the Minister, Bamforth, began to persuade him to change his religion and, as he said, to come out of Babylon; to whom he answered that he came not now to dispute but to offer his life for the Catholic faith and protested unto the people that he came not into England for any treasons . . . but only for the saving of souls.

Richard Holtby's Relation of Fr. Wharton,
28 March 1600

Fr. Joseph Lambton[1]

[1592]. Paid to a Frenchman which did take forth the seminary priest's bowels after he was hanged, 20s.; for coals which made the fire at the execution of the seminary priest, 6d.; and for a wright's axe,

---

[1] Executed at Newcastle, 23 July 1592.

which headed the seminary, 4s. 6d.—5s.; for a hand axe and a cutting knife, which did rip and quarter the seminary priest, 14d., and for a horse which trailed him from off the sledge to the gallows, 12d.—2s. 2d.; for four iron stanchels, with hooks on them, for the hanging of the seminary's four quarters on the four gates, 3s. 8d.; for one iron wedge for riving wood to make the fire on the moor, 18d.; and for a shovel to the fire, 2s.; to a mason for two days' work, setting the stanchels of the gates fast, 10d. a-day, 20d.; for carrying the four quarters of the seminary priest from gate to gate, and other charges, 2s.; for fire and coals for melting the lead to set the iron stanchels of the gate fast, 8d.

Newcastle Corporation Accounts

Fr. John Ingram

[August 1594]. 'Paid for charges at the execution of the seminary priest in Gateshead, John Ingram 2s. 6d. Paid for bringing his quarters off the gibbets, 18d., and for a pannier which brought his quarters to the town, 4d.—22d.'

Ibid.

Fr. William Waterson

[7 January 1593]. 'Paid to William Sever, sergeant, which headed William Waterson, the seminary priest, for his pains, 20s.; to two labourers for making a room for the making of the fire, 12d.; for an apron to the leech, 6d.; for a spade, 6d.; for one pound of tow, 4d.; for coals, 6d.; for two 'girdes to a water sea,' 2d.; for a boy going of an errand, 2d.; three labourers for carrying home of the gear, 3d.; for a horse which drew the sled to the gallows and back again, 18d.; one labourer for hanging up the three quarters and head of the priest, 9d.; for two halters, 2d.; for carrying the gear a-field, 12d.; for John Partus' pains taken, 12d.; William Sever for his arles[1] for quartering the priest, 12d.; Sandrs. Cheisman's man for putting the pinnacles for hanging the priest's head on the bridge, 6s.; for straw, candle, drink, and string which bound the seminary's arms before he was executed, 9d.; for a cat-band and a staple for the door that the priest burnt in prison, 6d.; for drink which John Letherington, the prisoner, had before he executed the priest, 2d.'

Ibid.

[1] Earnest-money.

MARY QUEEN OF SCOTS

After this she, being supported by Sir Amyas' two gentlemen aforesaid, and Melvin carrying up her train, and also accompanied with the Lords, knights and gentlemen aforenamed, the sheriff going before her, she passed out of the entry into the great hall, with her countenance careless, importing thereby rather mirth than mournful cheer, and so she willingly stepped up to the scaffold which was prepared for her in the hall, being two foot high and twelve foot broad, with rails round about, hanged and covered with black, with a low stool, long cushion, and block, covered with black also. Then, having the stool brought her, she sat her down; by her, on the right hand, sat the Earl of Shrewsbury and the Earl of Kent, and on the left hand stood the sheriff, and before her the two executioners; round about the rails stood knights, gentlemen and others.

Then, silence being made, the Queen's Majesty's commission for the execution of the Queen of Scots was openly read by Mr. Beale, Clerk of the Council, and these words pronounced by the assembly, 'God save the Queen.' During the reading of which commission the Queen of Scots was silent, listening unto it with as small regard as if it had not concerned her at all, and with as cheerful a countenance as if it had been a pardon from Her Majesty for her life; using as much strangeness in word and deed as if she had never known any of the assembly, or had been ignorant of the English language.

Then one Dr. Fletcher, dean of Peterborough, standing directly before her, without the rail, bending his body with great reverence, began to utter this exhortation following: 'Madame the Queen's most excellent Majesty,' etc., and iterating these words three or four times, she told him, 'Mr. Dean, I am settled in the ancient Catholic Roman religion, and mind to spend my blood in defence of it.' Then Mr. Dean said, 'Madame, change your opinion and repent you of your former wickedness, and settle your faith only in Jesus Christ, by him to be saved.' Then she answered again and again, 'Mr. Dean, trouble not yourself any more, for I am settled and resolved in this my religion, and am purposed therein to die.' Then the Earl of Shrewsbury and the Earl of Kent, perceiving her so obstinate, told her that sithence she would not hear the exhortation begun by Mr. Dean, 'We will pray for your Grace, that it stands with God's will you may have your heart lightened, even at the last hour, with the true knowledge of God, and so die therein.' Then she answered, 'If you will pray for me, my Lords,

I will thank you; but to join in prayer with you I will not, for that you and I are not of one religion.'

Then the Lords called for Mr. Dean, who, kneeling on the scaffold stairs, began this prayer, 'O most gracious God and merciful Father,' etc., all the assembly, saving the Queen of Scots and her servants, saying after him. During the saying of which prayer, the Queen of Scots, sitting upon a stool, having about her neck an *Agnus Dei*, in her hand a crucifix, at her girdle a pair of beads with a golden cross at the end of them, a Latin book in her hand, began with tears and with loud and fast voice to pray in Latin; and in the midst of her prayers she slid off from her stool, and kneeling, said divers Latin prayers: and after the end of Mr. Dean's prayer, she kneeling, prayed in English to this effect: 'for Christ his afflicted Church, and for an end of their troubles; for her son; and for the Queen's Majesty, that she might prosper and serve God aright.' She confessed that she hoped to be saved 'by and in the blood of Christ, at the foot of whose crucifix she would shed her blood.' Then said the Earl of Kent, 'Madame, settle Christ Jesus in your heart, and leave these trumperies.' Then she little regarding, or nothing at all, his highness' good counsel, went forward with her prayers, desiring 'that God would avert his wrath from this island, and that he would give her grief, and forgiveness for her sins.' These, with other prayers, she made in English, saying she forgave her enemies with all her heart that had long sought her blood, and desired God to convert them to the truth; and in the end of the prayer she desired all saints to make intercession for her to Jesus Christ, and so kissing the crucifix, and crossing of her also, said these words, 'Even as thy arms, O Jesus, were spread here upon the cross, so receive me into thy arms of mercy, and forgive me all my sins.'

Her prayer being ended, the executioners, kneeling, desired her Grace to forgive them her death: who answered, 'I forgive you with all my heart, for now, I hope, you shall make an end of all my troubles.' Then they, with her two women, helping of her up, began to disrobe her of her apparel; then she, laying her crucifix upon the stool, one of the executioners took from her neck the *Agnus Dei*, which she, laying hands of it, gave to one of her women, and told the executioner that he should be answered money for it. Then she suffered them, with her two women, to disrobe her of her chain of pomander beads and all other her apparel most willingly, and, with joy rather than sorrow, helped to make ready herself, putting on a pair of sleeves with her own hands which they had pulled off, and that with some haste, as if she had longed to be gone.

All this time they were pulling off her apparel, she never changed her countenance, but with smiling cheer she uttered these words, 'that she never had such grooms to make her unready, and that she never put off her clothes before such a company.'

Then she, being stripped of all her apparel saving her petticoat and kirtle, her two women beholding her made great lamentation, and crying and crossing themselves prayed in Latin. She, turning herself to them, embracing them, said these words in French, *Ne crié vous, j'ay promé pour vous,* and so crossing and kissing them, bade them pray for her and rejoice and not weep, for that they should now see an end of all their mistress's troubles.

Then she, with a smiling countenance, turned to her menservants, as Melvin and the rest, standing upon a bench nigh the scaffold, who sometime weeping sometime crying out aloud, and continually crossing themselves, prayed in Latin, crossing them with her hand bade them farewell, and wishing them to pray for her even until the last hour.

This done, one of the women having a Corpus Christi cloth[1] lapped up three-corner-ways, kissing it, put it over the Queen of Scots' face, and pinned it fast to the caul of her head. Then the two women departed from her, and she kneeling down upon the cushion most resolutely, and without any token or fear of death, she spake aloud this Psalm in Latin, *In te Domine confido, non confundar in aeternum,* etc. Then, groping for the block, she laid down her head, putting her chin over the block with both her hands, which, holding there, still had been cut off had they not been espied. Then lying upon the block most quietly, and stretching out her arms, cried, *In manus tuas, Domine,* etc. three or four times. Then she, lying very still on the block, one of the executioners holding of her slightly with one of his hands, she endured two strokes of the other executioner with an axe, she making very small noise or none at all, and not stirring any part of her from the place where she lay; and so the executioner cut off her head, saving one little gristle, which being cut asunder, he lifted up her head to the view of all the assembly, and bade *God save the Queen.* Then, her dressing of lawn falling off from her head, it appeared as grey as one of threescore and ten years old, polled very short, her face in a moment being so much altered from the form she had

---

[1] A silk veil hung over the pyx as it was suspended above the altar.

when she was alive, as few could remember her by her dead face. Her lips stirred up and down for a quarter of an hour after her head was cut off.

Then Mr. Dean said with a loud voice, 'So perish all the Queen's enemies'; and afterwards the Earl of Kent came to the dead body, and standing over it, with a loud voice said, 'Such end of all the Queen's and the Gospel's enemies.'

Then one of the executioners pulling off her garters, espied her little dog which was crept under her clothes, which could not be gotten forth but by force, yet afterward would not depart from the dead corpse, but came and lay between her head and her shoulders, which being imbrued with her blood, was carried away and washed, as all things else were that had any blood was either burned or clean washed; and the executioners sent away with money for their fees, not having any one thing that belonged unto her. And so, every man being commanded out of the hall, except the sheriff and his men, she was carried by them up into a great chamber lying ready for the surgeons to embalm her.

The Manner of the Queen of Scots' Death

Mr. Swithin Wells

For even in his way to his execution, seeing by chance an old acquaintance of his, he could not forget his wonted mirth, but saluted him in these words, Farewell, dear friend (saith he), farewell to all hawking, hunting and old pastimes. I am now going a better way.

Life and Death of M. Edmund Gennings

Fr. Edmund Gennings

'I must obey God rather than men, and must not in this case acknowledge a fault where none is. If to return into England priest and to say Mass be Popish treason, I here confess I am a traitor: but I think not so. And therefore I acknowledge myself guilty of these things, not with repentance or sorrow of heart, but with an open protestation of inward joy. . . .'

Which words Mr. Topcliffe hearing, being much troubled therewith, scarce giving him leave to say a *Pater noster*, had the hangman turn the ladder, which in an instant being done, presently he caused him to be cut down, the blessed martyr in the sight of all the beholders being yet able to stand on his feet, and casting his eyes towards heaven, his senses were very little astonished, in so much as the hangman was forced to trip up his heels from under him to make him fall on the block. And being dismembered, through very pain, in the hearing of many with a loud voice uttered these words, Oh, it smarts, which Mr. Wells hearing replied thus: Alas, sweet soul, thy pain is great indeed but almost past, pray for me now, most holy saint, that mine may come. He being ripped up and his bowels cast into the fire, if credit may be given to hundreds of people standing by and to the hangman himself, the blessed martyr uttered (his heart being in the executioner's hand) these words, *Sancte Gregori, ora pro me*, which the hangman hearing, with open mouth swore this damnable oath, 'God's wounds. See, his heart is in my hand, and yet Gregory is in his mouth. O egregious Papist!' Thus the afflicted martyr even to the last of his torments cried for the aid and succour of saints and especially of St. Gregory, his devoted patron and our country's apostle, that he might pass the sharpness of that torment.

Life and Death of M. Edmund Gennings

Fr. John Sandys

I told you before that Mr. Sandys, who was martyred at this Gloucester, was bloodily butchered. I will here set down some particulars. When they had condemned him, they could find none for any money to murder him; they could hire no knife or other instrument in all the town to mangle him. At last they found a most base companion, who yet was ashamed to be seen in that bloody action, for he blacked and disfigured his face, and got an old rusty knife full of teeth like a sickle, with which he killed him.

The holy martyr had requested the High Sheriff (who was Paul Tracy of Stanwaye) to suffer him to hang until he died. He then granted the request, yet caused him to be cut down as soon as he was cast off the ladder. The holy man was nothing past himself, but said, 'O, Mr. Sheriff, you have not kept your promise.' Unto which Mr. Tracy replied not, but commanded his men to pull down the traitor, the hangman to bowel him, and himself laid first hands on him. The hangman did his bloody office, the holy Martyr ever catching his ragged knife in his bare hands, thereby to save himself, but it was even pulled out most forcibly, wherewith they cut and mangled his sacred hands most pitifully. When he had pulled from him his bowels, the blessed saint cried ever with St. Stephen, 'Lord, forgive my persecutors,' and so fell asleep in the Lord.

GRENE, *Collections*

29

Each in the Other's View

THE POPE'S CHURCH

As in the restoring of this second temple many old men did weep, because it was not so great, gorgeous, costly, and glorious as the first was; so now in the restoring of the gospel many weep, when they see not the churches so well decked and furnished as before. The pope's church hath all things pleasant in it to delight the people withal: as for the eyes, their god hangs in a rope,[1] images gilded, painted, carved most finely, copes, chalices, crosses of gold and silver, banners, etc. with relics and altars; for the ears, singing, ringing, and organs piping; for the nose, frankincense sweet; to wash away sins (as they say) holy water of their own hallowing and making; priests an infinite sort, masses, trentals,[2] diriges, and pardons, etc. But where the gospel is preached, they knowing that God is not pleased but only with a pure heart, they are content with an honest place appointed to resort together in, though it were never hallowed by bishop at all, but have only a pulpit, a preacher to the people, a deacon for the poor, a table for the communion, with bare walls, or else written with scriptures, having God's eternal word sounding always amongst them in their sight and ears; and last of all, they should have good discipline, correct faults, and keep good order in all their meetings. But as they wept to see this second house no more costly nor pleasant to the eye; so our poor papists weep to see our churches so bare, saying they be like barns, there is nothing in them to make curtsey unto, neither saints nor yet their old little god. But hereafter it appears, whether of these churches God is more delighted withal. For although these ceremonies in the

[1] The pyx, or box with the consecrated wafer, hung up by a cord over the altar.
[2] Requiem Masses.

old law were given by Moses for the hardness of the people, to keep them exercised, that they fall not to idolatry of the gentiles; yet is there no mention of any of these in the New Testament, nor yet commandment now, neither to us nor them, but forbidden to be used at all, both for us and them. We be no longer under shadows, but under the truth: Christ hath fulfilled all, and taken away such dark kind of ceremonies, and hath placed the clear light of his gospel in his church to continue to the end.

James Pilkington, Bishop of Durham, 1562

LIKE A WASTE BARN

That church is more pleasant in the sight of God, where the gospel is preached, God's majesty and his mercy declared, than where all the ceremonies of Moses or the pope do shine so gloriously to the sight of the world. Let the papists examine well . . . whether their copes, chalices, vestments, crosses of gold and silver, their singing, ringing, censing, their images, relics, pardons, conjured waters, etc., be more pleasant service to the Lord our God, than where the trumpet of God's word sounds in our ears, to stir us up to the praising of God, and pulling down of our own crooked froward nature and stomachs. . . . Let us then be ashamed of these lewd sayings: 'What should I do at the church? I may not have my beads: the church is like a waste barn: there is no images nor saints, to worship and make curtsey unto: little god in the box is gone:[1] there is nothing but a little reading and preaching, that I cannot tell what it means: I had as lief keep me at home.' This is a woeful saying.

Ibid.

SPIRITUAL ADULTERY

Esau, because he would not obey but displeased his parents, married divers wives of the heathens round about him, contrary to God and example of all his good forefathers: so our papists, abhorring lawful marriage, follow carnal whores; and living in spiritual adultery, worship false gods, images, stocks and stones, the works of man's hands, . . . gadding from country to country a pilgrimage, to buy pardons, and rob Christ of his due honour.

Ibid.

[1] See note on previous page.

DILEMMA OF THE BISHOP OF COVENTRY AND LICHFIELD

If I correct them for religion, they sit out the excommunications willingly, and are glad they have so good occasion to be cut off from the church, thinking to avoid the penalty of the statute, because we forbid them *ingressum ecclesiae*, when indeed they meant not to come there at all, though they had been bidden never so much. For if by the ecclesiastical censures they be excommunicated out of the church, they think it no reason to punish them for not coming, when by ourselves, and by our own laws, they are forbidden to come. And so they make our excommunications to serve their turn.

William Overton, Bishop of Coventry to the Privy Council,
20 May 1582

A VICAR'S LAMENT

I have moved to abolish . . . abuses, but I cannot be hard. I digged of late in my own grounds and found a great number of alabaster images, whom I destroyed, as this bearer can declare; and for such cause we lose the love of idolaters.

Nicholas Daniel, Vicar of Preston, to Bishop Downham,
Low Sunday 1574

NO MUMMING OF MASSES

The merits of my works, were they never so just,
   I here forsake and them resign to such as in them trust.
There is no mumming Mass can make amends for me,
   Nor of the saints, departed hence, I trust in none but thee.
No pardon can me purge, but thy pardon alone,
   Nor yet no pilling pilgrimage made unto stock or stone.
No Psalter nor yet Psalms said to thy creatures;
   No ring of bells, no organ pipes, nor song that my soul cures.
Thy blood hath bought my soul and booteth all my bale,
   And not man's works nor chanted charms devised in Mammon's
   dale.

ROBERT BURDET, *The Refuge of a Sinner, 1564-5*

THE TYRANNOUS YOKE OF DOCTRINE

Then, we condemn as a tyrannous yoke . . . whatsoever men have set up of their own inventions, to make articles of our faith, or to bind men's conscience by their laws and institutes. . . . Of which sort are the doctrines of the supremacy of the see of Rome, purgatory, the mass, transubstantiation, the corporeal presence of Christ's body in the sacrament, adoration thereof; man's merits; free will; justification by works; praying in an unknown tongue, to saints departed, for the dead, upon beads; extolling of images, pardons, pilgrimages, auricular confession; taking from the lay-people the cup in the administration of the sacrament; prohibition of marriage; distinction of meats, apparel, and days; briefly, all the ceremonies and whole order of papistry: which they call the *hierarchy*; indeed, a devilish confusion, established as it were in despite of God, and to the mockery and reproach of all Christian religion. These, I say, with such like, we abjure, renounce, and utterly condemn.

Confession of faith of Ministers of Religion, 1571

AS THE POPE TEACHES

Why am I forbidden to communicate with Papists at their Mass? Surely, not so much for the evilness of the men themselves, as the wickedness of the order and the thing which they minister. For when thou comest to the communion with the Papists, and, according to St. Paul, would eat of that bread and drink of that cup, they will neither give thee bread nor wine according to Christ's institution, (for they say the substance is changed, and there remains no bread;) but they will give thee an idol of their own making, which they call their God. They come not together according to Christ's rule, to break the bread; but they creep into a corner, as the Pope teaches them, to sacrifice for the quick and the dead, to sell heaven, harrow hell, and sweep purgatory of all such as will pay. They come not to communicate with the people, but to eat up all alone. Therefore, because they have changed Christ's ordinance in his supper, broken his commandment, and set up their own device, we must not meddle with them in such things as they have done contrary to God and his word.

James Pilkington, Bishop of Durham, 1560

A CAVEAT FOR PAPISTS

Wherefore ye Papists all beware,
    forsake the Romish whore:
And fear the judgments of the Lord,
    which will you else devour.

Recant ye all your heresies,
  and leave your perverse way:
Wherein you walked so stubbornly,
  so long and many a day.

Love God, obey your sovereign,
  and pray for her estate:
Renounce ye all your maummetry,[1]
  Lest ye repent too late.

An Epitaph declaring the life and end of
D. Edmund Bonner, 1569

PILKINGTON ON PAPISTS

How hard a thing it is at this day to turn a papist, and specially to
see one that knew the truth once, if he fall to popery or other errors,
to rise again and believe the gospel, we have too many examples to
teach us. I fear the saying of the apostle may be verified on them: 'It is
impossible for them that were once enlightened and knew the truth,
if they fall away, to be renewed by repentance.' The Lord in his
mercy stay us that we fall not from him! for 'it is horrible to fall into
the hands of the living God' in his anger.

James Pilkington, Bishop of Durham, 1585

THE CHURCH PAPIST

A Papist is one that parts religion between his conscience and his
purse and comes to church not to serve God but the King. The fear
of the law makes him wear the mark of the Gospel which he useth,
not as a means to save his soul, but his charges. He loves Popery well,
but he is loth to lose by it, and though he is something scared by the
Bulls of Rome, yet he is struck with more terror at the apparitor.
Once a month he presents himself at the church to keep off the churchwardens . . . kneels with the congregation, but prays by himself and
asks God's forgiveness for coming thither. If he is forced to stay out a
sermon, he puts his hat over his eyes and frowns out the hour; and
when he comes home, he thinks to make amends for his fault by
abusing the preacher. . . . He would make a bad martyr, and a good
traveller, for his conscience is so large that he could never wander from

[1] The worship of images; idolatry.

it, and in Constantinople would be circumcised with a mental reservation. His wife is more zealous in her devotion and therefore more costly, and he bates her in tires what she stands him in religion.

Harleian Mss.

THE PLAGUE OF PRIESTS

Among these locusts—that is, amongst the innumerable troops of monks—none . . . have appeared more keen or better prepared and equipped for doing mischief than are the Jesuits at this present day.

WILLIAM WHITTAKER, *Disputatio de Sacra Scriptura*

PRIESTS AND APES

Cole, Archdeacon of Essex, preaching at Paul's Cross, anno 1565, the 11th day of November, likened the priests unto apes, for, saith he, they be both bald alike, but that the priests be bald before, the apes behind.

JOHN STOW, *Memoranda*

CREEPING VERMIN

The effect of their [priests'] labours is to bring the realm not only into a dangerous war against the forces of strangers . . . but into a war domestical and civil, wherein no blood is usually spared, nor mercy yielded, and wherein neither the vanqueror nor the vanquished have cause to triumph. . . . These are the most evident perils that necessarily should follow, if these kind of vermin were suffered to creep by stealth into the realm and to spread their poison within the same, howsoever, when they are taken, like hypocrites they colour and counterfeit the same with profession of devotion in religion.

LORD BURGHLEY, *The Execution of Justice in England, 1583*

JESUIT VULTURES

Sir Robert Napper, chief baron [of the Irish Exchequer] compared the Jesuits to vultures who, as Pliny writeth, were so subtle of smell, that they smell blood three days before the battle and would be three days before at the place of battle.

Journal of Sir Roger Wilbraham, 30 September 1593

Dr. King at Court

Dr. King preached lately at Court, and was very bitter against Jesuits and all priests. The Queen gave him great thanks, wishing all the *Kings* of Europe of his mind.

Anthony Rivers to Robert Persons, 17 March 1602

Fishers of Men

Jesuits come into rich men's houses, not to bring them salvation, but because there is something to be fished for. . . . So they are sent away naked and torn, like those presumptuous fellows that would have cast out devils in Christ's name without his leave, and the God of heaven will laugh them to scorn.

Sermon of Mr. Fenton at St. Paul's Cross, 21 November 1602

Nicolas Flute in Rome

He spent there the said six days, in which time he went about to see the Church of St. Peter and other places in the city, and saw many workmen building of the said Church and of the Pope's Palace; and saw in a new Church there the Pope, attended with many Cardinals and others, and saw him bless as he went in the said Church. He saw four or five young men go in the streets in black gowns and cornered caps, which were said to him to be Englishmen of a College there; but what they were he heard not, neither had he any words with them.

Examination of Nicolas Flute of Dartmouth before two
Justices of the Peace

Cambridge Men Abroad

After dinner we rode thirteen miles to Rome (of old the head-city of the world) through winding hills and pastures; and when we came to the first gate, we did meet many Englishmen on horseback, without boots, being all priests going to Madonna di Loreto. I was much afraid lest some of them, being scholars of Cambridge, should know me brought up in the same University; neither was the hearing of the English tongue, or the sight of Englishmen, ever before so unpleasing to me.

FYNES MORISON, *Itinerary*

PROTESTANT PILGRIMS IN JERUSALEM

Coming within a furlong of the gates, I, with my companion, Mr. John Burrell, went singing and praising God till we came to the west gate of the city, and there we stayed because it was not lawful for a Christian to enter unadmitted. My companion advised me to say I was a Greek, only to avoid going to Mass, but I, not having the Greek tongue, refused so to do, telling him even at the entry of the gate, that I would neither deny my country nor religion. Whereupon, being demanded who we were, Mr. John Burrell (answering in the Greek tongue) told them that he was a Greek, and I an Englishman. This gave him admittance to the Greek Patriarch, but I was seized on and cast in prison before I had stayed a full hour at the gate, for the Turks flatly denied that they had ever heard either of my Queen or country, or that she paid them any tribute. The Pater Guardian, who is the defender of all Christian pilgrims (and the principal procurer of my imprisonment, because I did not offer myself under his protection, but confidently stood to be rather protected under the Turk than the Pope) made the Turk so much my enemy that I was reputed to be a spy, and so by no means could I be released from the dungeon.

Now give me favour to tell you how it pleased God (the very day) to deliver me and grant me pass as a Protestant, without yielding to any other ceremony than carriage of a wax candle only, far beyond my expectation. Here let me remember you, that when I stayed at Ramoth in Gilead, where I wrote the eight letters for England by the caravan of Damasco, having so good leisure I went to a fountain to wash my foul linen, and, being earnest about business, suddenly there came a Moor unto me, who taking my clothes out of my hand, and calling me by my name, said he would help me. . . .

When this Moor saw me thus imprisoned in Jerusalem, my dungeon being right against the Sepulchre of Christ, albeit he wept, yet he bade me be of good comfort, and went to the Bashaw of the city, and to the Saniake,[1] before whom he took his oath that I was a mariner of a ship which had brought two hundred and fifty or three hundred Turks and Moors into Egypt from Algiers and Tunis, their journey being unto Mecca.

This Moor (in regard he was a Mussulman) prevailed so well with them that, returning with six Turks back to prison, he called me to the door and there said unto me that, if I would go to the house of the

[1] Chief Justice.

Pater Guardian and yield myself under his protection, I should be enforced to no religion but mine own, except it were to carry a candle; to which I willingly condescended.

So, paying the charges of the prison,[1] I was presently delivered, and brought to the guardian's monastery, where the pater, coming to me, took me by the hand, and bade me welcome; marvelling I would so much err from Christianity as to put myself rather under the Turks than his protection. I told him, what I did was because that I would not go to Mass, but keep my conscience to myself: he replied, that 'many Englishmen had been there, but (being Catholics) went to Mass, telling the Turks at the gate's entrance that they were Frenchmen, for the Turks know not what you mean by word Englishman'; advising me further, that when any of my countrymen undertook the like travel, at the gates of Jerusalem they should term themselves either Frenchmen or Britons, because they were well known to the Turks.

This, or such like conference, passed between us; and further he asked me, how old our Queen's Majesty was, and what was the reason she gave nothing to the maintenance of the Holy Sepulchre, as well as other kings and princes did? with divers other frivolous questions: whereto I answered accordingly. This day being spent even to twilight, Mr. John Burrell, who passed as a Greek without any trouble, came in unto us, being nevertheless constrained to this monastery, or else he might not stay in the city: for such sway do the Papists carry there that no Christian stranger can have admittance there, but he must be protected under them, or not enter the city. Mr. Burrell and I being together in the court of the monastery, twelve fat-fed friars came forth unto us, each of them carrying a wax-candle burning, and two spare candles beside, the one for Mr. Burrell, and the other for me. Another friar brought a great basin of warm water, mingled with roses and other sweet flowers, and a carpet being spread on the ground, and cushions in chairs set orderly for us, the pater guardian came and set us down, giving each of us a candle in our hands; then came a friar and pulled off our hose, and (setting the basin on the carpet) washed our feet.

So soon as the friar began to wash, the twelve friars began to sing, continuing so till our feet were washed; which being done, they went along singing, and we, with the guardian, came to a chapel in the monastery, where one of them began an oration in form of a sermon, tending to this effect: 'How meritorious it was for us to visit the Holy

---

[1] The prison of the Turks, where the travellers were lodged one night.

Land, and see those sanctified places where our Saviour's feet had trod.'

The sermon being ended, they brought us unto a chamber, where our supper was prepared; there we fed somewhat fearfully, in regard the strange cats have as strange qualities; but, committing ourselves to God and their outward-appearing Christian kindness, we fell to heartily, supped very bountifully, and (after praising God) were lodged decently. Thus much for my first entertainment in Jerusalem which was the 25th of March 1601, being our Lady-day in Lent.

Now follows what the friars afterward showed me, being thereto appointed by the pater guardian. Early the next morning we arose, and, having saluted the pater guardian, he appointed us seven friars and a trouchman: so forth we went to see all the holy places in the city which were to be seen, except those in *Sepulchra Sancta*, for that required a whole day's work afterward; and at every place where we came we kneeled down and said the 'Lord's Prayer.'

HENRY TIMBERLAKE, *Two English Pilgrims*

A Beggar's Cloak

The Papists' religion is like a beggar's cloak, where there are so many patches of policy sewed on, that none of the first cloth can be seen.

Diary of John Manningham, 12 February 1602

Quid Hi Inter Tantos?

Here were three seminary priests hanged and quartered the last week, but what is that among so many?

John Chamberlain to Mr. Dudley Carleton, 26 April 1602

A Friendly Warning

I am privately advertised that there is much evil intended against you and your family for recusancy, and that Robert Bainbrigg was put into the commission of purpose to sift you. The proceedings in this country are set down very sharp, and the presentments [are] to be made for the hundred in which you dwell upon the 11th of February before which time by my advice you shall not come to Sawley.

Mr. Harper to a Catholic friend, 24 January 1592

FAILURE OF GOSPEL-PREACHING

It was sad to consider, that notwithstanding the restoration of the
gospel under this queen, and that the bishops and officers of the church
did what they could in the exercise of discipline, for the restraint of
sin and wickedness, as adultery, fornication, profanation of the Lord's
day, wrongs done in matters testamentary, and the like; yet these
transgressions did abound very much.

JOHN STRYPE, *Annals*

LUCIFERIAN TRINKETS

Look into the laity of the Protestants, and tell me whether there
ever was such pride, especially in apparel? Did not all these new-
fashioned attires come in with your new religion? Your loose gowns,
your trains, your verdingales, your borders, your peringles, your
coronets, your wires, your ruffs starched white, blue, etc., your setting
sticks, your Venetian, French, Spanish and Switzers hose, your galle-
gascones, your scabilonians, your S. Thomas onions, your ruffs, your
cuffs and a thousand such new-devised Luciferian trinkets.[1] Is not all
spent now in pride and bravery which in Catholic time was employed
in housekeeping and in relieving the poor?

THOMAS HILL, *A Quatron of Reasons*

ASLEEP IN THE PEACE OF SIN

This time shall testify with me herein, and the very diversity that is
between these our corrupt conditions and the holy studies and endeavours of our forefathers shall testify: but the days that yet are to
come must needs most feel the smart of it, when these that have the
direction of other men's steps shall be gone, by whom for old discipline
wherein they were brought up, some signs and remnants of virtue be
continued in the world. For when they be spent and our yonkers that
never heard of the Church's discipline, but have had their full swing of
sin, with the instruction of a most wanton doctrine, shall be the
principal of the people, if this division so long continue (which God

---

[1] *verdingale* (or farthingale), a framework of hoops used for extending the skirts of
women's dresses; *setting stick*, a rod used for stiffening the plaits or 'sets' of ruffs; *galligas-
cones* (or galligaskins), loose hose or breeches; *scabilonians*, a contemptuous term for some
kind of garment.

orbid) into what terms shall truth and virtue be then brought. Methink I see beforehand the lamentable state of things and in a manner behold the fruit of our only faith, of this bold presumption of God's mercy, of removing the discipline of penance, of refusing the only ordinance of God for remission of our mortal sins. Evil are we now, but a thousand parts worse shall we be then, which in long nouseling[1] in this naughty learning of liberty shall be in perpetual woe and have no feel nor sense thereof. And all this must needs follow upon the lack of these outward acts and external ways of pardoning and punishing offences appointed either for man's present comfort and solace, or else to keep in awe the wantons of the world by the rod of outward discipline, which in the Church has ever especially been observed in the sacrament of penance. Have patience therefore a little and marvel not to see the ungodly flourish and feed himself with the wealth of the world: nothing being a more sure sign of wrath to come, nor more unlucky to a mortal man, especially to a Prince, than to have prosperity and good luck in wickedness, and so to be beset wholly with flatterers that rock him asleep in the peace of his sin, that he may neither hear his duty nor bear check or chastisement for the same.

WILLIAM ALLEN, *An Admonition to the Nobility* (*1585*)

THEY BUILD TO LIVE ALWAYS

But, to be plain with you, I fear many evils are hanging over our heads. For almost all are covetous, all love gifts. There is no truth, no liberality, no knowledge of God. Men have broken forth to curse and to lie, and murder, and steal, and commit adultery. And what Empedocles said of his Agrigentines, I may say also of my English: The English indulge in pleasures, as if they were to die tomorrow; while they build, as if they were to live always.

John Parkhurst to Henry Bullinger, 26 April 1562

GAZING AND STARING IN CHURCH

The Catholic Roman Church hath ever both in doing and speaking and every manner of way borne great respect and reverence towards God's holy saints and towards all holy things in regard of Him from whom proceedeth all holiness. . . . In every action and gest which

---

[1] *nouseling*: bringing the nose towards the ground, grovelling.

Catholics use in Church you see great reverence and humble veneration. But contrariwise amongst the Protestants, as all things are
profane, so are they most profanely used. They enter into their churches
with no greater reverence than they enter into taverns; they bow or
make reverence to nothing therein, for that they have made all sacred
things away; if any of them kneel, it is but upon thorns for full soon
are they up again, and then with their hats upon their heads they either
jangle or talk or walk or sit staring about them, as if they wanted to see
when the players would come forth upon the stage; or else the good
fellows go to the alehouse (where now and then they find the Minister
drinking his morning draught before he go to his service) to drink a
pot or two of nappy ale, that thereby they may better hold out the
service time, during which space they stand gazing and staring upon
the Minister as a country clown, which never was in London before,
doth gaze when he goeth down Cheapside at the goldsmiths' stalls,
or else they stare one upon another like as thieves do when they are
taken in a robbery, or else some of them walk without in the warm sun
and make their bargains, and generally you do see no more devotion
there than you do in a fair or market—no man or woman saying one
prayer, but all waiting for (that which they cannot have in that state)
'the peace of God'. The which being hastily chopped up, they rush and
gush out of the Church as water doth out of a mill pool, when the
flood gates are suddenly plucked up, no man moving lip or leg but
striving who shall be soonest at his pottage.

THOMAS HILL, *A Quatron of Reasons*

THE TREE OF OUR RELIGION

Now concerning the professors of our faith . . . we need not to
range far for examples of good life. For God be thanked, even our
adversaries themselves are so fully persuaded of our good behaviour
that if a man in company be modest and grave in countenance, if he
use no swearing, foul or unseemly speech, if he refuse to join in lewd
company and dishonest actions, he is strait suspected for a Papist:
and on the other side, if there be any ruffianly, quarrelous, foul-spoken
or lewdly conditioned, he is never mistrusted for a Papist but taken for
a very sound and undoubted Protestant. Let also the records of assizes
and sessions be searched and let it be but showed among so many
hundred Protestants as are yearly executed for felonies, murders,
rapes, extortions, forgeries and such like crimes, how few recusants

have been ever in so many years attached justly with such like offences. Let but the neighbours of Catholic and Protestant gentlemen be witnesses who live best and are readiest to all good deeds and works of charity. Let the jailers and keepers of prisons report what difference they find in the lives of Catholic and Protestant prisoners. And if all these say, as the truth is, that we go beyond the other in Christian duty, then may we by their own testimonies, avouch the tree of our religion to be good, seeing that, as Christ saith, 'an evil tree cannot bring forth good fruit'.

ROBERT SOUTHWELL, *An Epistle of Comfort*

Third Chronicle, 1580-1603

The Power of His Word

i. There are thought to be 20,000 Catholics more this year than the last, and nowhere of late years has the Lord given greater power and spirit to those who preach his word, be his name for ever blessed.

William Allen to the Rector of the English College, Rome,
23 June 1581

ii. The adversaries are very mad that by no cruelty can they move a single Catholic from his resolution, no, not even a little girl.

Robert Persons to Fr. Agazarri, 16 November 1580

The Poets Sang His Death

As concerning his death I can say nothing but by report of others, because I was not present at it, only I think good to relate that the same day the river of Thames, which daily floweth and ebbeth with the sea, did change his course, ceasing to flow or ebb all that day; which was so notorious that some poets employed their pens to make sonnets thereupon to celebrate the wonder, applying it to the martyrdom of Fr. Campion. And one of the sonnets was presently after set forth in music by the best musician in England, which I have often seen and heard.

THOMAS FITZHERBERT, *Recollections of Fr. Campion*

The Death of Leicester

Here lies the worthy warrior
That never bloodied sword:

Here lies the loyal courtier
That never kept his word.
Here lies his noble excellence
That ruled all the states,
Here lies the Earl of Leicester
Whom earth and heaven hates.

Contemporary epitaph on the Earl of Leicester

CATHOLIC BAPTISMS

Persons suffering their children to be baptised by any Jesuit, seminary or other massing priest shall forfeit £100 for every offence.

Burghley's Draft of Bill against Recusants, March 1593

EXAMPLE OF THE BETTER SORT

There are in many parts divers notorious recusants not yet reformed, whose presumption (they being of the better sort) draweth the inferior sort into no small boldness.

The State Civil and Moral of the County of Lancaster, 1590

A DIABOLICAL VISITATION

In this year [1595] at Eckington in Derbyshire, the minister being at his later service, the devil came to visit them; but first in the most terrible and warlike manner, he came down the steeple as though he had shot off guns; so that the minister's wife, fearing some conspiracies against her husband, called unto him to take heed of himself. He being altogether unarmed, called for assistance of the churchwardens, charging them very strictly to look who he was and take him. As they began to look for him, he came down so roughly, that in the bell-house he struck down two men. Then he went to the chancel so hotly that the officers thought it not good to lay hands on him. Back again he went from the chancel, so out of the church door invisible, much like a fiery bottle of hay all in burning flames of fire. The people were in such fear (as by report of some that were there) as words were not able to express. There was a young man stricken lame of all his limbs, but since he is recovered.

GRENE, *Collections*

THE DEATH OF WALSINGHAM, 6 APRIL 1590

Walsingham, being well at four o'clock in the afternoon, was dead before eleven of the same night. His body did presently savour so that no man was able to endure it, and very much ado they had to keep the body with all manner of spices until the next night, when, as it was secretly carried and buried in Paul's about midnight, one of those that carried him soon after died impoisoned with that most noisome smell.

An Ancient Editor's Note Book

COMFORT FOR THE DYING

If it were only possible for us to approach the dying, there is hardly a man who would not die a Catholic: for it suits them all to live as heretics, but to die Catholics.

Henry Garnet to Claude Aquaviva, 26 August 1587

ROYAL RAPACITY

Our expected Parliament is at a nonplus; the Queen will not have it; and for provision of money it is ordered that more of the crown lands shall be sold, and divers jewels in the Tower, as chalices, crucifixes, and such like, are set to sale to the goldsmiths.

Anthony Rivers to Robert Persons, 13 January 1601

OLD PRIEST AT LARGE, 1604

They present that there was one Mr. Smyth an old priest found in the house of the said Anne Holmes by Mr. Chaworth and Mr. Rookby.

*A List of the Roman Catholics in the County of York
in 1604*

INCREASE OF CATHOLICS

We are all well and follow our accustomed trade with good gain, for our customers (thanks be to God) do daily increase, which is perceivable even to our enemies and hath caused the Chief Justice to complain very bitterly to her Majesty now of late of the great multitudes of Catholics in this land.

Richard Blount to Robert Persons, 22 October 1600

THE QUEEN IN DECLINE

The ache of the Queen's arm is fallen into her side, but she is still, thanks to God, frolicky and merry, only her face showeth some decay, which to conceal when she cometh in public, she putteth many fine cloths into her mouth to bear out her cheeks, and sometimes as she is walking she will put off her petticoat, as seeming too hot, when others shake with cold.

Richard Blount to Robert Persons, 22 October, 1600

DEATH OF ELIZABETH I

i. This morning about three at clock her Majesty departed this life, mildly like a lamb, easily like a ripe apple from the tree, *cum leve quadam febre, absque gemitu*. Dr. Parry told me that he was present, and sent his prayers before her soul; and I doubt not but she is amongst the royal saints in heaven in eternal joys.

Diary of John Manningham, 24 March 1602 O.S.

ii. Her majesty being in very good health, one day Sir John Stanhope, being the vice-chamberlain, and secretary Cecil's dependant and familiar, came and presented her majesty with a piece of gold of the bigness of an angel, full of characters, which, he said, an old woman in Wales bequeathed her on her deathbed; and thereupon he discoursed how the said old woman, by virtue of the same, lived to the age of one hundred and twenty years; and in that age, having all her body withered and consumed, and wanting nature to nourish, she died, commanding the said piece of gold to be carefully sent to her majesty; alleging further that, as long as the said old woman wore it upon her body, she could not die.

The queen, upon the confidence she had hereof, took the said gold, and wore it about her neck. Now, though she fell not suddenly sick, yet daily decreased of her rest and feeding; and, within fifteen days, fell downright sick; and the cause being wondered at by my lady Scrope, with whom she was very private and confident, being her near kinswoman, her majesty told her (commanding her to conceal the same) that she saw, one night, in her bed, her body exceeding lean, and fearful in a light of fire. This sight was at Whitehall, a little before she departed thence to Richmond, and may be testified by another lady, who was one of the nearest about her person, of whom the queen demanded, whether she was not wont to see sights in the night, telling her of the bright flame she had seen. Afterward, in the melancholy of her sickness, she desires to see a true looking-glass, which, in twenty years before, she had not seen, but only such a one which of purpose was made to deceive her sight: which glass being brought her, she fell presently exclaiming at all those which had so much commended her, and took it so offensively, that all those, which had before flattered her, durst not come in her sight.

Now falling into extremity, she sat two days and three nights upon her stool, ready dressed, and could never be brought by any of her council, to go to bed, or eat, or drink: only, my lord admiral one time persuaded her to drink some broth. For any of the rest, she would not answer them to any question; but said softly to my lord admiral's earnest persuasions, that, if he knew what she had seen in her bed, he would not persuade her as he did. And secretary Cecil, overhearing her, asked if her majesty had seen any spirits; to which she said she scorned to answer him to so idle a question. Then he told her how, to content the people, her majesty must go to bed: to which she smiled, wonderfully contemning him, saying that the word *must* was not to be used to princes; and thereupon said, 'Little man, little man, if your father had lived, ye durst not have said so much: but thou knowest I must die, and that maketh thee so presumptuous.' And presently, commanding him and the rest to depart from her chamber, she willed my lord admiral to stay; to whom she shook her head, and, with a pitiful voice said, 'My lord, I am tied with a chain of iron about my neck.' He alleging her wonted courage to her, she replied, 'I am tied, and the case is altered with me.'

Then two ladies, waiting on her in her chamber, discovered, in the bottom of her chair, the queen of hearts, with a nail of iron knocked through the forehead of it; the which the ladies durst not pull out, remembering that the like thing was used to the old lady of Sussex, and proved afterwards for a witchcraft, for the which certain were hanged, as instruments of the same. The lady Elizabeth Guilford, then waiting on the queen, and leaving her asleep in her privy chamber, met her, as she thought, three or four chambers off, and, fearing she would have been displeased that she left her alone, came towards her, to excuse herself; and she vanished away; and when she returned into the same chamber where she had left her, found her asleep as before. So growing past recovery (having kept her bed fifteen days, besides three days she sat upon her stool), one day, when being pulled up by force, she stood on her feet fifteen hours, the council sent to her the bishop of Canterbury and other of the prelates, upon sight of whom she was much offended, cholerickly rating them, bidding them be packing, saying she was no atheist, but knew full well that they were hedge priests, and took it for an indignity that they should speak to her.

Now being given over by all, and at the last gasp, keeping still her sense in every thing, and giving, ever, when she spake, apt answers (though she spake very seldom, having then a sore throat) she desired to wash it, that she might answer more freely to what the council demanded; which was, to know whom she would have king:—but they, seeing her throat troubled her so much, desired her to hold up her finger, when they named whom liked her. Whereupon they named the king of France—the king of Scotland—at which she never stirred. They named my lord Beauchamp; whereto she said, 'I will have no rascal's son in my seat, but one worthy to be a king.' Hereupon, instantly she died.

Lady Southwell's relation

iii. I have no need to tell your Reverence what happened or the details of her dying. Nor, had I the wish, is there much that I could say, so completely was I cut off from converse with men and from news of those events. There was nothing I could learn apart from what my warder chose to tell me. But this I did witness. During those few days in which she lay dying beyond all hope of recovery, a strange silence descended on the whole city, as if it were under interedict and divine worship suspended. Not a bell rang out. Not a bugle sounded—though ordinarily they were often heard. About midnight on the Vigil of the Annunciation of the Blessed Virgin she breathed her last.

The next day about eight or nine o'clock the new King, James of Scotland, was proclaimed in the main street of London—with such precision and thoroughness had the Council calculated every detail. Then they came to the Tower, crying out and publishing the proclamation with great pomp. It was all done within view of my window, and I watched the style and order of the proceedings. Meanwhile couriers were despatched to Scotland. There was no delay. King James had determined not to tarry. In a short time he had settled with great expedition the affairs both of his kingdom and court, and was hastening to London.

WILLIAM WESTON, *Autobiography*

Abbreviations used in References

C.R.S.   Catholic Record Society.

C.S.P.   Calendar of State Papers.

Foley   *Records of the English Province of the Society of Jesus*, by Henry
            Foley, S.J.

Grene   Christopher Grene, *Collectanea* (Stonyhurst Manuscripts).

Morris   John Morris, S.J., *The Troubles of our Catholic Forefathers.*

Rambler   *The Rambler*, a weekly and later bi-monthly Catholic journal,
            1848–1862.

References

I
The Year of Change

Page

5 Henry Clifford, *The Life of Jane Dormer, Duchess of Feria* (edited by Joseph Stevenson, 1887), 90.

Archdeacon Sinclair, *Memorials of St. Paul's Cathedral*. Quoted in *The Mindes Delight*, by Hedley Hope-Nicholson (1928), 56-7.

Henry Clifford, *The Life of Jane Dormer, Duchess of Feria* (edited by Joseph Stevenson, 1887), 71-2.

6 John Strype, *Annals* (ed. 1824), vol. I, 1-2.

John Strype, ibid., 14-15.

7 John Strype, ibid., 42-3.

John Strype, ibid., 70.

Il Schifanoya to the Castellan of Mantua, 23 January 1559. C.S.P., Venetian, 1558-80, 16-17.

8 Dr. Nicolas Sander's Report to Cardinal Morone (1561), C.R.S., vol. I, Miscellanea, 31 (Translation).

Il Schifanoya to Ottaviano Vivaldino, Mantuan Ambassador with King Philip at Brussels, 30 January 1559. C.S.P., Venetian, 1558-80, 22-3.

9 Letter from London (6 February 1559) enclosed in a letter to Paulo Tiepolo, 17 February 1559. Ibid., 28.

Il Schifanoya to Ottaviano Vivaldino, 6 February 1559. Ibid., 27.

10 Venetian Ambassador's despatch, 21 March 1559. Cf. Magee, *English Recusants*, 24.

Il Schifanoya to Ottaviano Vivaldino, 28 March 1559. C.S.P., Venetian, 1558-80, 58.

John Strype, *Annals* (ed. 1824), vol. I, 283-4.

11 John Strype, ibid., 82.

Dr. Nicolas Sander's Report to Cardinal Morone, May 1561. C.R.S., vol. I, Miscellanea, 25-6 (Translation).

12 John Strype, *Annals* (ed. 1824), vol. I, 87.

John Strype, *Annals* (ed. 1824), vol. I, 284.

13 Il Schifanoya to Ottaviano Vivaldino, 25 April 1559. C.S.P., Venetian, 1558-80, 74.

Page

13 Paulo Tiepolo to the Doge and Senate, 4 May 1559. C.S.P., Venetian, 1558-80, 81.

Il Schifanoya to the Castellan of Mantua, 10 May 1559. Ibid., 84.

14 Richard Cox to Wolfgang Weidner, 20 May 1559. *Zurich Letters* (Parker Society), 27.

Ibid., 28.

John Jewel to Henry Bullinger, 22 May 1559. Ibid., 33.

Il Schifanoya to the Castellan of Mantua, 30 May 1559. C.S.P., Venetian, 1558-80, 94.

15 John Strype, *Annals* (ed. 1824), vol. I, 287.

Il Schifanoya to Ottaviano Vivaldino, 27 June 1559. C.S.P., Venetian, 1558-80, 105.

Dr. Nicolas Sander's Report to Cardinal Morone. C.R.S., vol. I, Miscellanea, 35-6 (Translation).

16 Nicolas Sander, *Anglican Schism* (ed. 1877), 284-5.

John Nichols, *The Progresses of Queen Elizabeth*, vol. I, 47.

17 John Jewel to Josiah Simler, 2 November 1559. *Zurich Letters* (Parker Society), 50.

2

The Bishops' Protest

18 John Strype, *Annals* (ed. 1824), vol. I, part II, 409-11.

20 John Strype, ibid., 399-400, 403-5.

21 John Strype, ibid., 414-15.

22 Abbot Feckenham in the House of Lords. *The Rambler*, New Series, vol. vii, 185-6.

3

Second Chronicle 1560-1577

23 John Strype, *Annals* (ed. 1824), vol. I, 200-1.

John Strype, ibid., 202-3.

John Strype, ibid., 120.

24 John Strype, ibid., 98.

John Jewel to Peter Martyr, 22 May 1560. *Zurich Letters* (Parker Society), 77.

John Strype, *Annals* (ed. 1824), vol. I, 254-5.

John Strype, ibid., 290.

25 John Strype, ibid., 210-11.

Henry Clifford, *The Life of Jane Dormer, Duchess of Feria* (ed. by Joseph Stevenson, 1887), 95-6.

26 Nicolas Sander, *Anglican Schism* (ed. 1877), 266-7.

Page

Dr. Nicolas Sander's Report to Cardinal Morone, 1561. C.R.S., vol. I, Miscellanea, 45-6 (Translation).

27 Nicolas Sander, *Anglican Schism* (ed. 1877), 317.

John Strype, *Annals* (ed. 1824), vol. I, 400.

John Strype, ibid., 400.

28 Dr. Nicolas Sander's Report to Cardinal Morone, 1561. C.R.S., vol. I, Miscellanea, 45 (Translation).

A. Wood, *History and Antiquities of the University of Oxford* (1796), vol. II, 149.

John Strype, *Annals* (ed. 1824), vol. I, 401.

29 John Strype, ibid., 374.

Anthony Wood, *Athenae Oxonienses*. Cf. Hedley Hope-Nicholson, *The Mindes Delight* (1928), 62.

30 John Strype, *Annals* (ed. 1824), vol. I, 390.

Stow's *Memoranda*, 1563 (Camden Society, New Series xxviii), 125.

Stow's *Memoranda*, January 1564, 128-9.

31 Nicolas Sander, *Anglican Schism* (ed. 1877), 285-6.

32 From a Visitation Book of Thomas Young, Archbishop of York, 29 October 1567. Surtees Society, vol. lxxxi, 344.

Archbishop Parker's report on the diocese of Chichester during the vacancy of the see, 1569. S.P. Dom. Eliz. lx, 71. Cf. Vic. Co. Hist., Sussex, vol. II, 25-6.

33 Sir Ralph Sadler, Chancellor of the Duchy of Lancaster to Sir William Cecil, 6 December 1569. S.P. Dom. Eliz. (Addenda), xv, no. 77.

William Harrison, *A Description of England* (in Holinshed's *Chronicle*) edited by Lothrop Withington (n.d.), 77.

Philip II of Spain to Geran de Spes concerning the Bull, *Regnans in Excelsis*. S.P. Simancas, 1569-78, 254.

34 Sir Robert Naunton, *Fragmenta Regalia* (1641).

John Northbrook, *A Brief and Pithy Sum of the Christian Faith* (ed. 1571). The Epistle Dedicatory.

35 Archbishop Grindal's Injunctions to the Laity, 1571. *Remains of Archbishop Grindal* (Parker Society), 140.

Archbishop Grindal's Injunctions to the Laity, 1571. Ibid., 134.

Edward Aglionby in the House of Commons, 11 April 1571. Sir Simonds D'Ewes, *Journals of all the Parliaments of Elizabeth* (ed. 1682), 161.

36 Edward Aglionby in the House of Commons, 21 April 1571. Ibid., 177.

John Strype, *Annals* (ed. 1824), vol. II, part I, 315.

37 The Queen's Commissioners to the Fellows of Magdalen. Gutch's *Collectanea Curiosa* (1781), vol. II, 280.

Archbishop Grindal's Visitation, 1576. *Remains of Archbishop Grindal* (Parker Society), 159-60.

Page

39 Edwin Sandys, Archbishop of York to the Privy Council, 28 October
1577. S.P. Dom. Eliz., cxvii, no. 23 in C.R.S., vol. 22, 3-4.

4

The Old Priests

40 John Strype, *Annals* (ed. 1824), vol. I, 80-1.
John Strype, ibid., 60.

41 John Cox to Peter Martyr (after 21 December 1559). *Zurich Letters* (Parker
Society), 66.
John Jewel to Peter Martyr, 1 August 1559. Ibid., 39.
John Cox to Peter Martyr, 5 August 1562. Ibid., 112.
John Scory, Bishop of Hereford, to the Privy Council, 1564. Camden
Miscellany, no. 9, 19-20.

42 Stow's *Memoranda* (Camden Society, New Series xxviii), 121.
Nicholas Bullingham, Bishop of Lincoln, to the Privy Council, 6
November 1564. Camden Miscellany, no. 9, 34.

43 John Scory, Bishop of Hereford, to the Privy Council, 1564. Ibid., 20-1.
John Scory, Bishop of Hereford, to the Privy Council, 1564. Ibid., 23.
Edwin Sandys, Bishop of Worcester, to the Privy Council, 27 October
1564. Ibid., 3.

44 The examination of Fr. Simon Southern before the Bishop of Winchester,
24 December 1582. S.P. Dom. Eliz., vol. clvi, no. 29-1.
Grene, *Collections*. Cf. Morris, *Troubles*, Third Series, 315.

45 Grene, *Collections*. Cf. Foley, *Records*, III, 232-3.
Archbishop Parker's report after visiting the diocese of Chichester during
the vacancy of the see, 1569. S.P. Dom. Eliz., lx, 71. Cf. Vic. Co. Hist.
Sussex, vol. II, 27.
Richard Barnes to Sir William Cecil, 27 October 1570. S.P. Dom. Eliz.,
lxxiv, 22, in C.R.S., vol. 22, 116.

46 S.P. Dom. Eliz., vol. clxxxiv, no. 33 (i). Examination of a priest, Sir
James Stonnes, ordained by Bishop Tunstall of Durham in the reign of
Henry VIII, and arrested in November 1585. He confessed he 'hath said
Mass as often as the time, place and company have given him leave, and
so is of mind to continue.'

5

The Image of Christ

47 John Strype, *Annals* (ed. 1824), vol. I, 260.
Heylyn, *History of the Reformation*, 124.
Richard Cox, Bishop of Ely to Peter Martyr (after 21 December 1559).
Zurich Letters (Parker Society), 66.

Page

47 John Jewel to Peter Martyr, 16 November 1559. Ibid., 55.

48 John Parkhurst, Bishop of Norwich, to Henry Bullinger, 20 August 1562. Ibid., 122.

Ibid., 129.

Stonyhurst MSS., Grene, *M*, 193-4.

49 An Ancient Editor's Note Book. Cf. Morris, *Troubles*, Third Series, 10.

The Sonnets of William Alabaster, edited by G. M. Story and Helen Gardner. (Oxford University Press, 1959), 7.

Edward Rishton, *Tower Journal*, Tierney-Dodd, vol. III, 155.

William Allen, *A Brief History of Twelve Reverend Priests* (ed. 1908), 68.

6

Wales, Ireland and Scotland

51 John Strype, *Life and Acts of Archbishop Whitgift* (ed. 1822), vol. I, 165-6.

52 Nicholas Robinson, Bishop of Bangor, to Sir William Cecil, 7 October 1567. P.R.O., Dom. Eliz., vol. xliv, no. 27.

53 Anonymous, *Report on Wales*, 1575 (MS. Lansd. 3, art. 4). Quoted in Henry Ellis, *Original Letters*, Second Series, vol. III, 49-50.

Richard Price of Brecknock to Lord Burghley, 31 January 1575. (MS. Lansd. 21, art. 32. *Orig.*). Henry Ellis, *Original Letters*, Second Series, vol. III, 47-8.

54 A Letter from Matthew Hutton, Archbishop of York, to John Whitgift, Archbishop of Canterbury, 20 May 1600. *The Correspondence of Dr. Matthew Hutton* (Surtees Society, vol. xvii, 1843), 154-5.

Stories from Scotland. C.S.P., Spanish, vol. iv, 591 (undated).

7

Compulsory Church-going

56 Robert Persons, *A Brief Discourse containing certain reasons why Catholics refuse to go to Church* (1580), 5-6.

Robert Persons to Fr. Agazarri, 17 November 1580. Quoted in Foley, *Jesuits in Conflict*, 164.

York Civic Records (Yorkshire Archaeological Society), vol. vii, 130, 131, 132, 133, 134, 135.

58 Answers of William Bowman and his wife to the Lord Mayor and aldermen of York, 20 November 1576. Ibid.

An Ancient Editor's Note Book. Cf. Morris, *Troubles*, Third Series, 21.

59 *William Weston* (Autobiography, translated by Philip Caraman), 148.

Page

60 Sir Simonds D'Ewes, *Journals of all the Parliaments of Elizabeth* (ed. 1682), 30.

61 Robert Persons to Claude Aquaviva, 17 November 1580. Cf. Richard Simpson, *Edmund Campion*, 244.

Ibid., 246.

Robert Persons, *A Brief Discourse containing certain reasons why Catholics refuse to go to Church* (1580), 55-6.

62 *Lives of Philip Howard and Anne Dacres* (ed. 1857), 170.

Edward Rishton, *Tower Journals*, Tierney-Dodd, vol. III, 152.

8

The Queen

64 Greenwich, 6 December 1559. G. B. Harrison, *Letters of Queen Elizabeth*, 29-31.

Queen Elizabeth to the House of Lords, 20 May 1585. Sir Simonds D'Ewes, *Journals of all the Parliaments of Elizabeth* (ed. 1682), 328-9.

65 Nicolas Sander, *Anglican Schism* (ed. 1877), 286-7.

John Nichols, *The Progresses of Queen Elizabeth* (1561), vol. I, 64-7.

67 Queen Elizabeth to James VI, King of Scotland. G. B. Harrison, *The Letters of Queen Elizabeth*, 182.

Queen Elizabeth to her Ambassador, Sir Francis Walsingham, 2 September 1571, reporting her discussions with Paul de Foix, French Ambassador, concerning her proposed marriage with Anjou. G. B. Harrison, ibid., 101.

68 John Baptista Castagna, late Archbishop of Rossano, Nuncio at Venice, to Ptolomy Galli, Cardinal of Como, 11 June 1575. C.S.P., Rome (1572-78), 207.

Sir John Harington, *Nugae Antiquae* (ed. 1779), vol. I, 4.

Sir John Harington, ibid., 30-1.

Robert Persons, Epistle Dedicatory to *A Brief Discourse containing certain reasons why Catholics refuse to go to Church* (1580).

69 Richard Shacklock, *The Hatchet of Heresies* (1565), Preface.

Diary of John Manningham, 12 February 1602 (Camden Society, vol. xcix), 130-1.

70 Robert Markham, to John Harington, 1598. *Nugae Antiquae*, vol. II, 291-2.

Sir Robert Sydney to John Harington, 1600. Ibid., 255.

Henry Garnet to Robert Persons, 19 November 1594. Stonyhurst, *Anglia*, i, no. 82.

Journal of Paul Hentzner's Travels in England. Cf. W. B. Rye, *England as seen by Foreigners* (1865), 104-5.

Page

71 Sir Robert Cecil to Sir George Carew, 24 October 1602. C.S.P., Carew (1601-3), 362.

Anthony Rivers to Robert Persons, 13 January 1601. Foley, *Records*, I, 8.

9

Ministers and Preachers

72 The humble Petition of the Commons to the House of Lords, 25 February 1585. Sir Simonds D'Ewes, *Journals of all the Parliaments of Elizabeth* (ed. 1682), 357.

John Strype, *The Life of Bishop Aylmer* (ed. 1821), 190.

73 Anon., *A Brief Admonition unto the new made Ministers of England* (1565), A. iv-v.

John Stow, *Memoranda* (Camden Society, New Series, vol. xxviii), 127.

Anon., *A Brief Admonition unto the new made Ministers of England* (1565), B. i-ii.

74 Thomas Hill, *A Quatron of Reasons* (1600), 84-5.

75 James Pilkington, Lord Bishop of Durham, Preface to *Exposition upon the Prophet Aggeus*, 1562. *Works*, vol. 3 (Parker Society), 6.

John Strype, *Life and Acts of John Whitgift* (ed. 1822), vol. I, 15.

10

Anabaptists and Others

76 John Stow, *Memoranda* (Camden Society, New Series, vol. xxviii), 115.

Ibid., 143.

77 John Strype, *Annals* (ed. 1824), vol. II, part I, 355.

John Strype, ibid., 562-4.

78 John Strype, ibid., 486-7.

Raphael Holinshed, *Chronicles*, iii, 1354, col. 2, l. 62.

John Strype, *Life and Acts of Archbishop Whitgift* (ed. 1822), vol. I, 472.

79 Robert Southwell to Claude Aquaviva, 26 August 1587. Arch. S.J., Rome, Fondo Gesuitico, 651.

11

Persecution

80 William Allen, *A True and Sincere Defence of English Catholics* (1584), 218.

William Allen, *Admonition to English Catholics*, quoted in A. C. Southern's *Elizabethan Recusant Prose, 1559-1582*, 270-1.

Page

81 George Gardiner, Dean of Norwich, to John Parkhurst, Bishop of Norwich, 8 April 1574. Strype, *Annals* (ed. 1824), vol. II, part I, 497-8.

William Allen to Alphonsus Agazarri, 23 June 1581. C.S.P., Dom. Eliz., vol. cxlix, no. 51 (Translation).

82 William Weston to Robert Persons, May or June 1586. Stonyhurst, *Anglia*, i, no. 28.

Edmund Campion to Claude Aquaviva, 17 November 1580. Cf. R. Simpson, *Edmund Campion*, 249.

William Weston (Autobiography translated by Philip Caraman), 31-3.

84 William Allen, *A True and Sincere Defence of English Catholics* (1584), 42-3.

Robert Persons to Claude Aquaviva, November 1580. Cf. R. Simpson. *Edmund Campion*, 245.

Proceedings against Mrs. Wiseman, 30 June 1598. C.R.S., vol. 5, 367.

85 Lady Babthorpe's *Recollections*. Cf. Morris, *Troubles*, First Series, 245-6.

An Ancient Editor's Note Book. Cf. Morris, *Troubles*, Third Series, 26.

Ibid., 30.

Stonyhurst MSS., Grene, *M*, 65.

Ibid., 65.

86 Robert Southwell, *An Humble Supplication* (ed. R. C. Bald), 33-4.

12

The Mass

88 Gregory Martin, *A Discourse of the Manifold Corruptions of the Holy Scriptures* (1582), 72-5, 97.

89 Norton's translation of Alexander Nowell's *Catechism*, 1570 (Parker Society), 215.

90 Ibid., 214.

Robert Persons to Fr. Agazarri, July 1581. Quoted in Foley, *Jesuits in Conflict*, 162.

John Jewel to Peter Martyr (no date). *Zurich Letters* (Parker Society), 24.

Life and Death of M. Edmund Gennings (1615), 63-4.

91 Relation of the sufferings of Mr. Thomas Woodhouse sent to Rome by Fr. H. Garnet and written by a fellow-prisoner. Arch. Col. Angl. Rome.

Presentments before Session of the Peace, Lancaster, 16 July 1590. Chetham Society, N.S., vol. lxxvii, Lancashire Quarter Sessions Records, I, 12.

Cf. *The Month*, August 1956, 106-7.

92 Dorothy Arundell, *Life of Fr. Cornelius*. Cf. Foley, *Records*, III, 445; *William Weston* (Autobiography, translated by Philip Caraman), 67.

Thomas Hill, *A Quatron of Reasons* (1600), 66-7.

93 Bernardino de Mendoza to the King of Spain, 26 June 1580. C.S.P. Spanish, vol. iii, 1580-86, 38.

Henry Garnet, *The Society of the Rosary* (1583), 204-6.

13

Douai and Rome

Page

94 Thomas Worthington, *A Relation of Sixteen Martyrs* (1601), 53-4.

95 Epistle to His Holiness [Clement VIII] of the English Priests united with the Archpriest, printed as Preface to *A Briefe Apologie* (20 July 1601).

96 Nicolas Sander, *Anglican Schism* (ed. 1877), 299-300.

Thomas Worthington, *A Relation of Sixteen Martyrs* (1601), 56-8.

97 *Life and Death of M. Edmund Gennings* (1615), 1 B, 42-3.

98 Report sent by Richard Bancroft to Robert Cecil, 27 April 1602. C.S.P., Dom. Eliz., vol. cclxxxiii, A, no. 86, II.

Bernardino de Mendoza to the King of Spain, 6 May 1583. C.S.P. Spanish, vol. iii, 1580-86, 471.

Anthony Munday, *The English Roman Life* (1590). Harleian Miscellany (ed. 1746), vol. vii, 137-40.

100 Robert Southwell, *An Humble Supplication* (ed. R. C. Bald), 7-8.

101 Robert Persons to Claude Aquaviva, November 1580. Cf. R. Simpson, *Edmund Campion*, 246.

John Chamberlain to Mr. Dudley Carleton, 27 May 1601. *Letters written by John Chamberlain* (Camden Society, vol. lxxix), 109.

102 Bernardino de Mendoza to the King of Spain, 1 October 1581. C.S.P. Spanish, vol. iii, 1580-86, 177.

Robert Persons, *The First Entrance of the Fathers of the Society of Jesus into England*. Stonyhurst MSS., Grene, *P*, I, 7-8.

103 Robert Persons, MS. *Life of Edmund Campion*. Stonyhurst MSS. Grene, *P*, 109-10.

Cardinal Allen to the Catholics of England, Rome, 12 December 1592, *Letters and Memorials of Cardinal Allen* (ed. T. F. Knox), vol. ii, 344-5.

14

Secret Arrivals

105 John Gerard, *Narrative of the Gunpowder Plot. The Condition of Catholics under James I*, 279-81.

106 *Life and Death of M. Edmund Gennings* (1615), 47-51.

108 William Allen to Fr. Agazarri. 23 June 1581. S.P. Dom. Eliz., vol. cxlix, no. 51 (Translation).

The Proclamation against Jesuits, 21 November 1591. *Proclamations*, pp. 298, 301. John Strype's *Annals*, vol. IV, 56, 62. Quoted in Harrison's *Elizabethan Journals*, vol. I, 76.

Page

129 Anthony Atkinson to Sir Robert Cecil, 24 October 1593. C.R.S., vol. V, 1584-1603, 221-2.

William Chaderton, Bishop of Chester, to Sir Francis Walsingham, 28 November 1583. Ibid., 46.

Recorded statement of Hilary Dakins, January 1595. Hat. Cal., v, 98.

Enclosure in letter from William Chaderton, Bishop of Chester, to the Earl of Derby, 23 May 1585. C.R.S., vol. I, 1584-1603, 111.

130 Hatfield Calendar, xi, 365.

C.S.P., Dom. Eliz., vol. clxv, no. 21.

Letter from Jasper Haywood to William Allen, 16 April 1583, from a deciphered copy in the Archives of the See of Westminster (*Records of English Catholics*, 352, 353). Foley, *Records*, IV, 679-80.

131 Robert Persons, *A Manifestation of Great Folly* (1602), 83-4.

16

The English Nuns

133 Dr. Nicolas Sander's Report to Cardinal Morone (May 1561). C.R.S., vol. I, 43 (Translation).

Chronicle of St. Monica's, edited by Adam Hamilton, O.S.B. (1906), vol. II, 166-8.

135 Stonyhurst MSS., Grene, P, 578.

English Benedictine Nuns in Flanders (1598-1687), C.R.S., vol. 6, 2-3.

136 *Chronicle of St. Monica's*, edited by Adam Hamilton, O.S.B., vol. I, 34-6.

138 Ibid. vol. I, 34.

Ibid. 96-8.

17

Exiles

140 Nicolas Sander, *Anglican Schism*, 261-3.

141 Robert Persons, *First Entry of the Fathers of the Society of Jesus into England*, Stonyhurst MSS., Grene, P, i, 5.

Maurice Baring, *Robert Peckham*, 279 (cf. A. J. C. Hare, *Walks in Rome*, vol. I, 226 for Latin inscription).

Lord Burghley to Sir Thomas Copley, 28 December 1574. *Letters of Sir Thomas Copley*, ed. by Richard Copley Christie (Roxburghe Club), 36.

Sir Thomas Copley to Lord Burghley, 25 February 1575. Ibid., 47.

142 Letter of Gregory Martin to his sisters. Gregory Martin, *Treatise of Christian Peregrination and Relics* (1583), Appendix.

William Allen, *An Apologie of the English Seminaries* (1581), 12a-13a.

Page

143 Nicolas Sander, *Anglican Schism*, 327-32.

145 R. Challoner, *Memoirs of Missionary Priests*, 109-10.

Arnold Harris Mathew and Annette Calthrop, *The Life of Sir Tobie Mathew* (1907), 76.

18

Controversy

147 William Allen, *A Defense and Declaration of the Catholic Church's Doctrine* (1565), 285-8.

149 William Allen, *A True and Sincere Defence of English Catholics* (1584), 35, 39.

151 Robert Persons, *A Declaration of the Trial made before the King of France upon the year 1600* (1604), 58-60.

152 William Allen, *A True and Sincere Defence of English Catholics* (1584), 45-8.

153 Thomas Harding, *Reioindre* (1577), sig. NNN1v.

154 Robert Persons, *The Warn-Word to Sir Francis Hasting's Ward-Word* (1602), 89-90.

Thomas Hill, *A Quatron of Reasons* (1600), 40-1.

155 Bishop Jewel to Henry Bullinger, 1 March 1565. *Zurich Letters* (Parker Society), 138-9.

James Pilkington, Bishop of Durham, to the Privy Council, 22 November 1564. Camden Miscellany, no. 9, 67.

John Strype, *Annals* (ed. 1824), vol. II, part I, 498.

156 Richard Cox, Bishop of Ely, to Rodolph Gualter, 4 February 1573. *Zurich Letters* (Parker Society), 281.

Richard Shacklock, Preface to his translation of Osorius' letter to Queen Elizabeth (1565).

Letter-Book of Gabriel Harvey, Camden Society (1884), 78.

157 John Strype, *The Life of Bishop Aylmer* (ed. 1821), 181.

Nicolas Sander, *Anglican Schism* (ed. 1877), 335.

19

Exhortation and Complaint

158 William Weston to Robert Persons, 10 May 1587. Arch. S.J., Rome, Fondo Gesuitico 651.

Robert Southwell, *An Epistle of Comfort* (1587), 124.

159 Robert Southwell, *The Triumphs over Death* (1596), in *Archaica* (ed. E. Brydges, 1815), 18.

Page

159 Edmund Campion to Richard Cheney, Bishop of Gloucester. Written at Douai in 1572. *The Rambler*, vol. viii, 60.

161 William Allen, *An Apologie of the English Seminaries* (1581), 105a-b.

162 Robert Southwell, *The Triumphs over Death* (1596), in *Archaica* (ed. E. Brydges, 1815), 17.
   Robert Southwell, ibid., 18.
   Robert Southwell, *An Epistle of Comfort* (1587), 203-4.
   Robert Southwell, *An Epistle of Comfort*, 97.

163 William Allen, *A True and Sincere Defence of English Catholics* (1584), 16-17.
   William Allen, ibid., 33.
   Robert Southwell, *An Humble Supplication* (ed. R. C. Bald), 40-1.

164 Robert Southwell to Claude Aquaviva, 31 August 1588, Christopher Devlin, *The Life of Robert Southwell, Poet and Martyr* (1956), 172.
   Verses among Blundell papers. *Crosby Records* (Chetham Society, New Series) vol. xii, 28-30.

165 Ibid. Concluding stanzas of verses entitled *A Cry for Relief* (c. 1592).

20

Practice and Belief

166 Robert Southwell, *Short Rules of Good Life*, *Works* (ed. 1620).
   Robert Southwell, ibid.

168 *The Life and Death of Philip Howard*, 105-11.

170 Lawrence Vaux, *Catechism* 1583 (Chetham Society, New Series) vol. iv, 9.
   Ibid., 15.

171 Ibid., 18.
   Ibid., 57-8.
   Ibid., 87-8.

172 Ibid., 83.
   Henry Fitzsimon, *Justification of the Masse*, chap. iii, 115. Quoted in Foley *Jesuits in Conflict*, 228.
   Gregory Martin, *A Treatise of Christian Peregrination* (1583), C-D.

173 Richard Young to the Lord Keeper, 23 December 1592. C.S.P., Dom. Eliz., vol. ccxliii, no. 93.
   Thomas Hill, *A Quatron of Reasons* (1600), 64-5.
   The State Civil and Ecclesiastical of the Co. of Lancaster, 1590. Chetham Miscellanies, v (Chetham Society, O.S., vol. xcvi), 5-6.

174 Sixteenth-century carol found among the Royal MSS., British Museum. Cf. *The Ransomer*, Christmas 1948, vol. xii, No. 7, 9.

Page

175 Boyes' Sandwich, 251, quoting John Weever, *Funeral Monuments*, 179. Cf. Edward Peacock, *A List of the Roman Catholics in the County of York in 1604* (1872), 33.

21

At Prayer

176 John Mush, *Life of Margaret Clitherow*. Cf. Morris, *Troubles*, Third Series, 393-4.

William Peryn, *Spiritual Exercises* (ed. 1557), f. Ri.

177 William Peryn, ibid., f. 1, lv.

William Peryn, ibid.

John Bucke, *On the Use of Beads* (1589), 77.

A Manual of Prayers (ed. 1595).

178 Robert Southwell, *Mary Magdalen's Funeral Tears*. Quoted in Christopher Devlin, *The Life of Robert Southwell*, 80.

Robert Southwell, *Works*, ed. 1620.

179 *A Manual of Prayers* (ed. 1595).

180 Swithin Wells. Cf. L. I. Guiney, *Recusant Poets*, 174.

181 Robert Persons, *A Christian Directory guiding men to their eternal salvation* (1673), 362-3.

Robert Persons, ibid., 438-40.

183 *The Sonnets of William Alabaster*, edited by G. M. Story and Helen Gardner. (Oxford University Press, 1959), 13.

Robert Southwell, *Short Rules of Good Life*. *Works* (ed. 1620).

185 Robert Southwell, ibid.

186 Prayer of Edward Throgmorton, student at the English College, Rome. Foley, *Records*, IV, 329.

187 Francis Tregian. Cf. L. I. Guiney, *Recusant Poets*, 197-8.

188 *A Manual of Prayers* (ed. 1595).

189 Ibid., 2.

From the Fifth Petition, *Jesus Psalter* (ed. 1575), quoted in A. C. Southern, *Elizabethan Recusant Prose, 1559-82*, 222-3.

190 From the Twelfth Petition. Ibid., 223.

Alexander B. Grosart, *The Complete Poems of Robert Southwell* (1872), 109.

22

Layfolk

192 Petition of loyal Catholics to the Queen, 1585. H.M.C., *Various*, vol. III, 40-1.

193 John Mush, *Life of Margaret Clitherow*. Cf. Morris, *Troubles*, Third Series, 387.

Page

193 An Ancient Editor's Note Book. Cf. Morris, *Troubles*, Third Series, 52. Stonyhurst MSS., Grene, *M*, 76.

The Correspondence of Dr. Matthew Hutton (1594), (Surtees Society, vol. xvii, 1843), 97-8.

194 Matthew Parker, Archbishop of Canterbury, to the Privy Council (1568). C.S.P., Dom. Eliz., vol. xlvii, no. 12.

195 Form of submission offered to John Southworth and rejected. C.S.P., Dom. Eliz., vol. xlvii, no. 12 no. 1.

196 Edmund Grindal, Bishop of London, to Sir William Cecil, 3 August 1569. *Remains of Archbishop Grindal* (Parker Society), 305.

Statement by Robert Colton of Wisbech. H.M.C., 12th Report, Appendix, Part iv, 334-6. (There the name is given as Dowlton, a misreading of Colton in the manuscript).

198 *Chronicle of St. Monica's*, edited by Adam Hamilton, O.S.B., vol. I, 82-4.

199 Fr. Pollard's Relation of the Persecution in the North, Stonyhurst, *Anglia*, iii, 100.

200 Foley, *Records*, IV, 539.
Cf. Foley, *Records*, III, 233-6.

201 *The Life and Death of Philip Howard, Earl of Arundel*, 212-14.

202 Richard Smith, *The Life of Lady Magdalen, Viscountess Montague*, translated into English by C.P. (1627), 26.
Richard Smith, ibid., 28-9.

203 Richard Smith, ibid., 29.
John Gerard, *Narrative of the Gunpowder Plot* (ed. by John Morris), 182-90.

207 Stonyhurst MSS., Grene, *M*, 144.
Stonyhurst MSS. Grene, *M*, 149a. Cf. *William Weston* (Autobiography, translated by Philip Caraman), 54.
John Gerard, *Narrative of the Gunpowder Plot*, 88-90.

209 An Ancient Editor's Note Book. Cf. Morris, *Troubles*, Third Series, 51.

23

Pursuivants

210 William Warford, *Relation of Martyrs*. Stonyhurst MSS., Grene, *M*.
Chronicle of St. Monica's, edited by Adam Hamilton, O.S.B., (1906), vol. II, 165-6.

211 An Ancient Editor's Note Book. Cf. Morris, *Troubles*, Third Series, 58.
Henry Garnet to Thomas Strange, 30 June 1601. Stonyhurst MSS., Grene, *P*, 553.

212 *Chronicle of St. Monica's*, edited by Adam Hamilton, O.S.B., (1906), vol. II, 114-15.

Page

213 Richard Welford, *History of Newcastle and Gateshead*, vol. iii, 71.

An Ancient Editor's Note Book. Cf. Morris, *Troubles*, Third Series, 19.

214 Ibid., 59.

Stonyhurst MSS., Grene, *M*, 145.

24

Prison

215 Laurence Vaux, from his prison in Westminster, to the prior of St. Martin's, 20 October 1580. *The Rambler*, December 1857, 412.

Bernardino de Mendoza to the King of Spain, 4 July 1581. C.S.P., Spanish, vol. iii, 1580-6, 139-40.

216 Richard Vaughan, Bishop of Chester, to Thomas Hesketh, 29 January 1598. C.S.P., Dom. Eliz. vol. ccxlvi, no. 32.

An Ancient Editor's Note Book. Cf. Morris, *Troubles*, Third Series, 33.

C.R.S., vol. 8, 29-30.

218 Bernardino de Mendoza to the King of Spain, 1 October 1581. C.S.P., Spanish, vol. iii, 1580-6, 177.

219 Certificate of Keeper of the Gatehouse, 21 November 1581. C.S.P., Dom. Eliz., vol. cl, no. 65.

Stonyhurst MSS., Grene, *M*, 19.

220 Relation of the sufferings of Mr. Thomas Woodhouse sent to Rome by Fr. Garnet and written by a fellow-prisoner. Arch. Col. Angl., Rome.

The Life and Death of Philip Howard, 112-21.

223 Dorothy Arundell, *Life of Fr. John Cornelius*. Foley, *Records*, III, 449.

Letter from Fr. John Bodey, in prison, 16 September 1593. Stonyhurst MSS., Grene, *N*, ii, 40-2.

224 Stonyhurst MSS., Grene, *M*, 55.

Cf. *William Weston* (Autobiography, translated by Philip Caraman), 227.

225 The Justices of Dover to Francis Walsingham. Dom. Eliz., undated, 1586. Foley, *Records*, III, 431.

226 C.S.P., Dom. Eliz., vol. cxviii, no. 49.

25

Trial

227 Fr. John Bennet to William Hughes, Bishop of St. Asaph, 1583. Foley, *Records*, IV, 504.

John Strype, *Life and Death of Archbishop Whitgift* (ed. 1822), vol. I, 578.

Evelyn Waugh, *Edmund Campion*, 205-6.

228 William Allen, *A True and Sincere Defence of English Catholics* (1584), 16.

Page

228 Foley, *Records*, III, 455.

229 John Mush, *Life of Margaret Clitherow*, Cf. Morris. *Troubles*, Third Series, 426-7.

Cf. Morris, *Troubles*, Third Series, 383-4.

230 Stonyhurst MSS., Grene, *M*, 56.

Stonyhurst MSS., *Anglia*, ii, no. 1.

John Morris, *Troubles*, Third Series, 204.

231 Stonyhurst MSS., Catalogue of Martyrs, *Anglia*, vii, no. 26.

The Examination of John Bennet, cf. Foley, *Records*, IV, 506.

Stonyhurst MSS., Grene, *M*, 22.

Stonyhurst MSS., Grene, *P*, 546.

26

Torture

233 William Allen, *A True and Sincere Defence of English Catholics* (1584), 29-30.

Ibid. 14-15.

234 Bernardino de Mendoza to the King of Spain, 12 August 1581. C.S.P., Spanish, vol. iii, 1580-6, 153.

Bernardino de Mendoza to the King of Spain, 11 December 1581. Ibid., 237.

Thomas Hill, *A Quatron of Reasons* (1600), 136-8.

235 Stonyhurst, *Anglia*, i, 66 and Grene, *N*, ii, 22-4.

236 *John Gerard* (Autobiography, translated by Philip Caraman), 107-11.

239 Stonyhurst, *Anglia*, ii, no. 27. Original in Italian.

William Allen, *A True and Sincere Defence of English Catholics* (1584), 10-11.

240 Stonyhurst MSS., Grene, *M*, 158.

241 Bernardino de Mendoza to the King of Spain, 4 December 1581. C.S.P., Spanish, vol. iii, 153.

William Allen, *Father Edmund Campion and his Companions* (ed. 1908), 13-14.

Edward Rishton, *Tower Journal*. Tierney-Dodd, vol. III, 150.

242 Ibid., 156, 157.

Ibid., 151.

Ibid., 155.

Ibid., 155.

243 Stonyhurst MSS., Grene, *M*, 82-3.

Letter of Alexander Briant. Cf. Foley, *Records*, IV, 357.

Stonyhurst MSS., Grene, *M*, 191.

244 Ibid., 15.

Ibid., 82.

27

The Eve of Execution

Page

245 Diego de Yepez, *History of the Reformation in England.*

247 Robert Southwell to Claude Aquaviva, 8 March 1590. *The Rambler,* New Series, vol. vii, 105.

248 John Gerard, *Catalogue of Martyrs.* Stonyhurst MSS., *Anglia,* vii, no. 26. Stonyhurst MSS., Grene, *M,* 26-7.
William Allen, *Father Edmund Campion and his Companions* (1908), 43.

249 Letter of Ralph Sherwin in the Tower to his friends on the eve of his execution, quoted in A. C. Southern's *Elizabethan Recusant Prose, 1559-82,* 278.

28

The Gallows

250 John Stow, *Annals* (1631), 750.
John Mush, *Life of Margaret Clitherow,* Cf. Morris, *Troubles,* Third Series, 430-2.

252 Stonyhurst MSS., Grene, *M,* 183.
Thomas Worthington, *A Relation of Sixteen Martyrs* (1601), 29-33.

255 Stonyhurst MSS., Grene, *M,* 65.
Ibid., 283.
Ibid., 5.

256 Stonyhurst MSS., Catalogue of Martyrs, *Anglia,* vii, no. 26.
Stonyhurst MSS., Grene, *F,* 3.
Henry Garnet to Claude Aquaviva, 17 March 1593. C.R.S., vol. I, p. 232 (Translation).
Contemporary account sent to Fr. Persons. Stonyhurst MSS., Grene, *M,* 107-8.

258 Stonyhurst MSS., Grene, *M,* 160.
Stonyhurst MSS., Grene, *N,* ii, 43.
Relation of Fr. James Young. Stonyhurst MSS., *Anglia,* vi, 117.

260 Henry Garnet to Robert Persons, 7 April 1598. Stonyhurst MSS., Grene, *P,* 548.
Stonyhurst MSS., Grene, *M,* 154.
Richard Walford, *History of Newcastle and Gateshead,* vol. III, 70-1.

261 Ibid., 87.
Ibid., 86-7.

262 *The Manner of the Queen of Scots Death,* 8 February 1586 (Lansdowne MS. 51, art. 46), quoted in Henry Ellis, *Original Letters,* Second Series, vol. iii, 114-18.

265 *Life and Death of M. Edmund Gennings* (1615). An Appendix concerning M. Swithin Wells, 108-9.

Page

265 *Life and Death of M. Edmund Gennings* (1615), 84-5.

266 Stonyhurst MSS., Grene, *M*, 145-6.

29

Each in the Other's View

268 James Pilkington, Lord Bishop of Durham, *Exposition upon the Prophet Aggeus*, 1562. *Works*, vol. III, (Parker Society), 129-30.

269 Ibid.

James Pilkington, Lord Bishop of Durham, *Exposition upon the Prophet Abdias*, 1563. *Works*, vol. III, (Parker Society), 256.

270 William Overton, Bishop of Coventry, to Privy Council, 20 May 1582. John Strype, *Annals* (ed. 1824), vol. III, part II, 217.

Nicholas Daniel, Vicar of Preston, to Bishop Downham, Low Sunday, 1574. *Lancashire Chantries*, vol. ii (Chetham Society, vol. lx), O.S., 206-7.

Robert Burdet, *The Refuge of a Sinner* (1564-5). Herbert L. Collmann, *Ballads and Broadsides of the Elizabethan Period* (Roxburghe Club, 1912), 44.

Confession of faith of Ministers of Religion, 1571. John Strype, *Annals* (ed. 1824), vol. II, part I, 139.

271 James Pilkington, Bishop of Durham, *An Exposition upon Aggeus*, 1560. *Works* (Parker Society), 171.

Thomas Brooke, the younger. From *An Epitaphe declaryng the lyfe and end of D. Edmund Bonner* (1569). Herbert L. Collmann, *Ballads and Broadsides of the Elizabethan Period* (Roxburghe Club, 1912), 42-3.

272 James Pilkington, Bishop of Durham, *An Exposition upon Nehemiah*, 1585. *Works*, vol. 3, (Parker Society, 1842), 448.

Description of a Church Papist, Harleian MSS. 1221, no. 5.

273 William Whittaker, *Disputatio de Sacra Scriptura* (Parker Society), *Epistle Dedicatory*. Quoted, Christopher Devlin, *The Life of Robert Southwell*, 156.

John Stow, *Memoranda* (Camden Society, New Series xxviii), 133.

Lord Burghley, *The Execution of Justice in England* (1583), f. B.i.

Journal of Sir Roger Wilbraham, 30 September 1593 (Camden Miscellany, vol. x), 9.

274 Anthony Rivers to Robert Persons, 17 March 1602. Foley, *Records*, I, 25.

From a sermon of Mr. Fenton (reader of Gray's Inn) at St. Paul's Cross, 21 November 1602. *Manningham's Diary* (Camden Society, vol. xcix), 88.

Examination of Nicolas Flute of Dartmouth before two Justices of the Peace on his return from abroad, 16 August 1594. Hatfield Cal., vol. IV, 582.

Fynes Morison, *Itinerary* (ed. 1617), 102.

275 A true and strange discourse of the travels of two English pilgrims, by Henry Timberlake. *Harleian Miscellany*, vol. I, 330-42.

Page

277 *Diary of John Manningham*, 12 February 1602 (Camden Society, vol. xcix), 131.

John Chamberlain to Mr. Dudley Carleton, 26 April 1602. *Letters written by John Chamberlain* (Camden Society, vol. lxxix), 125.

Mr. Harper to a Catholic Friend, 24 January 1592. Hatfield Cal., vol. IV, 175-6.

278 1573. John Strype, Annals (ed. 1824), vol. II, part I, 467.

Thomas Hill, *A Quatron of Reasons* (1600), 85-6.

William Allen, *An Admonition to the Nobility* (1585), 29-30.

279 John Parkhurst to Henry Bullinger, 26 April 1562. *Zurich Letters* (Parker Society), 108.

Thomas Hill, *A Quatron of Reasons* (1600), 129-32.

280 Robert Southwell, *An Epistle of Comfort* (ed. 1596), 92-3.

30

Third Chronicle

282 William Allen to the Rector of the English College, Rome, 23 June 1581. C.S.P., Dom. Eliz., vol. cxlix, no. 51 (Translation).

Robert Persons to Fr. Agazarri, 17 November 1580. Quoted in Foley, *Jesuits in Conflict*, 165.

Westminster Archives, vol. II, 185.

Richard Verstegan, *The True Causes of the Great Troubles* (1592), 54.

283 Bryan Stapleton, *Catholic Missions in Oxfordshire* (1906), 7.

The State Civil and Ecclesiastical of the Co. of Lancaster, 1590. Chetham Miscellanies, V (Chetham Society, O.S., vol. xcvi), 3.

Stonyhurst MSS., Grene, *F*, 5.

284 An Ancient Editor's Note Book. Cf. Morris, *Troubles*, Third Series, 59.

Henry Garnet to Claude Aquaviva, 26 August 1587. Arch. S.J. Rome, Fondo Gesuitico, 651.

Fr. Anthony Rivers to Robert Persons, 18 January 1601. Foley, *Records*, I, 7.

Edward Peacock, *A List of the Roman Catholics in the County of York in 1604* (1872), Wathe super Dearne, 8.

Fr. Richard Blount to Robert Persons, 22 October 1600. Stonyhurst MSS., Grene, *M*, 96.

285 Fr. Anthony Rivers to Robert Persons, 18 January 1601. Foley, *Records*, I, 24.

Diary of John Manningham, 24 March 1603. Camden Society, vol. xcix, 146-7.

A true relation of what succeeded in the sickness and death of queen Elizabeth, by Lady Southwell, maid of honour to Elizabeth I. Stonyhurst MSS., *Anglia*, iii, 77.

287 *William Weston* (Autobiography, translated by Philip Caraman), 221-2.

Biographical Notes

AGAZARRI, ALPHONSUS (1549-1602): born in Siena; Jesuit 1567; Rector of the English College, Rome; wrote the life of Edward Throckmorton.

AGLIONBY, EDWARD: Member of Parliament for Warwick (1571).

ALABASTER, WILLIAM (1567-1640): poet and divine; wrote *Roxana*; chaplain to Essex expedition to Cadiz (1596); became Catholic (1596); imprisoned; reverted to Protestantism.

ALLEN, WILLIAM (1532-1594): fellow of Oriel College, Oxford (1550); Principal of St. Mary Hall (1556); went into exile at Louvain (1561); visited Lancashire, and vigorously opposed occasional conformity (1562-5); principal founder of seminary at Douai (1570); helped also in foundation of seminary in Rome; Cardinal (1587).

ANDERSON, SIR EDMUND (1530-1605); Lincoln College, Oxford; studied at Inner Temple (1550); serjeant-at-law (1577); Lord Chief Justice of Common Pleas (1582); took part in trial of Babington and of Mary Queen of Scots, also in trials of Essex and Raleigh.

ANTHONY, ST. (*c.* 251-356): father of western monasticism; born at Como, Italy; retired to desert of Upper Egypt and collected disciples; personal friend of Athanasius, who wrote his life.

AQUAVIVA, CLAUDE (1543-1615): General of the Society of Jesus (1581-1615): previously Provincial of the Provinces of Naples and Rome.

AQUINAS, ST. THOMAS (1225-1274): Dominican philosopher; theologian; Doctor of the Church.

ARUNDEL, EARL OF, *see* HOWARD, BL. PHILIP.

ARUNDELL, DOROTHY: wife of Sir John Arundell of Lanherne, Cornwall; widowed at the time of Fr. Cornelius's arrest at Chideock Castle, Dorset (14 April 1594).

AYLMER, JOHN (1521-1594): tutor to Lady Jane Grey; in exile under Mary; Archdeacon of Lincoln (1562); Bishop of London (1577).

BABTHORPE, LADY (d. 1635): daughter of William Brimham of Knaresborough; married Sir Ralph Babthorpe; on death of her husband she entered St. Monica's convent, Louvain; professed (1621).

BALES, BL. CHRISTOPHER (d. 1590): born Coniscliffe, Co. Durham; educated at English College, Rome and at Rheims; ordained (1587); English mission (1588); executed 4 March 1590.

BANCROFT, RICHARD (1544-1610): educated Christ's College, Cambridge; prebendary of St. Paul's (1590); chaplain to Archbishop Whitgift (1592); Bishop of London (1597); Archbishop of Canterbury (1604); Chancellor of University of Oxford (1608); his works are principally directed against the puritans.

BANGOR, BISHOP OF, *see* ROBINSON, NICHOLAS (1566-1585).

BARNES, RICHARD (1532-1587): fellow of Brasenose College, Oxford (1552); Chancellor of York (1561); Bishop of Carlisle (1570); Bishop of Durham (1577).

BEESLEY, VEN. GEORGE (d. 1591): born in Lancashire; ordained at Rheims (1587); English mission (1588); captured; tortured by Topcliffe; executed with Fr. Montford Scott, 2 July 1591.

BELL, JAMES (fl. 1551-1596): reformer; fellow of Trinity College, Oxford (1556): assiduous translator of Protestant works.

BENNET, JOHN (1548-1625): at school at St. Asaph; studied at Douai; English mission (1580); worked in North Wales; arrested (1582); condemned to death, but reprieved and tortured in Ludlow Castle; banished, but returned; Jesuit (1586); died attending to London victims of the plague.

BICKERDICK, VEN. ROBERT (d. 1586): born near Knaresborough, West Riding, Yorks; apprentice; arrested for speaking in praise of the martyr, Fr. Ingleby; tried and found not guilty; later re-tried and condemned; executed at York in July 1586.

BIRD, BL. JAMES (1574-1593): gentleman; for some time a student at Douai; arrested and condemned for being reconciled to Church; executed in his native city, Winchester, 25 March 1593.

BLACKALL, CHRISTOPHER: Catholic gentleman of the Temple; rescued one of the quarters of a martyred priest; subsequently caught and imprisoned.

BLOUNT, RICHARD (1565-1638): studied at Oxford, Rheims and English College, Rome; priest (1589); English mission (1591); Jesuit (1596); superior of English mission (1617); first Provincial (1623); died in London.

BOAST, BL. JOHN (1544-1594): born at Dufton, Westmorland; fellow of Queen's College, Oxford; studied at Rheims; priest (1581) worked in north of England and in Scotland; sent to London for trial and torture; and back to Durham for execution, 24 July 1594.

BODEY, BL. JOHN (1549-1583): born at Wells; educated at Winchester (1562) and New College, Oxford (1568); studied law and later became schoolmaster in Hampshire. Arrested at Mapledurham. Executed at Andover, 2 November 1583.

BONNER, EDMUND (1500-1559): chaplain to Wolsey; Bishop of London (1539); refused oath of supremacy and deprived (1559); died in Marshalsea.

BRIANT, BL. ALEXANDER (1553-1581): educated at Hart Hall, Oxford and at Rheims; ordained (1579); imprisoned and tortured in the Tower; executed with Campion, 1 December 1581. Admitted into the Society of Jesus in prison.

BRISTOW, RICHARD (1538-1581): educated Christ Church, Oxford; fellow of Exeter College (1567); director of studies at Douai; shared with Gregory Martin work of translating the Bible.

BROMLEY, SIR GEORGE: high sheriff of Flintshire (1563); examined Fr. John Bennet on matters of religion.

BRUSHFORD, JOHN (b. 1559): native of Devon; entered English College, Rome (1581); priest (1584); English mission (1585); died in prison.

BUCKLEY (*alias* JONES), BL. JOHN (d. 1598): born Clynog Fawr, Caernarvon. At first a Conventual, then an Observant, at the Franciscan monastery at Ara Coeli in Rome (1591); English mission (1592-7); executed at St. Thomas Watering, 12 July 1598.

BULLINGER, HENRY (1504-1575): Zwingli's successor and pastor of Grossmunster, Zurich; voluminous writer; very hospitable to English refugees under Mary.

BULLINGHAM, NICHOLAS (1512-1576): fellow of All Souls, Oxford (1536); chaplain to Cranmer; in exile under Mary; chaplain to Archbishop Parker; Bishop of Lincoln (1560), and of Worcester (1571).

BURGHLEY, LORD, *see* CECIL, WILLIAM.

BURROWS, FRANCES (d. 1637): daughter of Anthony Burrows of Burrow-on-the-Hill, Leicestershire; niece of Lord Vaux, whose cousin Mrs. Brookesby brought her up; entered St. Monica's convent, Louvain; professed (1597) along with Fr. Garnet's sister, Eleanor; died 6 March 1637.

CAMPION, BL. EDMUND (1540-1581): Educated Christ's Hospital; fellow of St. John's College, Oxford (1557); speaker at Queen Elizabeth's state visit to the University (1566); crossed to Douai; became Jesuit (1573); returned to England (1580); executed at Tyburn, 1 December 1581.

CANTERBURY, ARCHBISHOPS OF, *see* PARKER, MATTHEW (1559-1575); GRINDAL, EDMUND (1575-1583); WHITGIFT, JOHN (1583-1604).

CAREW, SIR GEORGE (d. 1612): lawyer and diplomat; M.P. for various Cornish boroughs (1584-1601); a master in Chancery (1599-1612); knighted (1603).

CARLETON, SIR DUDLEY (1573-1632): educated at Westminster School and Christ Church, Oxford; travelled (1595-1600); ambassador's secretary at Paris (1602-3); knighted (1610).

CARLISLE, BISHOPS OF, *see* OGLETHORPE, OWEN (1557-1559); BARNES, RICHARD (1570-1577).

CECIL, WILLIAM (1520-1598): educated at Grantham school and St. John's College, Cambridge; M.P. for Stamford (1547); Secretary of State (1550-53; 1558-72); knighted (1551); Chancellor of Cambridge University (1559); created Baron Burghley (Feb. 1571); Lord High Treasurer (1572-98).

CHADERTON (CHATTERTON), WILLIAM (1540-1608); born at Manchester; fellow of Christ's College, Cambridge (1558); Lady Margaret Professor of Divinity (1567-9); President of Queens' (1568-79); Regius Professor of Divinity (1569-80); Bishop of Chester (1579-95); translated to Lincoln (1595); made great efforts to suppress recusancy.

CHAMBERLAIN, JOHN (1553-1627): letter-writer; entered Trinity College, Cambridge (1570); his letters date from 1598 to 1625.

CHESTER, BISHOPS OF, *see* SCOT, CUTHBERT (deprived 1559); DOWNHAM, WILLIAM (1561-1577); CHADERTON, WILLIAM (1579-1595).

CHEYNEY, RICHARD (1513-1579); courtier of Edward VI; canon of Gloucester (1558), and of Westminster (1560); Bishop of Gloucester (1562).

CHICHESTER, BISHOP OF, *see* SCORY, JOHN (1552).

CLEMENT, MOTHER MARGARET: daughter of Margaret Clement (née Giggs), kinswoman of St. Thomas More, and John Clement;

professed nun of St. Ursula's, Louvain, 11 October 1569; died at St. Monica's, 1612.

CLITHEROW, BL. MARGARET (d. 1586): daughter of Thomas Middleton, wax-chandler of York; married (1571) John Clitherow, butcher; imprisoned and executed for refusing to plead in her desire to save the conscience of the jury.

COLE, THOMAS (d. 1571): master of Maidstone school (1552); exiled under Mary; prebendary of St. Paul's and Archdeacon of Essex.

COLTON, ROBERT: later changed his name to Thomas; son of Robert Colton, a Wisbech joiner. A year before the events he records in the statement, he set out for the English College, Valladolid with nine other boys under a tutor; they were captured at Chester, sent to London on foot, and imprisoned in Bridewell. Three months later Fr. Garnet reports that they were still there and 'hardly used.' This makes his subsequent courage all the more remarkable.

COPLEY, SIR THOMAS (1534-1584): of Gatton, Surrey; a favourite of Elizabeth; became a Catholic, imprisoned, and later went abroad; died in Flanders.

CORNELIUS, BL. JOHN (1557-1594): born at Bodmin, Cornwall, of Irish parents; studied at Oxford; then English College, Rome; priest and on English mission (1583); arrested at Chideock, Dorset, where he was chaplain to Lady Arundell; executed at Dorchester, 4 July 1594.

COTTAM, BL. THOMAS (1549-1582): born in Lancashire; educated Brasenose College, Oxford; studied at Douai and Rome; priest (1579); English mission (1580); executed at Tyburn, 30 May 1582.

COVENTRY AND LICHFIELD, BISHOP OF, *see* OVERTON, WILLIAM (1579-1609).

COWLING, RICHARD (1563-1617); native of York; entered English College, Rome (1581); priest (1587); English mission (1588); Jesuit (1589); worked mostly in north of England.

COX, RICHARD (1500-1581): Headmaster of Eton; Dean of Christ Church, Oxford; canon of Windsor; in exile (1554-8); Bishop of Norwich (1559); Bishop of Ely (1559-80).

CROWE, VEN. ALEXANDER (d. 1587): born at South Driffield, North Riding, Yorks; shoemaker by trade; followed his trade at Rheims; entered seminary there; priest (1583); arrested and executed at York, 30 November 1587.

DACRES, ANNE, COUNTESS OF ARUNDEL (1557-1630); daughter

of Thomas Lord Dacres; married (1571) Philip Howard, Earl of
Arundel; after her husband's imprisonment(1585)lived at Arundel
House, London, where Robert Southwell was her chaplain.

DAVIES, VEN. WILLIAM (d. 1593): born at Croes-yn-Eirias, Caernarvon; studied at Rheims; priest (1585); worked in Wales;
arrested at Holyhead conducting four students to Valladolid;
executed at Beaumaris, 21 July 1593.

DEAN, BL. WILLIAM, (d. 1588): born at Linton in Craven W.R.
Yorks., convert minister; ordained at Rheims 1581; executed for
priesthood at Mile End Green 28 August 1588.

DE PERALTA, FRANCIS(1554-1622): Spanish Jesuit; rector of the English
seminary in Seville; author of a brief life of William Weston.

DICKENSON, BL. ROGER (d. 1591): born at Lincoln; ordained priest
at Rheims (1583); executed 7 July 1591.

DIGBY, SIR EVERARD (1579-1606): courtier; convert and friend of
John Gerard; involved in Gunpowder Plot; executed (1606);
father of Sir Kenelm Digby.

DORMER, JANE, Duchess of Feria (1538-1612): companion of Queen
Mary; married Count of Feria, who came to England with
Philip II; founded monastery near Villalva.

DOWNHAM, WILLIAM (1505-1577): fellow of Magdalen College,
Oxford (1543); canon of Westminster (1560); Bishop of Chester
(1561-77); reported frequently to Council for remissness in
enforcing Act of Uniformity.

DURHAM, BISHOP OF, *see* TUNSTALL, CUTHBERT (1530-1559);
PILKINGTON, JAMES (1561-1576); BARNES, RICHARD (1577-
1587).

ELY, BISHOP OF, *see* COX, RICHARD (1559-1580).

FECKENHAM, JOHN (1518-1585): last Benedictine abbot of Westminster; monk of Evesham; confessor to Queen Mary (1553),
and saved twenty-eight victims from the stake at one time; abbot
of Westminster (1556); sent to Tower by Elizabeth (1559); died
in prison at Wisbech castle.

FELTON, BL. JOHN: Catholic layman; affixed Pius V's bull of excommunication of Elizabeth to gates of bishop of London's
palace; executed (1570).

FERIA, DUCHESS OF, *see* DORMER, JANE.

FILBY, BL. WILLIAM (d. 1582): born in Oxfordshire; educated Lincoln
College, Oxford; studied for priesthood at Rheims; ordained
and sent to England 1581; executed at Tyburn, 30 May, 1582.

FITZHERBERT, THOMAS (1552-1640): educated at Oxford; imprisoned there for recusancy (1572); after release assisted Persons and Campion; on death of wife retired to Continent; ordained at Rome (1602); Jesuit (1607); Rector of English College (1618-40).

FITZSIMON, HENRY (1566-1643): educated Hart Hall, Oxford; Jesuit (1592); professor of philosophy at Douai; sent on mission to Dublin and arrested there (1599); imprisoned there and disputed with Ussher.

FLEETWOOD, WILLIAM (1535-1594): barrister, Middle Temple; M.P. for Lancaster in first two Parliaments of Elizabeth; made recorder of London (1571) through Leicester's influence; notorious for vigorous enforcement of laws against Catholics.

FULKE, WILLIAM (1538-1589): Puritan divine and friend of Thomas Cartwright; chaplain to Leicester; disputed with Edmund Campion in the Tower; published works against Allen, Stapleton and other Catholics.

GARDINER, GEORGE (1535-1589): fellow of Queens' College, Cambridge; prebendary of Norwich (1565); Dean (1573-89).

GARLICK, VEN. NICHOLAS (1555-1588): born Dinting, Derbyshire; educated Gloucester Hall, Oxford; schoolmaster at Tidswell; studied at Rheims; priest (1581); worked in Derbyshire; executed at Derby, 24 July 1591.

GARNET, HENRY (1555-1606): educated Winchester; entered Society of Jesus in Rome (1575); professor at Roman College; English mission (1586); succeeded Weston as superior the same year; arrested and executed (1606).

GENNINGS, BL. EDMUND (1567-1591): educated at Rheims: worked under name of Ironmonger in the north, at Lichfield and in London; arrested in house of Swithin Wells; executed 10 December 1591.

GERARD, JOHN (1564-1637): second son of Sir Thomas Gerard of Bryn; educated at Oxford, Douai and English College, Rome; priest and Jesuit (1585); English mission same year; arrested (1594); escaped from Tower (1597); returned to Continent (1606).

GILBERT, GEORGE (d. 1583): founder with Thomas Pound of Belmont of the 'Catholic Association' for the assistance of priests; later became a Jesuit and died in Rome.

GITTER, JOHN, *see* JETTER, JOHN

GLOUCESTER, BISHOP OF, *see* CHEYNEY, RICHARD (1562-1579).

GOLDWELL, THOMAS (d. 1585): chaplain to Cardinal Pole; Bishop of

St. Asaph (1555); escaped to Continent (1559); attended Council of Trent (1562); vicar-general to St. Charles Borromeo, Archbishop of Milan.

GREEN, RICHARD (fl. 1580-1606): studied at Rheims and English College, Rome; priest on English mission (1586); admitted into Society of Jesus, *c.* 1606.

GREGORY XIII (UGO BUONCOMPAGNI) (1502-1585): born Bologna; Cardinal (1565); succeeded Pius V (1572); endowed English College, Rome, and the Roman College, now Gregorian University; reformed calendar (1582).

GRENE, CHRISTOPHER (1629-1697): Jesuit priest and historian; assembled papers (*Collectanea*), concerning Elizabethan persecution now principally at Stonyhurst.

GRINDAL, EDMUND (1519-1583): exile under Mary; Bishop of London (1559-70); Archbishop of York (1570-75); Archbishop of Canterbury (1576-83).

HAMONT, MATTHEW (d. 1579): heretic; burnt at Norwich. On his case Philip van Limborch corresponded with Locke in 1699.

HARDING, THOMAS (1516-1572): educated at Winchester and New College, Oxford; named Warden by Edward VI; treasurer of Salisbury (1555); returned to Louvain under Elizabeth; carried on long controversy with Bishop Jewel.

HARRISON, WILLIAM (1534-1593): chronicler; Rector of Radwinter (1559-93); his *Description of England* (1577) printed in Holinshed's *Chronicles*.

HARVEY, GABRIEL (1545-1630): poet; fellow of Pembroke Hall, Oxford; acquainted with Spenser; wrote satirical verses that gave offence at court (1579).

HASTINGS, SIR EDWARD (d. 1573): first Baron Hastings of Loughborough; privy councillor and master of the horse under Queen Mary; Lord Chamberlain (1557); imprisoned for hearing Mass but released on taking the oath of supremacy.

HEATH, NICHOLAS (1501-1578): Bishop of Rochester (1539), Worcester (1543); imprisoned and deprived 1551; restored 1553; Archbishop of York (1555-9); deprived, imprisoned in Tower.

HENRY II OF FRANCE (1519-1559): married Catherine de Medici (1533); King (1557); took violent measures against French Protestants; recaptured Calais.

HENRY III OF FRANCE (1551-1589): son of Catherine de Medici; assassinated at St. Germain by fanatic, Jacques Clement.

HENTZNER, PAUL: German traveller in England at the end of Elizabeth's reign; his journal has been published under the title, *A Journey into England in the Year of 1598.*

HEREFORD, BISHOP OF, *see* SCORY, JOHN (1559-1585).

HESKETH, THOMAS: attorney of the court of wards and liveries, Gray's Inn.

HEYWOOD, JASPER (1535-1598): son of John Heywood, epigrammatist; page of honour to Princess Elizabeth; fellow of All Souls; Jesuit (1562); sent to England (1581); deported (1585); died at Naples.

HILARION THE GREAT, ST. (*c.* 291-373): born nr. Gaza; became Christian at Alexandria; visited St. Anthony; returned to set up monastery nr. Majuma; died in cave at Paphos.

HILL, THOMAS (1564-1644): Benedictine monk; ordained at Rome (1594); in English mission (1597); condemned to death (1612); reprieved and banished (1613); died at St. Gregory's monastery, Douai.

HOLFORD, BL. THOMAS (1541-1588): born at Aston, Cheshire; son of a minister; reconciled (1579); studied at Rheims; priest (1583); arrested as he was leaving the house at Swithin Wells; executed at Clerkenwell, 28 August 1588.

HOLT, WILLIAM (1545-1599): fellow of Oriel College, Oxford (1568); studied at Douai (1574-6); Jesuit (1578); in Scotland (1581-2); Rector of English College, Rome (1586-7).

HOLTBY, RICHARD (1553-1640): student at Cambridge; tutor at Hart Hall, Oxford (1576) where Alexander Briant was his pupil; crossed to Douai (1577); priest (1578); on English mission in north (1579-81); Jesuit (1583). For fifty years he successfully eluded arrest, although the most prominent priest in the north.

HORNER, BL. NICHOLAS (d. 1590): born Grantley, West Riding, Yorks; tailor, condemned for making a jerkin for Fr. Bales; executed at Smithfield, March 1590.

HOWARD, BL. PHILIP, EARL OF ARUNDEL (1557-1595): eldest son of Thomas Howard, 4th Duke of Norfolk; at court of Elizabeth; became Catholic (1584); imprisoned for rest of his life (1585); condemned to death but not executed.

HUGHES, WILLIAM (d. 1600): fellow of Christ's College, Cambridge (1557); chaplain to Thomas, 4th Duke of Norfolk; Bishop of St. Asaph (1573-1600); Welsh scholar and author.

HUMPHREY, LAWRENCE (1527-1590): in exile under Mary; Regius

Professor of Divinity, Oxford (1560); President of Magdalen (1561-90).

HUTTON, MATTHEW (1529-1606): fellow of Trinity College, Cambridge; Master of Pembroke Hall (1562-7); Dean of York (1567); Bishop of Durham (1589); President of the North (1596-1600); Archbishop of York (1596-1606).

INGLEBY, VEN. FRANCIS (d. 1586): 4th son of Sir William Ingleby of Ripley, Yorks; scholar of Brasenose (1562); Inner Temple (1577); Rheims (1582-4); English mission (1584); worked in Yorkshire; executed at York, 3 June 1586.

INGRAM, BL. JOHN (1565-1594): born at Stoke Edith, Hereford; studied at Rheims and English College, Rome; priest (1589); worked partly in Scotland; tortured in London, but sent to Newcastle-on-Tyne for execution, 26 July 1594.

JETTER, JOHN (d. 1585): studied at Rheims and Rome; ordained and sent on English mission; died in prison.

JEWEL, JOHN (1522-1571): in exile under Mary at Strassburg and Zurich; Bishop of Salisbury (1560-71); principal controversialist on side of the Reformers.

JOHNSON, LAURENCE, *see* RICHARDSON, BL. LAURENCE.

KETT, FRANCIS (d. 1589): clergyman; condemned for heresy (1588); burnt alive.

KING, JOHN (1559-1621): prebendary of St. Paul's and chaplain to Queen Elizabeth (1599); Dean of Christ Church, Oxford (1605); Bishop of London (1611-21).

KIRBY, BL. LUKE (d. 1582): born Richmond, Yorks; studied at Douai and Rome; priest (1577); English mission (1578); captured (1581); tortured; executed, 30 May 1582.

LAMBTON, VEN. JOSEPH (1569-1592): born Malton-in-Rydall, Yorks; educated at Rheims and Rome; English mission (1592); arrested on landing; executed 23 July 1592.

LANGDALE, THOMAS: Jesuit; English mission (1582); apostatised and entered the service of the Government abroad.

LINCOLN, BISHOPS OF, *see* BULLINGHAM, NICHOLAS (1560-1571); CHADERTON, WILLIAM (1595-1608).

LONDON, BISHOPS OF, *see* BONNER, EDMUND (1539-1559); GRINDAL, EDMUND (1559-1570); SANDYS, EDWIN (1570-1576); AYLMER, JOHN (1577-1594).

MANNINGHAM, JOHN (d. 1622): student of Middle Temple; his diary (1602-3) of considerable value for the period.

MARTIN, GREGORY (d. 1582): scholar of St. John's College, Oxford; tutor to sons of Thomas Howard, 4th duke of Norfolk; escaped to Douai (1570); priest (1573); translated Bible (Douai version) with help of Richard Bristow and others.

MARTYR, PETER (PIETRO VERMIGHI) (1500-1562): celebrated theologian; born at Florence; lectured on scripture at Naples and Oxford (1548); canon of Christ Church (1551); on accession of Mary returned to Continent; died at Zurich, 12 November 1562.

MATHEW, SIR TOBIE (1577-1655): courtier, diplomat and writer, son of Tobie Mathew, Archbishop of York; became Catholic in Italy (1606); ordained priest (1614).

MENDOZA, BERNARDINO DE: soldier; Spanish ambassador in England (1574-84).

MERCURIAN, EVERARD (d. 1580): elected General of the Society of Jesus (1573) in succession to St. Francis Borgia; Belgian by birth; responsible for sending Campion and Persons to England (1580).

MILLER (MILNER), BL. RALPH (d. 1591): born in Hampshire; maintained wife and eight children by manual labour; arrested for assisting priests; offered his life if he went to church; executed at Winchester, 7 July 1591.

MONTAGUE, LADY (1538-1608); daughter of 3rd Lord Dacre of Graystock; lady of honour to Queen Mary; married Viscount Montague of Battle and Cowdray (1556); her houses were strong rallying-points for Catholics in Sussex and Kent.

MORISON, FYNES (1566-1617): traveller; chief secretary to Sir Charles Blount (1600); published account of travels and of Irish war.

MORONE, GIOVANNI (1509-1580): Cardinal (1542); Pope's Legate at Council of Trent (1545); Cardinal Protector of England; had much to do with administration of English College, Rome.

MUSH, JOHN (1552-1617): educated Douai and Rome; priest and spiritual director of Margaret Clitherow, whose biography he wrote; opposed appointment of Blackwell as archpriest.

NEVILLE, LADY MARGARET: daughter of Charles Neville, 5th Earl of Westmorland (attainted for treason, 1571); captured with John Boast; tried, and, under pressure from Matthew Hutton, Bishop of Durham, renounced her profession of Catholicism.

NORTON, THOMAS (1532-1584): lawyer; M.P. for Galton (1558); remembrancer of City of London (1571); official 'censor' of Queen's Catholic subjects (1581) and conducted their examination under torture; poet, and translator of Nowell's 'Middle Catechism'.

NOWELL, ALEXANDER (1507-1602): exile under Queen Mary; dean of St. Paul's (1560); principal of Brasenose College, Oxford (1582); author of three Catechisms.

NORTHBROOK, JOHN (fl. 1568-1579): preacher against plays; theological writer.

NORWICH, BISHOP OF, *see* COX, RICHARD (1559); PARKHURST, JOHN (1560-1575).

NUTTER, VEN. ROBERT (1550-1600): born Burnley, Lancs; Brasenose College, Oxford (1564); Rheims (1581-4); English mission; arrested, tortured and banished (1585); returned and again arrested; entered Dominican Order; executed at Lancaster, 26 July 1600.

OGLETHORPE, OWEN (d. 1559): fellow of Magdalen College, Oxford; Bishop of Carlisle (1557-9); crowned Elizabeth, but was deprived.

OLDCORNE, BL. EDWARD (1561-1606): native of York; studied at English College, Rome; Jesuit (1588); entered England with John Gerard; arrested, tortured and executed at the time of the Gunpowder Plot.

OSBORNE, EDWARD: studied at Rheims; priest (1581); captured by Topcliffe (1582); he denied his faith, but repented and did penance at Rheims.

OVERTON, WILLIAM (1525-1609): fellow of Magdalen College, Oxford; Bishop of Coventry and Lichfield (1579-1609).

OWEN, BL. NICHOLAS (d. 1606): Jesuit lay-brother, known as 'Little John'; helped John Gerard to escape from Tower; companion of Henry Garnet; died under torture.

PARKER, MATTHEW (1504-1575): chaplain to Anne Boleyn; Master of Corpus Christi, Cambridge; supported Lady Jane Grey; Archbishop of Canterbury (1559).

PARKHURST, JOHN (1512-1575): fellow of Merton (1529); in exile under Mary; Bishop of Norwich (1560).

PATTINSON (PATENSON), BL. WILLIAM (d. 1592): native of Durham; studied at Rheims 1584-9; worked in Cornwall and Dorset; condemned for his priesthood; executed at Tyburn, 22 January 1592.

PECKHAM, ROBERT (d. 1567); member of Council under Queen Mary; went into voluntary exile in Rome and died there.

PERSONS, ROBERT (1546-1610): fellow of Balliol (1568); Jesuit (1575); came to England with Edmund Campion (1580); Rector of English College, Rome (1597); controversialist.

PERYN, WILLIAM (d. 1558): prior of Great St. Bartholomew in Smithfield; opposed Henry VIII; went to Continent; returned under Mary.

PILKINGTON, JAMES (1520-1576): fellow of St. John's College, Cambridge; President (1550); in exile under Mary; Master of St. John's, Cambridge (1559-61) and Regius Professor of Divinity (1559); Bishop of Durham (1561-76).

PIUS V, ST. (MICHELE GHISLIERI) (1504-1572): Dominican friar; inquisitor of the faith in Milan; Bishop of Sirtri (1556); elected Pope (1566); organised crusade against Turks; excommunicated Elizabeth, 1570.

PLASDEN, BL. POLYDORE (d. 1591): born at Battle, Sussex; educated at Brasenose College, Oxford; studied at Rheims and Rome; priest (1588); captured at house of Swithin Wells; executed at Tyburn 10 December 1591.

PLOWDEN, EDMUND (1518-1585): Serjeant-at-Law under Queen Mary; offered Chancellorship by Elizabeth, but rejected it.

RICHARDSON (*alias* JOHNSON), BL. LAWRENCE: (d. 1582): born Great Crosby, Lancs; fellow of Brasenose College, Oxford; crossed to Douai (1573); priest (1577); worked in Lancashire; arrested (1581); executed with three other priests, Thomas Cottam, Luke Kirby and William Filby at Tyburn, 30 May 1582.

RIGBY, BL. JOHN (d. 1599): born gentleman; born at Harrock Hall, near Wigan, Lancs.; reconciled to Church by John Gerard; executed at St. Thomas Waterings, Southwark on 21 June, 1599.

RISHTON, EDWARD (1550-1586): fellow of Brasenose (1572); studied at Douai; banished as priest (1581); died of plague (1586).

RIVERS, ANTHONY (fl. 1601-1606): Jesuit; companion to Fr. Henry Garnet; resided in London (1601-3) and wrote series of valuable letters containing much news on current events.

ROBINSON, NICHOLAS (d. 1585): fellow of Queen's College, Oxford (1551); vice-president (1561); ordained priest under Mary (1557); Archdeacon of Merioneth (1563); Bishop of Bangor (1566-85); Welsh scholar.

ROBINSON, VEN. CHRISTOPHER (d. 1598): born Woodside, four miles from Carlisle: studied at Rheims; priest (1592); witnessed and described martyrdom of John Boast; executed at Carlisle, 19 August 1598.

ROWSHAM, VEN. STEPHEN (d. 1587): born Oxfordshire; educated Oriel College; minister at St. Mary's Oxford; crossed to Rheims; ordained and sent on English mission (1581); executed at Gloucester about Easter (1587).

ST. ASAPH, BISHOPS OF, see GOLDWELL, THOMAS (1555-1559); HUGHES, WILLIAM (1573-1600).

ST. DAVID'S, BISHOP OF, see YOUNG, THOMAS (1559-1561).

SALISBURY, BISHOP OF, see JEWEL, JOHN (1560-1571).

SAMOSATENUS, PAULUS: Paul of Samosata on Euphrates; Bishop of Antioch in third century.

SANDER, NICOLAS (1530-1581): New College, Oxford; Regius Professor of Theology at Louvain; controversialist; papal nuncio to Ireland (1579).

SANDYS, EDWIN (1516-1588): Master of St. Catherine's Hall, Cambridge (1549); Vice-chancellor (1553); supported Lady Jane Grey, but exiled after imprisonment; Bishop of Worcester (1559-70); London (1570-76); Archbishop of York (1576-88).

SANDYS, VEN. JOHN (d. 1586): born in diocese of Chester; studied at Rheims; priest (1584); his execution at Gloucester (11 August 1586) was horribly protracted and cruel.

SCHIFANOYA, IL: A Mantuan resident in England; his letters are addressed to the Mantuan ambassador at the court of Brussels and to the castellan of Mantua; he was in the service of Sir Thomas Tresham (d. 1558), then resided with Mgr. Priuli, the executor of Cardinal Pole; he had therefore good opportunities for observing English affairs.

SCORY, JOHN (d. 1585): Dominican friar at Cambridge (c. 1530); chaplain to Cranmer and Ridley; Bishop of Rochester (1551), Chichester (1552); deprived by Mary, but recanted and worked in London diocese; Bishop of Hereford (1559-85).

SCOT, CUTHBERT (d. 1564): Master of Christ's College and Vice-chancellor of Cambridge (1554); Bishop of Chester (1556); deprived by Elizabeth; imprisoned in Fleet (1559-63); retired to Louvain.

SCOT, VEN. MUMFORD (d. 1591): born in Norfolk; studied at Douai; priest (1577); executed 1 or 2 July 1591. His execution was horribly protracted.

SCOTUS, DUNS (*c.* 1265-1308): known as 'Doctor Subtilis'; schoolman; Franciscan friar; taught philosophy in Oxford and Paris.

SHACKLOCK, RICHARD (fl. 1515): fellow of Trinity College, Cambridge; priest in exile at Louvain; published translation of Hosius' *De Heresibus* and other works.

SHERWIN, BL. RALPH (1550-1581); born nr. Longford, Derbyshire fellow of Exeter College, Oxford; studied at Douai and Rome; priest (1577); English mission (1580); protomartyr of English College, Rome.

SHIRLEY, SISTER ELIZABETH (d. 1 September 1641), daughter of Sir John Shirley of Shirley, Leicestershire. Professed nun of St. Ursula's, Louvain, 1596.

SLACK, RICHARD: schoolmaster; ordained Rheims (1579); English Mission (1581); imprisoned in Tower, then exiled (1585); lectured at Douai.

SHERWOOD, BL. THOMAS (d. 1578): student at Douai; arrested on a visit to England in order to raise money to continue his studies; tortured in Tower; then tried and executed at Tyburn, 7 February 1578.

SIMLER, JOSIAH (1530-1576): Swiss historian, pupil of Bullinger; professor of theology at Zurich in succession to Peter Martyr (1563).

SMITH, RICHARD (1566-1655): Bishop of Chalcedon (1625); author of controversial works.

SOUTHCOTE, SIR JOHN (1511-1585): judge; serjeant-at-law (1559); raised to Queen's Bench (1563); sat as assessor at trial of Norfolk (1572).

SOUTHWELL, BL. ROBERT (1561-1595): born at Horsham St. Faith, nr. Norwich; studied at Douai and Rome; Jesuit (1578); English mission with Henry Garnet (1586); chaplain to Countess of Arundel; captured and tortured by Topcliffe; executed at Tyburn, 21 February 1595.

SOUTHWORTH, SIR JOHN (d. 1595): of Samlesbury Hall, Lancashire; knighted (1547); high sheriff of Lancashire (1562); imprisoned for recusancy in Salford gaol (1568-70); he refused to sign the form of submission and is said to have suffered more in fines and imprisonment than any other layman in Lancashire.

STANNEY, THOMAS (1558-1617); student at English College, Rome (1581-85); Jesuit (1597); chaplain to Countess of Arundel (1603); arrested and exiled (1606); died at St. Omer.

STONOR, LADY (CECILY): daughter of Sir Leonard Chamberlayne of Shirburn Castle, Oxon; married Sir Francis Stonor of Stonor Park; died probably in prison after 1592.

STOW, JOHN (1525-1605): chronicler and antiquarian; suspected of partiality for the old faith; most accurate historian of his century.

STRYPE, JOHN (1643-1737): ecclesiastical historian and biographer; acquired fine collection of original documents now in the Harleian and Lansdowne collections.

SUTCLIFFE, MATTHEW (1550-1629): fellow of Trinity College, Cambridge (1574); Dean of Exeter (1588); published a large number of controversial works directed against Catholics.

SUTTON, VEN. ROBERT (d. 1587): born at Burton-upon-Trent; parson of Lutterworth; converted by his brothers; studied at Douai; priest (1578); worked nine years in Staffordshire; executed near Skilmore, Stafford, 27 July 1587.

THROCKMORTON, EDWARD (1562-1582) son of Sir John Throckmorton of Coughton; entered the English College, Rome (1580); died there, after being admitted into the Society (1582).

TIEPOLO, PAULO: Venetian Ambassador with King Philip in Flanders and Spain (1559-61).

TIMBERLAKE, HENRY (d. 1626); traveller; visited Jerusalem 1602; member of the Company of Merchant Adventurers formed 1612.

TOPCLIFFE, RICHARD (1532-1604): persecutor of Catholics; M.P. for Beverley (1572) and Old Sarum (1586); racked prisoners in his own house, particularly Robert Southwell.

TREGIAN, FRANCIS (1548-1608): Elizabethan courtier; imprisoned for 28 years, and his property confiscated, for harbouring Cuthert Mayne (1577); retired to Spain, where he died.

TUNSTALL, CUTHBERT (1474-1559): friend of Thomas More; Bishop of London (1522-30) and Durham (1530); refused oath of supremacy and deprived by Elizabeth.

'TURNER OF BOULOGNE,' Richard Turner (d. 1565): chaplain to Cranmer; prebendary of Windsor; in exile at Basle under Queen Mary; restored (1559).

VAUX, LAURENCE (1519-1585): B.D., Corpus Christi College, Oxford (1556); withdrew to Louvain (1564); published *Catechism* (1567); Augustinian canon (1572); on English mission (1580); prisoner in London (1580-85).

VAVASOUR, DOROTHY (d. 1588): wife of Thomas Vavasour, doctor of physic, of York; many years a prisoner in York castle; died there 1588.

VIVALDINO, OTTAVIANO: Mantuan ambassador in Brussels (1558-59).

WALDEGRAVE, SIR EDWARD (1517-1561); privy councillor and master of the wardrobe (1553); chancellor of duchy of Lancaster (1557-58); recusant prisoner in the Tower (1558-61).

WALSINGHAM, SIR FRANCIS (1530-1590): educated King's College, Cambridge (1548-50); abroad during Queen Mary's reign; M.P. for Banbury (1559); collected foreign information for Sir William Cecil; chief of secret service in London (1559); envoy to Paris (1570-72); Secretary of State (1573-90); knighted (1577); secured conviction of Anthony Babington (1586) and Mary Queen of Scots (1587).

WARFORD, WILLIAM (1560-1608): scholar, then fellow of Trinity College, Cambridge; studied at Rheims (1582) and Rome; priest (1584); Jesuit (1585); penitentiary at St. Peter's; at English College, Valladolid, where he died.

WATERSON, BL. EDWARD (d. 1593): Londoner; converted abroad; studied at Rheims, priest (1592); arrested at Newcastle soon afterwards; tried with Joseph Lambton; maltreated and starved; executed at Newcastle, 7 January 1593.

WATKINSON, BL. ROBERT (1579-1602): born at Hemingborough, York, and educated at Castleford; studied at Douai and Rome (1598-1602); ordained in March and executed at Tyburn the following month on 20 April.

WATSON, JOHN (1520-1584): fellow of All Souls, Oxford (1540); Chancellor of St. Paul's (1558); Archdeacon of Surrey (1559); Dean of Winchester (1570); Bishop of Winchester (1580-84).

WATSON, WILLIAM (1559-1603): born at Durham; employed in seminary at Rheims as servant; later became student; ordained (1586); missioner in England the same year; at various times arrested; betrayed Jesuits and others, and wrote against them; finally executed at Winchester for plotting against James I, 9 December 1603.

WEIDNER, WOLFGANG: pastor at Worms; friend and correspondent of English reformers.

WELBEY, VEN. HENRY (d. 1588): layman; born Gloucester; he was arrested on shipboard in Chichester harbour (1580), condemned for aiding priests; executed Mile End, 28 August 1588.

WELLS, BL. SWITHIN (1536-1591): Catholic layman; kept school at Monkton Farley, Wilts; moved to house in Gray's Inn Lane (1585); executed with Edmund Gennings, 10 December 1591.

WESTMINSTER, ABBOT OF, *see* FECKENHAM, JOHN.

WESTON, WILLIAM (1550-1615); educated Christ Church, Oxford; Jesuit (1575); English mission (1584); received Earl of Arundel into Church; captured (1586); exiled (1603); Rector of English College, Valladolid.

WHARTON, VEN. CHRISTOPHER (d. 1600): born at Middleton, nr. Ilkley, Yorks; fellow of Trinity College, Oxford (1564); studied at Rheims; priest (1584); arrested at Carlton Hall, Leeds (1599); executed at York, 28 March 1600.

WHITAKER, WILLIAM (1548-1595): Regius Professor of Divinity, Cambridge (1580-95); Master of St. John's College (1586-95); canon of Canterbury; controversialist.

WHITE, BL. EUSTACE (1536-1591): born Louth, Lincs; convert to Catholicism; studied at Rheims and Rome; priest (1588); betrayed at Blandford, Dorset; imprisoned, tortured and starved in Bridewell; executed at Tyburn, 10 December 1591.

WHITGIFT, JOHN' (1530-1604): fellow of Peterhouse, Cambridge (1555); Lady Margaret Professor of Divinity (1563-67) and Master of Trinity College (1567-77), Cambridge; Regius Professor of Divinity (1567-69); Vice-chancellor (1570); Bishop of Worcester (1577); Archbishop of Canterbury (1583-1604).

WILBRAHAM, SIR ROGER: Solicitor-General in Ireland and Master of Requests. His journal covers the years 1593-1616, and contains much parliamentary and legal gossip for the last ten years of Elizabeth.

WINCHESTER, BISHOP OF, *see* WATSON, JOHN (1580-1584).

WISEMAN, JANE (d. 1610): wife of Thomas Wiseman of Braddocks, Essex (d. 1585) and mother of Sir William Wiseman; four of her daughters entered English convents abroad; arrested (1595) for harbouring priests; condemned to death, but reprieved; remained in prison until accession of James I.

WODEHOUSE, FRANCIS (d. 1605): gentleman of Breccles, west Norfolk; a squire of considerable wealth; his mansion is one of the finest extant examples of Elizabethan domestic architecture in East Anglia; he suffered severely from fines and was compelled to sell his house; died in poverty at Cawston in March 1605.

WOODHOUSE, BL. THOMAS (d. 1573): Marian priest (ordained 1558);

imprisoned in Fleet, London (1561); executed 12 years later, 19 June 1573.

WORCESTER, BISHOPS OF, *see* SANDYS, EDWIN (1559-1570); BULL-INGHAM, NICHOLAS (1571-1576); WHITGIFT, JOHN (1577-1583).

WORTHINGTON, THOMAS (1550-1626): professor of theology at Douai College (1590); President of Douai (1599); retired (1613); entered Society of Jesus; died in Staffordshire.

YORK, ARCHBISHOPS OF, *see* HEATH, NICHOLAS (1555-1559); YOUNG, THOMAS (1561-1568); GRINDAL, EDMUND (1570-1576); SANDYS, EDWIN (1576-1588); HUTTON, MATTHEW (1596-1606).

YEPEZ, DIEGO DE: Hieronymite Father: confessor to Philip II of Spain; Bishop of Tarazona; his *Historia particolar de la persecucion de Inglaterra* (1599), a valuable source of information on priests in England.

YOUNG, RICHARD (d. 1594): J.P. for Middlesex; assisted Topcliffe in persecution and examination of Catholics.

YOUNG, THOMAS (1507-1568): exile under Queen Mary; Bishop of St. David's (1559); Archbishop of York (1561).

Index of Subjects and Places

Index of Persons

Index of Books

(Short Titles)